C0-ATD-419

This book   nt

A 6n

STAND STRONG IN THE LORD

BTQ 2188 .E16S   ST. JOSEPH'S UNIVERSITY   STX
Stand strong in the Lord;

3 9353 00151 4288

Stand Strong in the Lord

Spiritual Conferences on the Interior Life

William Eberschweiler, S.J.

Translated by
SISTER MARY ALOYSI KIENER, S.N.D.
Notre Dame College
Cleveland, Ohio

With FOREWORD by the
Right Reverend Msgr. Martin B. Hellriegel, M.A., L.H.D.

A division of St. Paul Publications
STATEN ISLAND 14, NEW YORK

NIHIL OBSTAT:

Anthony F. Alexander,

Censor Deputatus

IMPRIMATUR:

✠Edward F. Hoban

Archbishop - Bishop of Cleveland

April 15, 1962

BX2182
E/16 S

Library of Congress Catalog Card Number 62-17038

Copyright 1962, by Society of St. Paul, N. Y., N. Y.
Printed in U. S. A., by Society of St. Paul, N. Y., N. Y.

To all who participate

in the

"Royal Priesthood" of Christ

in the

Mystical Body.

OTHER BOOKS

by SISTER MARY ALOYSI KIENER, S.N.D., PH. D.

Jesus, the Model of Religious - 2 vols.

John Henry Newman, the Romantic, the Friend,
the Leader

Splendor and Strength of the Inner Life

A Light to my Paths

The Rosary and the Soul of Woman

Praying with the Poverello

"Draw Near to Him"

"This is the Victory"

In the Light of Christ

"Hearts Shall Be Enlightened"

The Heart of Mary, Sacrificial Altar of Christ's Love

"Bought at a Great Price"

FOREWORD

Notwithstanding the dust and soot of human frailty which from time to time besmirch the beautiful countenance of Christ's Bride, "the Church without spot or wrinkle,"[1] there are hopeful signs of a great renaissance, "an awakening of the Church in the souls of men."[2]

The primary aim of the Vatican Council II, as Pope John desires, is the rejuvenation of the Church in all her members, clerical, religious and lay, so that her inner beauty and glory may shine forth again through her members and compel the "other" sheep of the Good Shepherd to embrace that "one, holy, catholic, and apostolic" fold of security, peace and life.

Are not such world-wide movements as the Biblical, Liturgical-Sacramental, the Retreat and Christian Family apostolate happy signs of that *divine revolution* going on at the present time in the bosom of that living and life-imparting organism, which is Christ's Body and the Extension of the divine Head? Surely, a conscious return to the living Word of God; a joyous return to the "primary and indispensable source of the true Christian spirit,"[3] the liturgy, with active participation in it; an earnest effort to renew the spiritual life by the annual retreat and the

---

1 Eph. 5:22.
2 Guardini.
3 St. Pius X.

monthly recollection days; the sincere efforts which are being made to intensify spirituality in seminaries and convents, in clergy and faithful, in home and school, all of these movements and many others must unleash the tremendous, world-transforming energy of the Mystical Body and bring about an "incorporation of all things in Christ,"[4] a rebirth of that spirit of the martyrs and athletes of Christ before whom a pagan world exclaimed in amazement: "A new mankind has risen among us."

Among the pioneers of the present-day renewal of the Church in the souls of men are two worthy sons of St. Ignatius of Loyola who, while laying foundation stones for this renovation during the first two decades of this century, were considered by some as "startling," if not "revolutionary"; men whom the Lord graced with pentecostal vision and courage, and who must never be forgotten. They are Father Joseph Kramp and Father William Eberschweiler to whom the Christian world owes a deep debt of gratitude.

The beginning of the twentieth century witnessed a growing "eucharistic piety." The accent, however, rested primarily on *tabernacle, adoration,* and *holy hour.* Without minimizing the value of this development, Father Joseph Kramp endeavored, in season and out of season, to restore the divinely-willed order by placing the accent where it belongs, namely on the *Eucharist* as *Sacrifice* and *Meal.* In his book "Eucharistia" (1924), he showed that, in accordance with the institution and the ancient tradition of the Church, the purpose of the Eucharist is not in the first

4 St. Pius X.

place its cult, but rather the corporate celebration of the Sacrifice with the reception of holy Communion. Today we take such things for granted. But let us not forget the pathfinders and bridgebuilders!

In like manner Father Eberschweiler—whom the Lord called to His heavenly Kingdom in the Advent of 1921— seemed to many, like the Advent preacher John the Baptist, "as a voice crying in the wilderness." There were some who called his book, "Gnade und Tugend," *abstruse* and *nebulous.* The fact that as Christians we share the very life of Jesus Christ, as the branch shares the very life of its vine; and that the purpose of the sacramental activity of the Church is to bring this Christ-life in us to full maturity so "that we may have it more abundantly,"[5] was, unhappily, not fully present in the consciousness of the Christian world at the opening of this century.

While reading his book with its four precious chapters, I was reminded of the four rivers that irrigated the garden of Eden, supplying life, growth, and fruitage. We are indebted to this pioneer who, more than twenty years before the appearance of the immortal encyclical "On the Mystical Body," opened to posterity four mystic rivers to carry the waters of Christ—so strikingly pointed out in the encyclical —into the minds and hearts of prayerful readers, priests, religious, and faithful.

We are very thankful to Sister Mary Aloysi Kiener, S.N.D., for giving to the English speaking world an elegant translation under the appealing title, STAND STRONG IN THE LORD. The book in its English garb is a tribute

---

5 John 10:10.

to Father Eberschweiler, S.J., a well deserved monument to his pioneering and to everyone who loves to "drink from the water that I will give him, a fountain of water, springing up into life everlasting."[6]

Martin B. Hellriegel, M.A., L.H.D.
Pastor of "Holy Cross," St. Louis, Mo.

Exaltation of the Holy Cross
September 14, 1961

---

6 John 4:4.

TRANSLATOR'S NOTE

The deep spirituality of this work on the interior life, by the late Father Eberschweiler, S.J., and its positive challenge made the preparation of an English translation a labor of love.

Strong in the power of God's grace, with firm reliance on the workings of Divine Providence, the author would have us realize the depths of God's mercy and the sublimity of intimate union with the Eucharistic Christ in meeting the problems of Christian living.

Reverend William Eberschweiler, S.J., who died at Exaten in the Netherlands, December 23, 1921, in the odor of sanctity, had for many years filled the office of Spiritual Father with dignity and Ignatian energy and dedication in the various Houses of the Society of Jesus.

Perfect conformity to the Will of God and implicit trust in His paternal designs, evidence the strength of his own surrender to the movements of divine grace, his love of the cross, and apostolic zeal for souls. Regularly addressed to his Confreres and the Scholastics of the Society, these conferences - *Stand Strong in the Lord* - should be a source of inspiration and a powerful incentive to the countless souls who today long for genuine progress in Christlike living and holiness.

The late Reverend Walter Sierp, S.J., who edited the original series in 1931, believed that they might appeal to the Reverend Clergy at large and to all who aspire to priestly perfection. Religious, both men and women, may find them an asset in their houses of formation, for the training of the younger members.

The layman himself will find ample compensation in a prayerful reading of these words of eternal truth of a loyal servant of God, himself a perfect exemplar of the splendor and strength of the spiritual life.

Feast of the Immaculate Heart of Mary
August 22, 1961

Notre Dame College
Cleveland, Ohio

CONTENTS

PART THREE

ZEAL FOR SOULS—THE MOST EXCELLENT FRUIT OF THE INTERIOR LIFE

PART FOUR

MEANS FOR CULTIVATING THE INTERIOR LIFE

PART ONE

THE INTERIOR LIFE
ITS VITALITY AND GRANDEUR

"O God, my God, to Thee do I watch at break of day. For Thee my soul hath thirsted."

—*Ps.* 62:2

CHAPTER I

THE INTERIOR LIFE

> *"Be perfect, then, as your Heavenly Father is perfect."*[1]
> *"Unto the praise of the glory of His grace."*[2]

In these beautiful words Our Divine Saviour proposes to us for our interior life no less a model than God Himself. This mysterious life comes from heavenly heights into this mundane world. How aptly the words of St. James inform us: "Every best gift, and every perfect gift is from above, coming down from the Father of Lights, with whom there is no change or shadow of alteration. For of His own will hath He begotten us by the word of truth, that we might be, as it were, the first fruits of His creatures."[3]

1. THE INTERIOR LIFE—"BORN . . . OF GOD"[4]—ITS VITALITY AND GRANDEUR

It is a free gift of God's eternal bounty, a life "born . . . of God."[5] It is nothing short of a participation of the divine

---

1 Matt. 5:48.
2 Eph. 1:6.
3 James 1:17, 18.
4 John 1.
5 John 1:13.

life, aglow with joy in the Lord. It is an awareness of something in my soul that cannot be expressed in words. "For as the Father has life in Himself, so He hath given to the Son also to have life in Himself."[6] The Son came from heaven to bring it to us. "I am come that they may have life, and may have it more abundantly."[7] St. Paul exhorts us to treasure this infinite gift and to "put on Christ."[8] What a serious challenge! But the interior man is aware of the strengthening of supernatural powers in putting on Christ.

In Baptism we were reborn in this divine life out of the water and the Holy Spirit. Its vital principle, its inner essence, is sanctifying grace. The Church teaches that God, who has marvellously created our human nature, has still more marvellously renewed it. Grace transforms the very being of our soul. According to St. Peter, God "hath given us most great and precious promises: that by these we may be made partakers of the divine nature."[9] The powers of this fruitful life, however, are faith, hope, and love; in fact, the whole treasure of virtues, full of life and light, infused into us by the Holy Spirit in Baptism. And that we may make a more facile use of these faculties, God enriches this life, over and above, with the Seven Gifts of the Holy Spirit.

Provided they are not neglected through dissipation or laxity and lukewarmness, and thus lie dormant, they preserve to us the life of grace in the most intimate union with the ultimate source of all life. This makes the soul

---

6 John 5:26.
7 John 10:10.
8 Gal. 3:27.
9 2 Peter 1:4.

receptive for every inspiration of the Holy Spirit, and thus aids the supernatural life to its loftiest perfection. "Every best gift, and every perfect gift, is from above, coming down from the Father of Lights, with whom there is no change, no shadow of alteration."[10]

As both the origin and the nature of the interior life lie wholly outside the realm of what is earthly, so it finds its nourishment only outside this realm, in the supernatural. The holy Sacraments are the fountains that nourish this fruitful lifestream. There it is born, purified, clarified, increased; there it finds refreshment. After the Blessed Eucharist, prayer, meditation, and intimate converse with heaven are the domestic hearths of intense spiritual happiness, where in the depths of our soul we perceive words that, as Our Lord declares, are the "Bread of Life."[11]

This life is strengthened and fortified through the practice of virtue and good works, avoiding even the smallest wilful sin, through the complete fulfillment of the holy Will of God. In short, by walking on the ways of justice, we grow into the likeness of Christ. *"In semita justitiae vita."* "On the path of justice there is life."[12] In one word, the true interior life is of God: *"ex Deo nati sunt."* ". . . born of God."[13] A life in and with God: *"Vita vestra est abscondita cum Christo in Deo."* "Your life is hidden with Christ in God;"[14] a life for God: *"In laudem gloriae gratiae suae."* "Unto the praise of the glory of His grace."[15]

---

10 James 1:17.
11 Matt. 4:4.
12 Prov. 12:28.
13 John 1:13.
14 Col. 3:3.
15 Eph. 1:6.

It is the most faithful imitation of the life of the only begotten Son of the Father full of grace and truth, of the life of Jesus Christ. And the more faithfully we possess it, with all the more truth can we say with St. Paul: "It is now no longer I that live but Christ lives in me."[16]

2. PRESERVATION AND GROWTH OF THE INNER LIFE

Is it, perhaps, only he who withdraws from all outward activity and spends days for himself alone, in prayer and recollection who is interior? Oh, then our Divine Saviour in His public life would not have been our highest and most perfect exemplar in this regard. Yet His inner life shone with a special radiance in the most glorious divine light during those years. The Apostles without exception would have fallen short; St. Francis of Assisi, St. Ignatius, St. Vincent de Paul and hosts of eminent leaders in the Church, strong in the midst of worldly concerns, would not have been spiritual men. Nor could a Xavier and the hosts of missioners to distant pagan lands be justly remembered by posterity as truly interior souls of genuine spirituality. Yet they were such in the most magnificent way, and for that very reason their apostolate was crowned with tremendous success. Christ inspired their most varied and difficult activity.

Indeed, if solitude, retirement, and seclusion were the essence of the inner life, religious who combine a life of outward activity with the contemplative spirit, would be forced to renounce their aspirations to the inner life. Still more would this hold for seculars. No, indeed, the true

---

16 Gal. 2:20.

inner life never fundamentally excludes outward expenditure of one's best efforts. The deepest kernel of the interior life is grace and virtue; these are capable of flowering anywhere and of bearing richest fruit.

Every life is characterized by a threefold striving: for preservation, for growth and increase, and finally for activity. This may be observed at all levels of life, even the lowest in the plant world. Every plant seeks to preserve its life, to increase it to full growth, to unfold the highest flowering and fruition. In all the phases of natural life, we notice that the more perfectly life is lived at a certain level, the more perfectly this triple striving shapes itself.

This striving is peculiar, also, in the supernatural life, the life of grace. In the first place it seeks to preserve itself in our hearts, defends itself from within against enemies and aggressors; it desires, further, to grow and wax strong. We must grow mightily in interior strength through the Holy Spirit, be firmly rooted and grounded in love, as St. Paul observes: "... to be strengthened by His Spirit with might unto the inward man."[17] Finally, it desires to manifest itself in acts of devotion and piety, and to continue its innate activity through apostolic work.

In the supernatural life, far more than in the natural, this fruitfulness depends upon our personal efforts, our striving, our concentrating on the operations of divine grace in our souls. The question as to who leads a truly interior life, may, therefore, be answered briefly. It is he who endeavors to preserve unspotted in his heart grace and virtue, radiating true inner stability; who strives in-

---

17 Eph. 3:16.

cessantly to strengthen this life more and more in him, through Christ. In short, it is he who seeks to impregnate all his actions with the supernatural quality of virtue and sanctifying grace, and to ennoble and dignify them. The greater our zeal in this triple endeavor, the more our interior life will shine forth in genuinely spiritual souls, in men and women according to the Heart of God.

3. THE MOST EXCELLENT MEANS OF FOSTERING THE INTERIOR LIFE

In the first place, we must be zealously intent upon preserving wholly intact the grace which makes us children of God and the virtue which the Holy Spirit has infused into our soul. We must diligently use the means necessary for the preservation of this precious life.

a) *The most excellent of these means are at our disposal*

They are foremost those that help us guard against every sin; the custody of the heart, the spirit of prayer, the persevering practice of mortification. The means to combat sin and fortify us against relapses are especially operative in the worthy and regular reception of the Sacrament of Penance; in the practice of the particular examen for the definite rooting out of faults and imperfections; fostering the spirit of penance and atonement, in the mind of the glorious Encyclical *"Reparation to the Most Sacred Heart of Jesus,"* of Pius XI, as well as other tried and efficient means.

b) *Cultivating the spirit of prayer*

"*Sis devotus et quietus, et manebit tecum Jesus.*" "Be devout and recollected, and Jesus will abide with you," we read in the *Imitation*. "Very quickly, on the contrary, can you drive Jesus away and lose His grace, if you dissipate yourself in externals." The spirit of prayer, the atmosphere or mood of recollection and reserve are indispensable for the preservation of the inner life and the gaining of ascendancy over the worldly spirit that surrounds us.

One who still craves worldly honors and pleasures freely offered on all sides, whose longings and volitions gravitate towards the earthly, who dissipates himself in every fashion, seeking to gratify his sensual, worldly leanings, will never succeed in acquiring a taste for heavenly goods. He will never become a truly interior man, but will remain a slave of external things with a base, materialistic outlook.

Where shall we find the entire hollowness of the pure earthly joys, where learn to despise the vanities and the nothingness of the world? Only there where the instability, the misery and the worthlessness of all this is clearly discernible in the supernatural light, and where it manifests itself without deception: in prayer and meditation, in converse with Him who has created all things as a means for our spiritual advancement, who gently admonishes us: "Seek first the kingdom of God and His justice, and all else will be given unto you." Hear St. Paul: "All that matters is that Christ is being made known."[18]

Only there where the wealth and the lovableness of

18 Phil. 1:18.

these wonderful gifts reveal themselves to us shall we learn to esteem, admire, and love this kingdom of God and His justice, which the world disdains and therefore cannot esteem. In prayer, close to the Heart of Jesus, where we behold and taste the sweetness of the Lord, as far as this is possible here below, this special light will be ours. Paul points to the most beautiful reality when he states, "there is nothing but Christ in any of us."[19]

In prayer, the light of faith shines more brightly in the depth of our souls. In its gentle brilliance we view everything with different eyes. God draws us upward to Himself; there the worldly spirit, this foremost enemy of the inner life, succumbs and takes to flight. On this lofty height of nearness to God, on the quiet eminence of aloneness with Him, the genuinely spiritual man pitches his permanent tent, in order to secure and preserve his most precious possessions. Even in the midst of storms of worldly living, tossed about by the exigencies of daily toil, he finds in prayer and silent, thoughtful reverie and communion with God, a haven in which he may dwell securely in holy love.

c) *The practice of mortification*

We have to safeguard the inner life of grace still against another far more dangerous foe. With St. Paul we will admit: "I see another law in my members, warring against the law of my mind."[20] Even if we dislike to hear it, it is nevertheless true that there is a perennial combat between light and darkness, between the flesh and the spirit. Human

---

19 Col. 3:11.
20 Rom. 7:23.

nature stained by actual sin, on the one hand, and grace urging us ever upwards on the other, cannot be friendly companions along the way. One of the two must disappear. In one who fails to understand what is of the spirit, the life of grace will eke out but a miserable existence, or even fall a prey to sinful concupiscence. But he who realizes with the Apostle what is of the spirit, must needs energetically seek to promote it, though difficulties encumber the way. He will utilize with resolute determination and dexterity the weapons that alone can safeguard the life of grace against our most insidious foe—that other law in our members—and help us achieve the victory.

"For if you live according to the flesh, you will die; but if by the Spirit you put to death the deeds of the flesh, you will live . . . For whosoever are led by the Spirit of God, they are the sons of God."[21] Obviously the man who leads an interior life must also practice mortification; he must present a bold and determined front to oppose the unjustifiable desires and strivings that stem from the depths of sensuality and pride, of self-will and haughtiness in demanding consideration. This he does, not as worldlings might think, because he wills neither to live nor to let live, but on the contrary, because he wishes to preserve true life in every respect and help it to its finest fruition; therefore he prunes away all weeds and tries to pull them up roots and all.

4. GROWTH IN THE LIFE OF GRACE

Our Divine Saviour tells us that He came not only that through Him we may have life, but that we may have it in

---

21 Rom. 8:13, 14.

greater abundance and live His life in us in the fullest measure. Sanctifying grace should grow and wax strong in us. "He that is just, let him be justified still; and he that is holy, let him be sanctified still."[22] This striving to grow, to develop to the fullness of life, is, as we have seen, the second dominant motive force dwelling in every human being.

a) *How is the supernatural life of grace increased in us?*

The same Holy Spirit who bestowed it upon us gratuitously in Baptism as a gift of love, unfolds it also in our souls, heightens its splendor and its fulness more and more, unto our maturity in Christ Jesus. Even if all this is unmerited and gratuitous grace and goodness of God, Jesus nevertheless willed our cooperation. We should at least open our hearts without the slightest hindrance to the reception of grace. In order to further the growth of this supernatural life, Our Lord instituted the holy Sacraments, which as theologians say in virtue of the power dwelling within them effect an increase of grace *ex opere operato*. Out of His abundance, He further imparted to our life of grace the strength and the vitality to merit new graces ourselves, and to draw from the inexhaustible riches of Christ, the increase of grace *ex opere operantis*.

If we would lead a perfect life, we must above all highly esteem and zealously utilize the most excellent nourishment of this life—the Bread of the Strong. It is the Most

---

22 Apoc. 22:11.

Blessed Sacrament of the Altar, which Jesus has left us under the semblance of food; in a special way it is known as the Bread of Life, and is such in reality.

How happy we should be in the ease with which we may partake frequently of this surpassing heavenly Food. In our very midst Jesus, our most loving Redeemer, has set the Table of His grace for us. Day after day He extends to us the friendly invitation: "Come, eat my bread and drink the wine which I have mingled for you."[23] "Come to Me, all you who labor and are burdened, and I will give you rest."[24] In order to heed this invitation we need only make a small sacrifice of time and convenience. All the more, however, must we be intent upon doing everything in our power to make it possible for this mystic nourishment of life to exert its fullest efficiency.

b) *Characteristics of the man who leads an interior life*

He provides above all for a wholesome hunger, for a sincere, ardent desire to eat of the Most Adorable Flesh and Blood of Jesus. It is far from him to think of this Sacred Banquet only when the time of immediate preparation has come. The greatest solicitude and zeal in the day's actions in anticipation of that moment testify eloquently to a heart filled with holy longing for Him who is our life, our delight, the center of all our thoughts and affections, of all our actions and omissions. What is the immediate result?

---

23 Prov. 9:5.
24 Matt. 11:28.

The interior man will experience the truth of Our Lady's glorious canticle: "He hath filled the hungry with good things." Every Holy Communion will bring to him an overwhelmingly great increase of sanctifying grace and growth in the inner life; perhaps not always with palpable delights, yet in a far higher degree than if he had prepared negligently. The interior man understands not only how to hunger and thirst for the Food of Life, but also to taste and relish It, in fervent thanksgiving, in union with His Saviour. In His glorious Presence, he will seek no other delights than to make known His glory "as it shines on the face of Christ Jesus."[25]

c) *Self-activity in the life of grace*

Self-activity is the third striving peculiar to every life, to life in general. True life tends to penetrate and strengthen everything within its reach. The healthier and fuller the life in a tree, the more thoroughly will it interpenetrate all that belongs to the tree, from the tiniest rootlet to the last leaflet on the topmost pinnacle.

Something similar happens in the supernatural life, the inner life of the soul. Where it is vigorous and sound, it will make an effort to invest everything within reach with the supernatural and true interior worth and validity. What means will insure success to this endeavor? They are the virtues; they represent the strength and vigor by means of which sanctifying grace absorbs all our thoughts, inclinations, and affections, as well as our words and works, and

---

25 2 Cor. 4:6.

assimilates them into our own being and essence. Sanctifying grace supernaturalizes them and invests them with
genuine values that render them pleasing to God and
meritorious for eternity.

One who desires to lead a vigorous interior life, giving
of self, will devote himself tirelessly to the acquisition of
solid virtues, as well as to the diligent practice of those
acquired. This can be done by utilizing in generous measure the occasions that are inseparable from his office, his
environment, and his occupations. This he regards as the
perfect accomplishment of God's holy Will and the essence
of all virtue.

d) *Conformity to the Divine Will*

In order to walk more securely, the interior man con-
centrates above all on the virtues most needful for his
character and inclinations, his position and assignments.
A genuine life of union with God, accordingly, consists
solely in doing to the best of one's ability the most holy
Will of God, how He wills it and why He wills. We do this
from the loftiest motives, namely for love of God, because
He wills it, for His divine pleasure and infinite complacence.

Then the words of the Psalmist will be realized:
"Blessed is the man whose help is from Thee; in his heart
he has disposed to ascend by steps, in the vale of tears,
in the place which He has set. For the lawgiver shall give
a blessing; they shall go from virtue to virtue: the God of
gods shall be seen in Sion."[26]

---

26 Ps. 83:6-8.

And that other word from Proverbs will likewise find fulfilment: "But the path of the just, as a shining light, goeth forwards and increases even to perfect day."[27] This light not only shines, but it gives light to all; it dispenses blessings. The mystery of the apostolate is the transforming of all exterior work into virtuous actions, in closest union with God our Saviour. Jesus Himself said: "He who remains in Me brings forth much fruit." What a glorious word! Union with Jesus, we know, flowers forth from grace and the virtue of love. Only in this manner do we remain in Him, and only thus can we yield fruit for the eternal harvestings of God.

5. FRUITFULNESS OF THE INTERIOR LIFE

Fulfilling our life's work in the supernatural spirit, consists essentially in our endeavor to be good children of our Heavenly Father, by striving to resemble Him more and more in order to become perfect, "Be perfect, then, as your Heavenly Father is perfect."[28]

a) *What is the actual life in the Divinity?*

Is it not the interior life? That life which the Infinite God leads from all eternity, and in which the Son is begotten of the Father from all eternity, and the Holy Spirit proceeds from both? Is it not the inner life which the Most Blessed Trinity has led for an eternity before anything

---

27 Prov. 4:18.
28 Matt. 5:48.

existed outside the Triune God? The inner life in which for a whole eternity the Trinity was infinitely perfect, infinitely active, infinitely happy and blessed, even before there was any outward manifestation, as it were, of an exterior life?

And after God has revealed Himself outwardly, called a world into being, and then consummated the marvellous and amazing work of the Redemption, what should be the outward effect of this Divine Activity? Nothing less than bringing rational beings to a participation in the interior life, which the Triune God leads in Himself, and thus, through understanding and love, to immerse them in that marvellous life-stream which floods the depths of the Godhead. "Your life is hid with Christ in God."[29] Truly, "*omnis gloria filiae regis ab intus.*" "All the glory of the king's daughter is within in golden borders."[30] Here we see what it means to live like God.

b) *The power of Christ dwelling in me*

To work beneficently for others, we must also take on a likeness to our Heavenly Father in our activity. Now, whence is the perfection and the efficiency of divine action? It resides in this that God, independent of anything outside Himself, possesses in Himself the plenitude of power. We, too, should like to do great things, achieve deeds worthy of the Most Adorable Trinity. A laudable ambition! The more we grow in the inner life, the more power and

---

29 Col. 3:3.
30 Ps. 44:14.

strength we harbor in ourselves, the more activity, unction, and solidity we shall be able to pour out upon our task. St. Ignatius was deeply convinced of this fact. The efficacy of all exterior means for the work of the salvation of souls, he traces back to the inner motive force or impulse of the soul of the apostle himself. When he exhorts his Sons to devote themselves wholeheartedly to the practice of solid virtue and to a genuine interior life, he advisedly adds several motivating principles to his injunctions. He would have them zealously espouse the interior advantages, especially love and the pure intention in divine service, intimacy with God in their spiritual exercises, genuine zeal for His glory, for Him who created and redeemed souls—all these invest the outward performance with its unique efficacy. In fact, a man fostering the spiritual life will always do great and noteworthy deeds, perhaps not in the eyes of the world, but certainly before God. In all circumstances the fostering of the spiritual life will bring enrichment of the inner life.

c) *Enrichment of the inner life*

There will be times when he is beset with many cares, in divers ways. Will he, then, enlist all his faculties as the special work requires it? He most assuredly will because the love of God prompts him. Love is a far more powerful lever and incentive to the full utilization of all the gifts of nature and of grace than any other consideration. Added to this is the fact that having wholly immolated self-will, he is not impeded, nor does he forfeit the blessings of obedience. He pierces the veil and sees the light.

Finally, vanity and pride in him have yielded to true

humility; the desire to please himself and others immoderately has given way to his heart's intent of looking to the pleasure of God alone. In this way, the influence and cooperation of divine grace in all his actions and omissions will be neither endangered nor minimized. Holiness must be directed straight to the Heart of God.

There will be a time when outward success is lacking, when even among those nearest to him he is denied the respect and consideration he desires, and which are justly his due. Will he waver? Whereas others, who neglect to do God's holy Will in these things and grow indifferent to the practice of virtue, will, perhaps, suffer a total collapse, outwardly as well as inwardly, to their great harm, he will keep his eye fixed on the goal. At such times, the interior man, accustomed to look solely to God and the intrinsic excellence of a virtuous life, will experience the greatest inner success. Outwardly, too, the structure of Christian living will know the power of God's beneficent grace. The life of the spirit is the life of sanctifying grace, which is measured by charity.

At times exterior activity is cut off, or other work intervenes with little natural appeal. The spiritual man will not seek refuge in self-pity and sadness or dejection, for he is a discerning man. While others sit idly by bemoaning their fate and discontent, the spiritual-minded man serves his great God with the utmost fidelity and alacrity. He will approve himself a soldier on the spiritual battlefields.

He has at his command what he seeks—God and His holy Will, opportunities at every turn for the exercise of humility, of obedience and total self-surrender. Not a day or hour passes in which he neglects to pray for the salvation of souls; with great alacrity he offers his works, sufferings and sacrifices for the apostolic intentions of the Church and the interests of the Sacred Heart. There are times when sickness cripples all outward activity. Others, perhaps, gather stuff for the purgatorial flames, by yielding to impatience and self-pity, but the spiritual man perfects himself on his bed of pain. His acts of total surrender will be transmuted into purest gold, a joy to the angels of God. In how far the natural life is diminished, in so far the supernatural grows in him with fresh vigor. The exterior faculties may be atrophied, yet the inner powers seek to carry out the designs and the holy Will of God with fervor and generosity. Faith, hope, and charity unite him ever more closely with the Triune God, the Author of all life.

Finally comes the hour of death. The sands of time are running out and the portals of eternity open wide. Heaven awaits him. Through his zealous custody of the life of union with the Mind and Heart of God, he earned not only the merest admittance to the heavenly realms; we may assume him qualified to appear in the Divine Presence, his heart aflame with love of his Lord and Creator. He is, therefore, able to behold God for all eternity more perfectly and to love Him with a love purified of earthly dross, and to glorify Him more joyously with the angels and saints. Now he enters wholly and entirely into the joys of his Lord, and participates to amazing depths in the inmost essence of the Godhead Himself.

For all eternity he can manifest himself as a man of the inner life in God, as one who has truly grasped the full significance of the word: "For the greater honor and glory of God," who has constantly envisioned it and has now attained to the full Beatific Vision. What a glorious aim!

To this end Jesus desires to lead us: "I am come that they may have life, and may have it more abundantly."[31]

Let us enter into His designs, for He would draw all things to His infinitely loving Heart. Let us more and more be guided by faith, persevere in our dedicated life in and with Christ, winning souls to Him in selfless labor.

---

31 John 10:10.

CHAPTER II

THE GLORIOUS RICHES WHICH THE HOLY SPIRIT IMPARTS TO OUR SOUL

> *"With Me are riches and glory, glorious riches and justice."*[1]
> *"Do you not know that you are the temple of God and that the Spirit of God dwells in you?"*[2]

The sublime word St. Paul addresses to the Corinthians is for us as well. "For holy is the temple of God, and this temple you are."[3] A temple of the Holy Spirit! Who can comprehend this truth! Where a sublime and heavenly Guest has taken up His abode, He replenishes everything with His glory. He bestows His celestial, blissful gifts in abundance. All that the Eternal Wisdom speaks of Himself holds in equal measure of the Holy Spirit, who proceeds from Him. "With Me are riches and glory, glorious riches and justice."

These treasures we shall ponder briefly in order to become fully aware of the magnitude of the divine gifts bestowed upon us, to esteem them justly and fittingly, and be deeply grateful for them in heartfelt joy. Animated with

---

1 Prov. 8:18.
2 1 Cor. 3:16.
3 1 Cor. 3:17.

this interior joy, we shall willingly employ these supernatural gifts in the service of the Most High, that they may
yield fruits of every virtue and promote the salvation of
mankind.

1. THE GIFTS OF LOVE BESTOWED UPON US BY
   THE HOLY SPIRIT

a) *Sanctifying grace*

The Holy Spirit presents us, above all, with *sanctifying
grace*. O gift of gifts! With it, He imparts to us a *new,
supernatural, divine life*. Through it, St. Peter reminds us,
we enter into a certain *communion with the divine nature*.
We are, indeed, and will remain human beings; we are
infinitely below the Divinity Itself. Still, we are actually
elevated above the whole realm of the natural creation;
we have entered into the *divine order of living*, and participate in the inner life peculiar to God Himself.

Since this participation in the divine nature imparts a
mysterious generation in God, we enjoy a certain equality
of birth with the Son of God, with Christ Jesus, who became the firstborn through the Incarnation among many
brethren. "Whosoever are led by the Spirit of God, they
are the Sons of God . . . Whom He foreknew, He also pre-
destinated to be made conformable to the image of His
Son, that He might be the firstborn among many brethren."[4]

Sanctifying grace is grace of sonship, of a filial adoption,
making us wonderfully conformable to the Son of God.
With the Son, the Holy Spirit enters into us, with the wis-

---

4 Rom. 8:14, 29.

dom of God, His Love. Now it is the Spirit of God in whom we cry, "Abba, Father!"[5] "And because you are sons, God hath sent the Spirit of His Son into your hearts, crying, 'Abba, Father'!"[6] We are children of God not in one sense only, nor because of outward adoption as sons, but in virtue of an interior resemblance with the Son of God, effected in us through sanctifying grace.

Our soul will be replenished with the features that render us pleasing to the Heavenly Father, the features that win for us His paternal love and qualify us to participate in an "inheritance incorruptible and undefiled . . . that cannot fade," as the Apostle styles it, "which is reserved in heaven for us."[7] "What gratitude," exclaims St. Gregory of Nyssa, "could be commensurate with such a blessing! What words, what expressions or thoughts could be adequate to praise such an unsurpassed grace worthily? Man rises above his own nature, since from being mortal he becomes immortal; being frail and defective, he becomes perfect and imperishable; from a man of a day and a creature of time, he becomes an eternally living being; in short, a mere human being is transmuted into God. For since he was deemed worthy to be made a child of God, he will, surely, participate in the Father's dignity and become the heir of all paternal goods and benefits."[8]

Truly this is wealth! *Mecum sunt divitiae.* More precious than all earthly riches, which are passing and of value only for this earthly life. Compared with sanctifying

---

5 Rom. 8:15.
6 Gal. 4:6.
7 1 Peter 1:4.
8 de beatitud. c. 7.

grace, according to the testimony of the Eternal Truth, all gold is as worthless sand, and silver is but dross. This is honor! "Et gloria!" Honor not due to worldly greatness. What, indeed, would be comparable to the dignity of a child of God, to the divine pleasure, the love and friendship of the Triune God?

Not satisfied with transforming us through grace into new creatures in Christ Jesus, the Holy Spirit imparts to us both the power and the means of living according to the new state of surpassing greatness, to perfect ourselves in it, and to enable us to attain to the blissful vision of God. These are of great diversity. They are precious and will easily promote sanctity in us, if zealously used. "*Mecum sunt opes superbae et justitia.*" "With me are superabundant goods and justice." If we use them in keeping with their worth, then, as St. Paul declares, we shall be transformed into the likeness of Christ, from clarity to clarity, through the Spirit of God.

b) *New supernatural gifts and virtues*

These marvellous powers are first of all the infused, supernatural virtues of faith, hope, and charity, as well as the moral virtues, preeminently Christian prudence, temperance, justice, and fortitude. As sanctifying grace transmutes the essence of our soul and endows it with a similitude to the divine nature, so these infused virtues transmute the faculties of our soul and qualify it for an activity resembling the divine.

These virtues do not of themselves, as a matter of course, remove or weaken our evil tendencies and our human frailties, but they are none the less precious gifts, heavenly powers. Endowed with them, we are enabled even here below in the land of exile, to confer with God as our Father, and always attain to a more intimate union with Him, the object of our soul's aspiration for eternal bliss. We can live at peace with our neighbor as brothers in Christ, as domestics of God and fellow-citizens of the saints, as St. Paul puts it in Ephesians.[9] We may now be dear to the demands of corrupt nature and walk in the spirit that deals the death blow to the works of the flesh and yields the fruits of heavenly modesty and meekness, humility, temperance, and chastity.

Naturally, the use of these faculties will not prove so easy and agreeable, as long as our earlier evil tendencies and customs still persist. But they, in turn, give us the light and strength to overcome these obstacles and to remove them from our path, and finally help us achieve ease, stability, and joyousness in the service of God, as it befits the children of God. This process is all the easier because those supernatural virtues are not the only kind of faculties or powers which the Holy Spirit imparts to our soul. *"Mecum sunt opes superbae."* Where He dwells, there are supernatural goods and inestimable riches at our disposal.

A goodly number of even more excellent gifts await us there. "And the spirit of the Lord shall rest upon him: the spirit of wisdom, and of understanding, the spirit of counsel and of fortitude, the spirit of knowledge and of obedience. And he shall be filled with the spirit of the fear of the Lord."[10] What the prophet foretells here of the Incarnate Son of God finds its fulfillment in a special way also

---

9 Eph. 2:19.
10 Isa. 11:2, 3.

in us, who through sanctifying grace have been made living members of Jesus Christ. The Seven Gifts of the Holy Spirit then became our property. They are at home, in very truth, in our soul. Marvellous, most precious treasures, indeed!

"*Opes superbae!*" In them we possess new, supernatural aptitudes, in virtue of which our soul is easily moved by the Holy Spirit to the most sublime acts and activities. They are, in a certain sense, the heavenly mainspring in the supernatural virtuous acts and invest them with a marvellous energy and resiliency. They are comparable to the seven lamps on the seven-branched golden candelabra in the temple at Jerusalem, which alternated day and night in burning before the Ark of the Covenant to the honor of God. They burn partly by day, that is, in the performance of our good works and, in part by night; that is in time of temptation or stress, in order to preserve us from the snares of sin and to unmask the deceits of Satan.[11]

The chalices of the lamps in the temple (as savants assert), were moulded into the shape of an ear; likewise, the gifts of the Holy Spirit endow our soul with an excellent spiritual ear, enabling it to perceive the inspirations of the sweet Divine Guest more readily and allow them to penetrate the interior. What could be compared with these precious gifts!

Inseparably united with sanctifying grace, they are our property. If we do not always perceive their wonderful influence, it is not that these gifts are lacking, but rather that our evil tendencies, too readily indulged, have fettered them. Let us endeavor, by faithful, persevering self-denial

---

11 Scheeben: *Glories of Divine Grace.*

to afford these divine powers more freedom in our heart, that we may be of those of whom it is said: "They shall renew their strength, they shall take wings as eagles, they shall run and not be weary, they shall walk and not faint."[12]

Should weariness and insecurity threaten us, He, of whom the prophet speaks, stands at our side. "The Lord is the everlasting God (who hath created the ends of the earth). He shall not faint, nor labour, neither is there any searching out of His wisdom. He giveth strength to the weary, and increaseth force and might to them that are not."[13] He gives it in abundance. And how is this accomplished, we may ask. The Holy Spirit, Sanctifier, Holiness Itself imparts it.

a) *The Actual Graces*

Through the actual, helping graces, the good thoughts and incentives, the Holy Spirit offers us this rich abundance. *"Mecum sunt divitiae et opes superbae."* Oh, the goodness, love and generosity of our God! This heavenly Gardener, to speak figuratively, is not satisfied in having transformed a miserable, creeping growth of northern moss into a noble vine and given it new, rich, and vital energies and powers. He also transplants it into a correspondingly milder climate, where the slumbering germs, moistened by heavenly dew and rain, irradiated by heavenly light, refreshed with heavenly warmth, are able to unfold and yield a plentiful harvest of the noblest fruits.

It is not enough for this Supreme King to have gathered

---

12 Isa. 40:31.
13 Isa. 40:28, 29.

poor, forsaken, depraved children of the streets into the bosom of His own family, to have allotted to them a princely income. He will also Himself be the Educator and train them to a mode of life befitting their state. He wills to cultivate princely sentiments and actions, to encourage, to help and give support.

Finally to abandon figurative speech: the infinite God, having endowed us through sanctifying grace with a new nature in the likeness of His own, and in the infused virtues and the gifts of the Holy Spirit given us new strength corresponding to His infinite perfections—after all these gracious acts, *He wills to cooperate in the activity with a new, supernatural assistance.* He is ready to fortify us incessantly with that strength which, according to the Council of Trent, always precedes the good works of the just, accompanies them and follows them, renders them pleasing to God and meritorious.[14]

Most assuredly, after the Holy Spirit has taken up His abode in our soul through sanctifying grace, He knocks incessantly upon our heart to stimulate us to do good. He speaks to us, in order to teach us all truth, admonishes us to perfect works, restrains us from sin, strengthens us in the hour of danger, and supports us when we vacillate and are about to succumb. If we heed His voice, it will be verified in us what Moses of old sang of his people: "The Lord led him about, and taught him, and he kept him as the apple of his eye. As the eagle enticing her young to fly, and hovering over them, he spread His wings and hath taken him and carried him on his shoulders."[15]

---

14 Sess. 6. c. 16 de justif.
15 Deut. 32:10, 11.

Provided we are willing, we can walk the ways of God securely, without stumbling against a stone. We can make rapid strides and attain to the degree of perfection which God in His goodness has destined for us. Grace is not lacking us. A veritable wealth is at our disposal and in the midst of these heavenly treasures, the spirit of God Himself. "Know you not that the Spirit of God dwelleth in you?"[16]

2. OUR GRATEFUL RETURN OF LOVE TO THE HOLY SPIRIT

What do we owe our most opulent, benign Heavenly Spirit for all His precious gifts?

a) *Gratitude, first and foremost*

"It is truly meet and right," Holy Church exhorts us daily, "proper and availing to salvation, that we should always and everywhere give thanks to God." Our thanksgiving will be commensurate with our esteem and appreciation of these wonderful gifts. The more we cleanse our heart of all attachment to creatures, the more fully will be our appreciation of these superb benefits. "But the sensual man perceiveth not these things that are of the Spirit of God."[17] *"Animalis homo non percipit ea, quae sunt Spiritus Dei,"* St. Paul writes. He does not perceive it because such a gift must be judged spiritually.

If through detachment we become spiritual men, we shall perceive it more and more. The pronouncements of Holy Writ will then no longer be mere words. In the depths

---

16 1 Cor. 3:16.
17 1 Cor. 2:14.

of our heart we will catch the sweet echo in praise of God's gracious gifts. "I preferred (heavenly wisdom and grace) her before kingdoms and thrones, and esteemed riches nothing in comparison of her. Neither did I compare unto her any precious stone. I loved her above health and beauty, and chose to have her instead of light: for her light cannot be put out. All good things came to me together with her, and innumerable riches through her hands."[18]

Thus we become aware, silent, and experience in ourselves the inexpressible worth of the gifts the Holy Spirit has deposited in our soul. Self-evidently, then, our heart turns in grateful and loving appreciation to the Divine Dispenser of such treasures. With St. Paul we sing and make melody: "Singing and making melody in your hearts to the Lord,"[19] because of the superabundant gifts He has apportioned to us.

We rejoice in these gifts which, as the Wise Man says in the Old Testament, are nothing less than a breath of the strength and power of God, a pure outpouring of the magnificence of the Almighty, goods that surpass by far the splendor of the sun and the glory of the starlit sky. They ravish even the eye of God, win the friendship and love of the whole heavenly court. And the reality is of still greater magnitude and glory than all the images are able to represent it.

Oh, give thanks to the benign Giver who so generously lavishes His gifts. Let it be fulfilled in us what the prophet foretold of the New Jerusalem: *"Invenietur in ea . . . gratiarum actio, et vox laudis"* "Joy and gladness shall be

---

18 Wis. 7:8-11.
19 Eph. 5:19.

found therein, thanksgiving and the voice of praise."[20] Did
not the mighty Spirit of God through His grace build up
our soul from all its ruins into a veritable city of God, in
whose interior He Himself dwells? Has He not transformed
the desert into a paradise of pleasure and turned her
wilderness into the garden of the Lord? Does He not
continue to lavish solicitous care upon His garden, to protect His city, to govern it, improve its status and well-
being? "The Lord ruleth me: and I shall want nothing."[21]
This we must proclaim, and from it must arise our thanksgiving and ceaseless song of praise.

> b) *"Gaudium et laetitia invenietur in ea"*
> *Joyousness, indeed, is the second thing*
> *we owe the Holy Spirit*

Does sadness harmonize with the dignity of a child
of God? The Holy Spirit made us such through sanctifying
grace. "Behold," exclaims the Beloved Disciple, "Behold
what manner of charity the Father hath bestowed upon us,
that we should be called, and should be the sons of God![22]
How can moodiness and despondency fraternize with the
glorious talents, the marvellous forces and powers, which
have been infused into us together with the love of God?
Is not the slightest degree of these virtues and the seven
gifts of infinitely greater worth than the loftiest natural
endowments and talents? Finally, can narrowness and
pusillanimity be made to harmonize with the actual graces
generously offered us, with the uninterrupted actual assist-

---

20 Isa. 51:3.
21 Ps. 22:1.
22 1 John 3:1.

ance He deigns to bestow on us in whom we can do all things?

But corrupt nature, not yet wholly dead, the evil tendencies that again assert themselves, the temptations that annoy us so much, the fatigues and difficulties and hardships that lie in wait for us at every turn, are a constant challenge to our best efforts. In the midst of all this, can one still be cheerful and buoyant of spirit? We may sorrow, if we choose, and lament over it at the right time and in the right spirit, with the sorrow of which Jesus speaks: "Blessed are the sorrowful for they shall be comforted." This sorrow, however, is far removed from despondency, from impatience and anger, or narrowness and timidity.

It rather elevates and expands the heart, infuses new courage and confidence. It bears within itself the germ of holy joy and good cheer, which follow it upon every step. It never loses sight of the superabundant gifts which, in spite of our dire misery, are gratuitously bestowed on us and remain our own property. It clarifies our spiritual outlook and shows the ways and means of extracting profit even from all this abjection and misery, and of augmenting our treasure of virtues and merits for eternity.

Would that we could always view the matter in this bright light! Interior joy and comfort would render the service of God more agreeable. What shall we reply to this suggestion? It is our privilege to strive for this grace. The measure of our spirit of faith and of consolation sufficient to lift our spirits to self-sacrifice in spite of mishap and reverses, is within our grasp under all circumstances. Our only care must be to see that the Holy Spirit is always free to execute His sublime office of loving Comforter in our hearts. We presently indicate the means.

c) *The faithful utilization of grace is the*
most efficacious means to this noble end

We owe it to our Benign Giver. These precious gifts bestowed on us so generously deserve to be cherished with the greatest solicitude. They help us over seemingly insurmountable difficulties and aid us to attain to the eternal delights of heaven, to enjoy a lofty participation in the bliss of the Triune God. How this can be done may be said in a few words. We need but walk faithfully in the path of our holy Vows and the Holy Rule. There is no better, more perfect means of cooperating with grace for us, fortified by obedience and charity and confidence in God strong enough not to be shaken by obstacles and temptations. The Holy Spirit will shine into our soul and fill it with light and life, if we call upon Him. He directs and guides us in this endeavor without doubt, as it were, surpassing Himself in doing His utmost to advance the soul by His copious graces to a high degree of perfection He will pray in us, who is Holiness Itself.

Day by day, He will be ready to hold out new and even greater spiritual incentives and efficient graces. In this way He would give us strength and energy for our mission and lead us from step to step up to the perfection that qualifies us to accomplish great things for God and the salvation of souls.

This perfection will finally earn for us a high degree of glory in eternity in the measure in which we are able to make sacrifices and deny ourselves. This resplendent glory will afford us the inexpressible happiness of joining through endless ages with the angels and saints, glorifying the Triune God forever and forever.

CHAPTER III

THE LOVE OF GOD

> *"Look to him that you may be radiant with joy."*[1]
> *"I have come to cast fire on the earth, and what will I but that it be kindled?"*[2]

In these words our Divine Saviour has in the mind of Holy Church, for the Office of the feast of the Sacred Heart, expressed His ardent desire to see the fire of the love of God kindled in the whole world. His entire earthly life, His bitter passion and death, everything served His supreme aim. His continued life in the Blessed Eucharist, from day to day, until the end of time, serves this one divine purpose and aim. "I have come to cast fire on the earth, and what will I but that it be kindled?"

1. KINDLING THE FIRE OF LOVE IN OUR HEARTS

How can we in a special way give joy to His Sacred Heart? Obviously by responding to His Heart's intense love and zealously striving to be a true apostle of sacrifice and prayer. Jesus wills to kindle the fire of love and fan it into flame. With the greatest joy we will cherish it in our

---

1 Ps. 33:6.
2 Luke 12:49.

hearts. "I press on towards the goal," in the spirit of St. Paul "to the prize of God's heavenly call in Christ Jesus."[3]

a) *There is nothing more precious than this love*

The gifts of nature are manifold and rich; the marvellous gifts of grace are numerous, but the crown of all is love. Health and strength are to be treasured, culture and knowledge are valuable. Still more precious are the manifold virtues that adorn the heart, yet all are surpassed by love.

What gold is among the metals, the diamond among the gems, that is love among all the gifts and graces which ennoble and dignify human nature. But still more, love is the consummation of everything else, it is perfection. For what should we, therefore, strive with greater zeal than for love? What in all the world should we wish to possess and acquire in a higher degree than love? "But above all these things," we read in Colossians, "have charity, which is the bond of perfection."[4]

b) *Without love or charity, all else is useless*

What should it profit us without love? Nothing, absolutely nothing. This is no exaggeration. Hear the dynamic Paul:[5]

> *"If I should speak with the tongues of men and of angels, but do not have charity,*

---

3 Phil. 3:14.
4 Col. 3:14.
5 1 Cor. 13:1, 2, 3.

I have become as sounding bass or a tinkling cymbal.
And if I have prophecy and know all mysteries and all
knowledge,
And if I have all faith so as to remove mountains, yet
do not have charity, I am nothing.
And if I distribute all my goods to feed the poor,
And if I deliver my body to be burned, yet do not
have charity, it profits me nothing."

These are the words of a St. Paul, who as few others took up this divine fire into his heart, knew its tremendous power from experience, and illumined by its light clearly sensed the true value of all things, and was competent to judge of them correctly; for him love is all-surpassing. What signficance must we attribute to the admonition which the Apostle, aglow with love, attaches to the words: *"Sectamini caritatem!" "Aim towards love!"*

Indeed, we want it; we will not be content with the measure of love that is ours by God's grace, but will strive effectively to increase it more and more in our hearts. Enlightened by a loftier light in holy ecstasy, Thomas a-Kempis tells us: "Nothing is sweeter than love, nothing stronger, nothing higher, nothing wider, nothing more pleasant, nothing fuller or better in heaven or on earth; for love is born of God and cannot rest but in Him, above all created things. One who loves, knows the cry of this voice of love. A loud cry in the ears of God is that ardent affection of the soul which says: "Oh, Thou art all mine, and I am wholly Thine, my God, my Love!"[6] For such love we must expend the utmost. St. Paul says we will be rooted

6 Imit. Bk. 3, ch. 5.

and founded in charity," that we "may be filled with all the fulness of God."[7]

Let us ponder it well. Charity replenishes us "unto the fulness of God." What else could it mean but that our soul is enriched through love with all of God's good gifts. In very truth, the words of Sacred Scripture apply to love: "Now all good things came to me together with her, and innumerable riches through her hands."[8]

According to St. Paul, all other virtues follow in the wake of charity. "Charity," he writes in his Epistle to the Corinthians, "is patient, is kind; charity envieth not, dealeth not perversely; is not puffed up; is not ambitious, seeketh not her own; is not provoked to anger, thinketh no evil . . . she rejoiceth not in iniquity, but rejoiceth with the truth; beareth all things, believeth all things, hopeth all things, endureth all things."[9]

Love is truly a marvellous power. "Love can achieve anything; and it doth perform and effect many things, where he that loveth not fainteth and falleth prostrate. . . . When weary, it is not tired; when straitened is not constrained; when frightened is not disturbed; but, like a vivid flame, and a burning torch, it mounteth upwards."[10] It breaks through all hindrances and lifts itself up beyond all creatures, unto the most intimate union with God, the Supreme Good, Eternal Beauty, Immeasurable Goodness.

O marvellous power of charity!

It comes from God, leads to God, unites us inseparably

7 Eph. 3:17 ff.
8 Wis. 7:11.
9 1 Cor. 13:4, 7.
10 Imit. Bk. 3. ch. 5.

with Him. Who then shall separate him that truly loves
from God? "Shall tribulation or distress? or famine? or
nakedness? or danger? or persecution? or the sword? ...
But in all these things we overcome, because of Him that
hath loved us,"[11] and whom we wish to love in return. No
harm can come to him, for the charity that fills his heart
transforms everything that the natural man regards as
misery and misfortune into purest gain. "We know," writes
St. Paul again, "that to them that love God, all things work
together unto good."[12]

It is easy to understand why the loving Heart of Jesus,
who so ardently wills our happiness, longs for nothing more
intensely, than to kindle His love in our hearts. "I am come
to cast fire on the earth: and what will I but that it be
kindled?"[13] We can readily see that all who truly love the
Lord can afford Him no greater pleasure than to open their
hearts wide to this newly-kindled fire. "*Amorem tuum
solum cum gratia tua mihi dones.*" Give me Thy love and
Thy grace, and I am rich enough, and desire nothing more.
How Jesus delights to answer this plea, provided it be
sincere! It may not be a mere petition, a mere longing or
wish. We must do all in our power to make it possible for
Jesus to fulfill our request.

2. SPECIAL MEANS OF KINDLING THE FIRE OF LOVE IN OUR
   HEARTS

We must first of all remove the obstacles to the love of
God, and then foster the most tender union with the

11 Rom. 8:35, 37.
12 Rom. 8:28.
13 Luke 12:49.

furnace of Love itself. For you know that a piece of damp wood does not ignite readily and yields much smoke. If you would have it flare up brightly, you must see that it is thoroughly dried. This is precisely true of our spiritual striving. Before the love of God can fill the soul it must first be prepared by the removal of all obstacles and foreign substances.

a) *The chief obstacle to the love of God*

St. John tells us what is the chief obstacle to the love of God. "If any man love the world, the charity of the Father is not in him."[14] Love of the world, attachment to its varied offerings, the disordered love of creatures, the sum total of all these is an obstacle to the love of God in our hearts. Therefore he exhorts us: "Love not the world, nor the things which are in the world."[15]

A religious may say: Thank God, I have left the world, and thereby laid low the greatest hindrance to the love of God in my heart. Certainly, through your entrance into the cloister you find detachment a simpler matter; it is easier, as a rule, to keep your heart free and unhampered, entirely devoted to God. Consider, though, that it will not suffice for you to have left the world exteriorly; you must take further precautionary steps to banish completely from your heart, the insinuations of the false and deceptive worldly loves.

It is possible for us to overcome all obstacles to the love of God and to keep the heart free enough for genuine love

---

14 1 John 2:15.
15 Ibid.

of God to dwell within, making of the soul an earthly paradise. It is feasible at the cost of sacrifice and oblation. Simultaneously, there may be much disordered attachment lurking in the background, holding fast to the tendrils of the unwary heart. If we try resolutely to conquer these delicate attachments and illusive affections more and more, and mercilessly take up the combat against venial sin, we are gaining strength. We may, however, actually kindle the divine fire to a blazing flame, provided we resolutely remove whatever may be harmful, even if not sinful, yet may lead to sin and prepare the soil for ultimate transgressions.

Cultivating the love of God in this way may seem wearisome and laborious, indeed. There is simply no other way. Love finds nothing burdensome. Self-love with its inordinate cravings for comfort and sensual gratifications, for honors and praise, clinging passionately to creatures and hoping for everything from them, relaxes its hold only reluctantly and after stout resistance. What can it avail? It must be so. In the *Spiritual Exercises* of St. Ignatius we read: "Everyone may be convinced that he makes progress in spiritual matters, especially in the love of God, only in so far as he abandons self-love, self-gratification, and self-will."

Still, this imperative is not so painful as our blind self-love in league with the tempter would make us believe. Or is it hard to forfeit a penny in exchange for a gold piece? Are the sacrifices we make and the inevitable denials even comparable with the increase of the love of God that is our gain?

What is the verdict of the Wise Man in Sacred Scripture regarding this love? "I preferred her before kingdoms and thrones, and esteemed riches nothing in comparison of her. Neither did I compare unto her any precious stone: for all gold in comparison of her, is as a little sand, and silver in respect of her shall be counted as clay. I loved her above health and beauty, and chose to have her instead of light: for her light cannot be put out."[16]

Let us, therefore, not allow our shortsightedness to rest on the trivial goods we are to forfeit. Let us fix our gaze rather on the immeasurable treasure, as the Holy Spirit styles it, which we are to gain. The love of God must be our all. Let us often pray, "Give me only Thy grace, and I am rich enough, am honored enough, and I desire naught else." This generates strength and courage and joyous dilation of the heart. In this spirit one gladly makes any sacrifice asked of him. The one who loves finds nothing hard and burdensome in the service of the loved one. Thus the heart, gradually freed more and more of all obstacles to the love of God, is capable of receiving in ever higher degree the fire that Jesus has come to bring to earth: "For the Lord bestows His benedictions there where He finds empty vessels,"[17] that is, hearts free of disordered love of the world and of self. "And the more perfectly," a-Kempis continues, " one foresakes the things below, and the more he dies to himself by contempt of himself, the more speedily grace cometh, entereth in more plentifully, and the higher it elevateth a heart that is free to higher union with God."[18]

---

16 Wis. 7:8, 9, 10.
17 Imit. Bk. 4, ch. 15.
18 Ibid.

b) *God is light, life, and love*

In order to attain to a great love of God it will not suffice to remove all hindrances; we must kindle the fire in our hearts to a bright, glowing flame. Where is this union with the furnace of Love Itself in its proper setting and atmosphere? Where is it found? It is in the Holy Eucharist, at the Holy Sacrifice of the Mass, where we gather daily about the Sacrificial Altar of the Lord, in order to become one with Him in loving immolation. It is in Holy Communion, where we partake of the Eucharistic Banquet of the Mass and rest on the Heart of Christ; there the soul is immersed in the infinite ocean of the love of His divine mercies. Finally, it is before the Tabernacle, where we gather in moments of leisure or under pressure of cares; there upon the Altar of His Merciful Heart incessantly burns the fire of love for us in order to kindle our hearts to brightest flame—these are the moments when the unquenchable flame of divine love conquers our hearts.

The Altar is, indeed, the hearth of the Love of God. Jesus becomes present here anew, so that united with us, He may love His and our Father, more and more. Of every holy Mass, the word rings true: "I have come to cast fire on the earth: and what will I but that it be kindled?" The flame of His love rises upward, raising our hearts aloft with a holy vehemence. Through Him, and in Him, and with Him, is to Thee, God the Father, in the unity of the Holy Ghost, all honor and glory.

But still more. Our Divine Saviour comes not only to love His Father in union with us. He comes personally to enkindle fire in our souls, in the most intimate union of hearts in Holy Communion. As often as Jesus enters our heart, He sets it aglow with new life and new love. We should hardly be able to recognize our soul, could we see it both before and after, in the light of profound faith and adoring love. The Triune God has anew and in an intensified manner set up His dwelling in our soul, and there He abides as in His Temple. But God is life, light, and love. This His life He lives in us, and His light shines in us, and His love glows in us, with greater splendor through each new union. This new love thus stems from God. And "We have known and have believed the charity which God hath to us. God is charity: and he that abideth in charity, abideth in God."[19]

Every morning in union with our Sacramental Saviour, we have tendered God our love in holy, joyful giving, and He has then personally given us a new increase of glowing love of God. He remains with us on the Altar in the Tabernacle, where the holy fire incessantly burns; from its glowing warmth we can again and again kindle the flame of our love as often as we choose.

There is, according to St. Magdalen of Pazzi, no more effective means of reaching perfection than this Most Holy Sacrament, the Sacrament of Love. And if you knew how to profit of this Treasure, she continues her exhortation to her daughters, you would in a very short time be replenished with heavenly love.

Well, then, *"Accedite et illuminamini!"* "Come ye to Him and be enlightened."[20] There on the Altar, the radiant Sun of our inner life is bright and resplendent. Let us regard not only its brilliance, its beauty, its warmth, nor

19 1 John 4:16.
20 Ps. 33:6.

forget that this Sun emits rays of light, of fire, and of love unto all hearts. As often as we kneel at the foot of the Altar, be it at Holy Mass or in intimate union with Him after Holy Communion; be it in moments of silent adoration and confidential whisperings with the Beloved at our Eucharistic Visits when day is done—in all these moments we are under the immediate touch of the rays of His love emanating from His Heart.

Our love will be kindled more and more as it approaches this fire of immeasurable warmth and mercy so that it may in truth be said of us: In His love we live, we move, and have our being. What a beautiful thought for contemplating love! And when after having been borne by love, we shall have finished our course, we shall be immersed in the immense ocean of the love of the Triune God. Uninterruptedly we shall gaze upon the splendor, the beauty, the magnificence of the highest, the Infinite Good. For all eternity we shall then praise that Heart whence flowed all the delights of love and will flow to us unceasingly without end.

CHAPTER IV

OF THE KNOWLEDGE OF JESUS CHRIST

> *"Now this is eternal life: that they may know Thee, the only true God, and Jesus Christ, whom Thou has sent."*[1]

1. THE SUBLIME KNOWLEDGE OF JESUS CHRIST

"Now this is eternal life: that they may know Thee, the only true God, and Jesus Christ, whom Thou hast sent."[1]

In these words of Christ's Prayer we find clearly and definitely enunciated the whole significance of the knowledge of Christ. In it consists our true life, our salvation for time and for eternity, our bliss, our All. Thanks be to God, we are so happy as to possess this knowledge already in an appreciable degree. This is a grace for which we shall never be able to render adequate thanks to God. It is also a grace that we must guard solicitously and daily seek to grow in it. To us applies the exhortation of St. Peter: *"Crescite vero in gratia et in cognitione Domini nostri et Salvatoris Jesu Christi.* But grow in grace, and in the knowledge of our Lord and Saviour Jesus Christ."[2]

---

1 John 17:3.
2 2 Peter 3:18.

a) *In order to heed this exhortation, we must cherish a great and effective desire for greater knowledge of Jesus*

Only what we ardently desire will be the object of our earnest striving and search. But who is Jesus? we may ask. He is the Book which the blessed spirits peruse for all eternity without probing its depths. Let us hear what the Archangel Gabriel said when announcing the conception and the birth of the Lord: "Behold," he said to Mary, "thou shalt conceive in thy womb, and shalt bring forth a son: and thou shalt call His name Jesus. He shall be great and shall be called the *Son of the Most High.*" And again, "The Holy which shall be born of thee shall be called the *Son of God.*" Jesus is, therefore, the Son of the Most High, the Son of God, not only a likeness but the most perfect image of the Father, one essence with the Father. He is the splendor of His glory, not only a reflection, but the representation of the whole glory itself, without the least diminution. "We saw His glory," St. John writes, "the glory as it were of the only begotten of the Father, full of grace and truth."[3] Jesus Christ, God of God, Light of Light, true God and true Man, an infinite, immeasurable Good. How ardently we should desire to know this surpassing Good! A slight desire would be wholly unworthy and a gross insult to the Lord.

b) *Let us hear the prophet Isaias*

No better description of the grandeur of Our Saviour could be devised than we have it from the lips of the

---

3 John 1:14.

"Evangelist of the Incarnation": "There shall come forth a rod out of the root of Jesse, and a flower shall rise up out of this root. And the spirit of the Lord shall rest upon Him: the spirit of wisdom, and of understanding, the spirit of counsel, and of fortitude, the spirit of knowledge and of godliness. And He shall be filled with the spirit of fear of the Lord. Justice shall be the girdle of His loins: and faith the girdle of His reins. He standeth for the ensign of the people. Him the Gentiles shall beseech, and His sepulchre shall be glorious. He shall set up a standard unto the nations, and shall gather together the dispersed of Juda from the four quarters of the earth.[4] "You shall say in that day: Sing ye to the Lord, for He hath done great things. Rejoice and praise, O thou habitation of Sion: for great is He that is in the midst of thee, the Holy One of Israel."[5]

Truly, Jesus it great in our midst. Even prescinding from the fulness of the Godhead that is His, Jesus is and will always be great and unspeakably wonderful, full of glory and grandeur in our midst, in His Most Holy Humanity. Titles of honor and renown have been bestowed upon princes and personalities of note. We may gather them all, all without exception and with far greater right confer them on Our Saviour. Yet with none of these designations shall we come even nigh exhausting the ineffable glories in which His Holy Humanity is resplendent and transfigured.

---

4 Isa. 11:1, 2, 5, 10, 12.
5 Isa. 12:5, 6.
6 Col. 2:9.

Jesus, all wise; Jesus, prudent, meek and gentle, and mild; Jesus, all good, all beautiful; Jesus, beneficent, most merciful; Jesus, strong and formidable; Jesus, most faithful and just; Jesus, great and victorious! O glorious Jesus, for Thee alone! Jesus, the inexpressible, *ineffabilis*, but for that reason also *totus desiderabilis*, to be desired, to be loved, with heart and soul. Thou deservest that all our desires, all thirst for knowledge be concentrated in the sublime knowledge of Thy Most Holy Person.

c) *Would it be possible to rest satisfied with the knowledge we already have?*

If such were our wish, this moderation on our part would indicate plainly that our actual knowledge of Christ Jesus is very light and meager. Why, we ask. It is peculiar desire the more we grow in it. *"Qui te gustant, esuriunt, qui bibunt adhuc sitiunt, desiderare nesciunt nisi Jesum, quem diligunt."* How could it be otherwise! It is an immeasurable Good, and as often as our soul taste of it, we realize anew that infinitely more is lacking.

We know Jesus, and to the Heavenly Father be eternal thanks for having called "us unto the fellowship of His Son";[7] for simultaneously enjoining upon us a great knowledge, love, and imitation of Jesus for our life's work. Still our actual knowledge of Jesus is none the less pitifully slight. Holy Church requires an entire year to give us, as it were, only the outlines of this Divine Model, merely the shadow of Jesus Christ. The angelic choirs, the hosts of the saints in heaven, fix their gaze inadvertently upon

---

7 1 Cor. 1:9.

this Book, *"in tuo lumine videbimus lumen."* In Thy Light
they behold Light. Day and night they scan its pages, and
will continue to read it for all eternity. They will be transported by its contents into eternal delights and eternal
ecstasy, without ever exhausting it.

There is One only who comprehends the whole content
of this Volume, only God is capable of probing its depths.
The beauty and splendor of its pages suffice in very truth
to fill the infinite Spirit of God entirely, and to constitute
the immeasurable immensity of the Beatitude of God.
"This is my beloved Son' in whom I am well pleased."[8]

The same Son of God, the same Godman, the same
Jesus, who is the Father's eternal delight, is He in whose
knowledge we should daily grow; *"crescite vero in cognitione Domini nostri et Salvatoris Jesu Christi."* Should we
not be animated by the most ardent desire? An object so
sublime deserves it truly.

2. THE TRUE NATURE OF THIS KNOWLEDGE

Our desire must be great, also, because of the nature
of this knowledge. The more a good is the work of grace,
the more God exacts on our part at least a sincere and
fervent desire to secure this priceless good.

An intimate knowledge of the Lord, however, is in a
special manner a work of grace. Our Lord Himself tells us,
"No man can come to Me, except the Father draw him."[9]
We have still greater need of support from above if we
would come very close to Jesus, know Him perfectly, be
really aware of all the Saviour means to us. Many have

---

8 Matt. 3:17.
9 John 6:44.

a wide knowledge of all that pertains to the Saviour, perhaps the most that may be said of Him theoretically, but in spite of it, of Jesus Himself they know very little, their knowledge is still mediocre. The *intima cognitio nostri Domini,* the most profound interior knowledge of Our Lord, as St. Ignatius designates it, is not so much the fruit of study as a gift of the Holy Spirit. There is a vast difference, therefore, between the knowledge of Jesus Christ that derives from study and that which comes to us in prayer, in meditation, taught by the Holy Spirit. *"Est magna differentia inter sapientiam illuminati et devoti viri et scientiam litterati atque studiosi clerici,"* says Thomas a-Kempis.

Though the man of prayer may not have so profound and extensive a knowledge of many things, to him will be given what transforms knowledge into true wisdom, namely, the intimate *"sentire et gustare,"* as spiritual writers style it. His whole soul is permeated by the object of his knowledge; his mind is bent on learning and growing stronger in this deeper insight. He becomes interior and tastes what Jesus means to us.

The *Heavenly Father* draws the man of profound interior prayer close to His beloved Son. *Jesus* unveils His Countenance to him, for he hearkens to the cry of his heart: *"ostende faciem tuam, et salvi erimus."* "Show us Thy Countenance, and we are saved." The *Holy Spirit opens the* eye of his soul and clarifies his gaze. Thus the man of interior prayer experiences something of what St. John declares of himself: "We saw His glory, the glory as it were of the only begotten of the Father, full of grace and truth."[10]

---

10 John 1:14.

This genuine intimate knowledge of Jesus Christ is nothing less than the work of the Most Blessed Trinity. The Three Divine Persons are animated by the intense desire to transmit it. Must we not also accept it with whole-souled readiness? Or at least cherish an insatiable longing for so precious a Good?

It is not necessary for us to envision extraordinary manifestations of the Saviour in our soul. It would surely be infinitely worthy of Christ if there were many souls to whom He could manifest Himself in a higher degree, souls who seek nothing outside of Jesus. These souls would through the most faithful, most persevering, magnanimous self-denial, be qualified to take Jesus into their hearts wholly and entirely, and finally be able to declare in the truest sense of the word: "With Christ I am nailed to the cross. I live, now not I, but Christ liveth in me."[11] I am for the moment not thinking of this superb degree of the knowledge and union with Jesus, though I do not exclude it altogether.

The degree of the knowledge of Jesus Christ which is obligatory of all religious and priests without exception, in virue of their noble calling to tend toward perfection, is so stringent as to exact an ardent desire on their part to attain it. Such a high degree is a grace, a grace to be treasured most highly. Since we have the happiness of serving God in the state of perfection, we have been vouchsafed many spiritual lights. Yet even the least conspicuous, the least among them, are graces, gifts, favors of the Lord to be greatly esteemed and treasured. All this is wholly and entirely a gift, a grace and a gracious gesture of God,

---

11 Gal. 2:19, 20.

Our Lord, a visitation of the Holy Spirit, who would guide us to the truth, to an ever more perfect knowledge of Jesus Christ, the Way, the Truth, and the Life. Is it not fitting for us to appreciate these graces as they deserve, and to hold communion with God in prayer, in holy longings? O Jesus, Come and show Thyself to us more and more!

3. THE WORKINGS OF GRACE IN THE SOUL

There is still a third reason for striving earnestly to acquire this comforting, tender, intimate knowledge of Jesus. It is found in the efficacious workings of this understanding penetration into the deeps of Divine Beneficence. In a beautiful medieval hymn, these effects are paraphrased: *"Quando cor nostrum visitas tunc lucet ei veritas, mundi vilescit vanitas et intus fervet caritas."* In truth, when God endows us with a deeper knowledge of Christ Jesus, the light of truth, of all truth, illumines the soul. What is still more, what is the main consideration, the actual objective: the knowledge of Jesus of which we are speaking, and which is the work of grace, attaches us in faithful love to His Most Holy Person. It fills our heart with a sound detestation of earthly things, with disesteem and contempt of things worldly. In short, it generates love and imitation of Christ.

Mere knowledge, no matter how profound, is unable to *kindle the heart,* much less to *transform* it, but the knowledge of Jesus Christ infused into our soul by the Holy Spirit possesses *creative power: et renovabis faciem terrae.* Thou wilt renew the face of the earth. It is not like the light of the moon and the stars, which only sparkles and shines, but rather like the light of the sun, which radiates warmth and evokes life wherever it penetrates. Where Jesus, the Sun of Justice, appears there love glows, there all virtues sprout, grow, and wax strong, and mature to a rich harvest of the most beautiful fruits pleasing to God.

Let us therefore place no barriers to our desires. Let us not heed our blind, corrupt nature, which is repulsed by the thought of the imitation of Our Lord and Saviour, constricts the heart, cools the heart's desires for the knowledge of Our Lord, and only too often tempts us to be content with the ignoble lassitude that is ours. Nature surmises that in the light of this knowledge her whole perverseness is not only brought to light, but that constant denial confronts her. This is actually the case, for it has been said: *"Christo confixus sum cruci.* With Christ I am nailed to the cross." But we read further: "I live, now not I, but Christ liveth in me."

This is the very thing we desired. We must strike out beyond the narrow confines of our self-love. We must rise above ourselves. In spite of the cowardice, the indifference, the opposition of our corrupt nature, we will ever more ardently long for the genuine knowledge of Jesus Christ. With St. Paul we will regard as disadvantage, detriment, and dross, everything that these disordered inclinations consider as gain, when compared with the all-surpassing knowledge of Jesus. To this knowledge all our wishes, our whole longing and our desires should tend with devoted love and enthusiasm.

These desires must be not only intense, but effectively active, overcoming hurdles and obstacles with great fervor and alacrity. Herein lies the foremost proof of the sincerity of our desire, for neither feeling nor sentiment but active cooperation with the means at our disposal testifies to the sincerity of our efforts to attain to the surpassing knowledge of Christ Our Lord.

We are familiar with these means and have several times touched upon them in these pages, but briefly they are: a) purity of heart; b) meditation on the Mysteries of Christ; c) faithful cooperation with the knowledge already acquired.

a) *Purity of soul—a cleansing of the heart*

This is not confined to the cleansing from sins. They constitute the darkness wherein the light, even if it be bright as the sun, does not penetrate. It must be a cleansing also of the roots of sin, of every inordinate tendency. These are like a fog through which the light of the sun penetrates only slightly as in a twilight dusk. To the extent that we conquer these tendencies by persistent self-denial, the eye of the spirit will be clarified, and we shall know Jesus ever better, understand Him better, become aware of Him in intimate union with Him, and experience here below the beautiful words, "Blessed are the clean of heart for they shall see God."

b) *Love of meditation on the Mysteries of Christ*

We know what treasures are hidden behind this seemingly insignificant exterior. Let us, therefore, endeavor, through the year to make these reflections in the spirit of St. Ignatius, when he teaches us: "*desiderando magis cognoscere Verbum aeternum incarnatum.*" We should make our meditation "with genuine desire to know more and more the Eternal, Incarnate Word of God."

According to the *Spiritual Exercises,* we should express this desire in a devout preparatory prayer. Before beginning the reflection, we should ask for the grace of a more intimate knowledge of Jesus and greater love of Him. Such a prayer will be heard. Nothing does the Heavenly Father bestow more gladly and more generously than the knowledge of His well-beloved Son in whom He is well pleased. He gave Him the solemn promise: *"Clarificavi et iterum clarificabo.* I have both glorified It, and will glorify It again."[12] This occurs in a special manner in the hearts of those finally, who

> c) *Faithfully cooperate with the knowledge already acquired*

This means that in so far as they are able and understand, they will *imitate Christ.* Only when the student has demonstrated his ability to sketch from the model at large with facility, will the master artist allow him to concentrate on the details of the figure. Jesus is the Divine Model whom the Heavenly Father holds up for our admiration and eventual imitation. Look at it, ponder it fervently, then act in accordance with your understanding and appreciation. To the extent that this is done and the once recognized traits find expression in us, God will deign to reveal to us new traits and characteristics. He will show us in ever brighter light His Son, so that, as St. Paul has it, "we are transformed into the same image from glory to glory."[13]

If we are faithful, we shall attain not only a mediocre

12 John 12:28.
13 2 Cor. 3:18.

knowledge of Our Lord and Saviour Jesus Christ, but shall eventually reach the state which St. Paul holds out to all, the plenitude of knowledge, that "being instructed in charity unto all riches of fulness of understanding unto the knowledge of the mystery of God the Father and of Christ Jesus: in whom are hid all the treasures of wisdom and knowledge."[14]

"If you follow Me perseveringly," said Our Lord to Saint Margaret Mary Alacoque, "I will reveal Myself to you that you may know Me." O blissful knowledge!

"In that day there shall be a fountain open to the house of David, and to the inhabitants of Jerusalem."[15]

---

14 Col. 2:2.
15 Zach. 13:1.

CHAPTER V

OF THE GROWTH OF CHRIST IN US

"I will hear what the Lord God will speak to me."[1]
"He who has My commandments and keeps them, he it is who loves Me."[2]

Through sanctifying grace Jesus is born in us; He must also grow in us and reign. This exacts of us the fostering of the inner life, which embraces a trinity: a life of recollection, a life in Christ Jesus, through love and the practice of virtue, and finally, since these are otherwise unattainable, by means of mortification.

We shall inspect the life of recollection and inwardness as prerequisites of growth in Christ Jesus. That grace may gain the upper hand and reign in us, we must heed her promptings and shun the turmoil of worldliness or the unruly demands of passion. The wealth of the inner life is Jesus Himself living in us by grace; the theological virtues, charity, above all; through the moral virtues: put ye on Our Lord Jesus Christ, His humility, His obedience, His patience . . . ; through the Seven Gifts of the Holy Spirit; through the actual graces of enlightenment and motivation.

---

1 Ps. 84.
2 John 14:21.

All this wealth is intimately related to Jesus; the unfolding of these graces and gifts forms the inner life, which is a participation in the life of Jesus. Mortification is essential for cultivating the interior life, avoiding the pitfalls of error and temptation, of selfishness and lassitude in God's service. The mystery of the inner life may be summarized as mortification and denial of self.

With grateful hearts we revert once more to the feast of the Nativity of Our Saviour, just recently celebrated. With heart and soul we joined in the Gloria of the angelic hosts, and again and again we taste the delights of the aroma of heavenly peace and good will that radiates from the Saviour's Crib to all men of good will. This peace should not pass away with the Christmastide, but permanently abide with us and grow to such proportions that we may be able to impart of its fulness to countless others.

This can easily be done. Our heart resembles the Crib of the Infant God. Through sanctifying grace, the Prince of Peace was born in it. Jesus must now grow in us, must wax strong and reign supreme in our hearts that with St. Paul we may say: "I live, now not I, but Christ lives in me."[3] Through a life of recollection or a true interior life this beautiful state will come to pass.

1. RECOLLECTION AND AN INTERIOR LIFE REQUISITES FOR THE GROWTH OF CHRIST IN US

Jesus will grow in us in the same measure as divine grace increases in the soul; as it becomes powerful, strong, and dominant; as it permeates all our actions, our thoughts and desires, guides and directs them. This is hardly pos-

3 Gal. 2:20.

sible for grace to achieve if we refuse to give the necessary
and fitting attention to grace, if we neither esteem it, nor
listen to its voice, and *fail to understand its directions*

   a) *The first requisite for the strengthening of grace,*
      therefore, is to have eye and ear alert for Jesus, for
      the sound of His whisperings of grace in our hearts

"*Audiam quid loquatur in me* Dominus. I will hear
what the Lord God will speak to me."[4] Recollection of
spirit is, therefore, absolutely necessary. But still more is
required. The voice of the Saviour is gentle and mild, the
guidance of His grace is serene and calm; its wishes and
demands are without impetuosity or noise: "*non in com-
motione Dominus.*" "The Lord is not in the wind, the Lord
is not in the earthquake."[5] If they are to be understood and
heeded, calm and tranquillity must prevail, the turmoil of
the exterior life must cease. "*Sileant omnes creaturae in
conspectu tuo. Tu mihi loquere solus,*" says a-Kempis.
"May all creatures be silent before Thy Countenance, O
Lord, Thou alone, speak to me."

Even if we must live among creatures, if their voice
penetrates to the outer ear, if the outward life makes heavy
demands, all this should be done only in so far as the
Lord wills it. Creatures should speak only in order to prepare the way for Christ, to call attention to Him and lead
us to Him. They should be as stars indicating the house
where the Child dwells, but disappearing as soon as we
have arrived. Solitude and a great stillness must ensue, as
in Bethlehem.

---

4 Ps. 84:9.
5 3 Kings 19:11.

Therefore the Holy Spirit observes that He will first lead us into solitude, and then speak to our hearts. And the wise man, who wishes to surrender himself completely to grace and entrust himself fully to the guidance of Eternal Wisdom, tells us that he will enter into his own interior and there abide with wisdom and seek repose. *"Intrans in domum meam conquiescam cum illa.* When I go into my house, I shall repose myself with her, for her conversation has no bitterness."[6]

We must act likewise. If Jesus, born in us by grace, is not to be ignored or neglected, or be lost to us again, we must be truly recollected, reserved, united with God. By lending ourselves to outward things inordinately without a careful survey of the spiritual premises, we may all too readily lose Jesus and His grace. But we may wonder whether such a life is not exacting and difficult, burdensome, and tedious? It is so just as long as we fail to discover the hidden treasures of an interior life; as long as we dwell only in the outer courts of our devotions; as long as we do not understand what it means to find Jesus in the depths of our heart and there to abide with Him.

b) *Two classes of persons find recollection difficult*

They live only exteriorly and devote themselves wholly to a dissipated life, motivated by mere natural impulses. They are in the first place those in whom the inner sanctuary is destroyed, in whose heart the abomination of desolation reigns in the Scriptural sense; in whose soul sin is much at home, and uncontrolled passions carry on

---

6 Wis. 8:16.

without check or hindrance. It is easily seen why such persons do not favor the abiding in their own spiritual house and entering into themselves, much less remaining there. The whole interior is unattractive, bare, unclean, and disconsolate, infested with sinful aims and aspirations. As long as they refuse to restore the kingdom of God in their souls, there can be neither peace nor joy, nor can happiness be found. They, consequently, have recourse to creatures, hoping vainly to find what their own dissipated heart is powerless to give. Without contentment, peace, and joy, they carry on from morning till night, day in, day out, without a trace of recollection or interior living, without the slightest effort of conforming their souls to that of our Divine Master.

The second class is somewhat better disposed. They at least have some desire to lead an interior life and make a somewhat ineffectual effort towards recollection, yet they find it tedious and boring. They remain as it were on the threshold of the interior life, at best reaching the ante-room. Since even there, naturally, the scene is again disarming and poor, and without warmth, they foolishly turn about to resort to creature comforts to find what their own heart could offer them in a high degree, if they only knew the art of finding it.

Among these we may find souls whose vocation demands recollection and the interior life without question. Even religious may be strongly inclined towards exterior estimates and interests, and remain such; therefore they achieve little that is worth while in the balances of perfection above what the ordinary Christian may easily have to his credit. We wonder how such a situation can be accounted for and how remedied.

There is a positive lack of determination, and the spirit of faith is conspicuous in gross neglect. Having grown up in the world and reached maturity in the midst of outward turmoil and easy living, where value is set only on what pleases the eye or the ear, what flatters the sensual appetites and the craving for honor, they find it almost unthinkable, even after having left the world, to disengage themselves from a certain hankering after worldly esteem and flitting honor. Since they are still too dependent upon their senses, they lack the power of refined judgment of values, their mind is befuddled and their heart retains its dubious taste for all that is natural and worldly in the extreme, without their doing the least violence to themselves.

A thorough break with the world, setting limits to our comfort and desires, would show us what wealth and treasures, what honors and delights reside in our own hearts, which have so often been the dwelling place of the Eucharistic Christ. Well does Thomas a-Kempis say: "Turn thee unto the Lord with thy whole heart and quit this miserable world, and thy soul shall find rest."[7] Forsake the world with all its vanities, learn to despise mere outward show thoroughly, and to devote yourself to true interior values, and you will rejoice in seeing the kingdom of God fill your heart.

c) *St. Ignatius recommends this mode of resolute procedure most forcefully to his spiritual Sons*

With their whole heart, not by half measures, they should turn away with genuine disgust, not only from one

---

7 Bk. 2. ch. 1:1.

or the other "false god," to which they cling, but simply from all that the world loves and feverishly seeks after— the vain desire for honor and specious renown, for a great name and worthless goods. Nothing will be lost thereby, but great will be our gain. Not in mere externals, in time-serving materialistic aims, but within our own hearts, giving up the world's enjoyments, embracing the practice of good works from supernatural impulses, will the kingdom of God be found.

Yet in the face of such incontestable truths, how slight is my awareness of it all! Not seldom the peace of my soul is disturbed by dryness and disconsolation, by misery and disorder, with a flagrant absence of interior thought and purity of intention. Still it remains true: *"Regnum Dei intra vos est!"* "The kingdom of God is within you." In Bethlehem there was naught but emptiness, abandonment, loneliness and poverty, and for the natural man it was devoid of comfort and joy. A stable, a hard crib, straw, poor swaddling clothes, verily nothing for the natural man, and yet there lies the Child with a whole heaven of divine treasures in His little Heart.

Our heart naturally resembles Bethlehem's stable in various ways in its inhospitable offerings. Nevertheless, this realization must not tempt us to abandon recollection and all interior striving. Let us not foolishly seek to compensate ourselves by distractions, nor lose ourselves in dissipation among external things and interests. Let us remain within, be watchful and open the eyes of faith. The Divine Child is there, *"Quis me separabit a caritate Christi!* Who shall separate me from the love of Christ! Yes, the Divine Child is there!

2. THE LIFE OF CHRIST IN US ENRICHES AND STRENGTHENS THE GROWTH OF THE INNER LIFE

The interior life is a God-centered life. It is Jesus Christ dwelling in us with an abundance of treasures worth more than all that could be found outside, worth more than the whole visible creation. Strong in closest union with God, the center of our soul-life, we feel the power to carry on perseveringly steeped in the alchemy of His love.

a) *A sublime truth!*

Through the incomparable gift of sanctifying grace, Jesus is really born in us, and it is ours to bring our lives into closer union with the holiness of the Triune God. This Divine Life in God was conferred upon us in baptism, and in Holy Communion it is daily increased. It is a participation in the Divine Nature, which elevates us to a dignity and a nobility high above the realm of kings and princes; makes us resemble God, whose kindliness and peace draw us ever closer to Him. We can understand why St. Paul cries out: " I count all things to be but loss for the excellent knowledge of Jesus Christ."[8] And "I count them but as dung, that I may gain Christ."[9] This is what earthly things are when pitted against the possession of Christ, in the light of grace, through God's overwhelming power.

---

8 Phil. 3:8.
9 Ibid.

b) *Together with grace, the three theological virtues of faith, hope, and charity, the moral virtues, and the Seven Gifts of the Holy Spirit are freely bestowed*

These exceptional treasures, sad to say, may lie dormant through life with a large portion of mankind, like a dead capital, perhaps; they have nevertheless been infused into each justified person together with sanctifying grace in baptism. We possess and harbor in our hearts precious treasures in comparison with which all the pearls and gems that adorn the robes of royalty, of the great, all the jewels and priceless stone that glitter in the crowns of kings and emperors, are even less than miserable glass, or than dust and refuse.

We further receive the comforting, sublime, excellent truths of faith, which open to us only in the inner light of grace and shine out as the most glorious gifts of grace and benefactions. Can anything more fascinating be imagined? A single one of these lights surpasses all merely natural knowledge and worldly news. Then think of the acts of virtue in which God deigns in a special manner to cooperate. How well we know that a single act of virtue surpasses in vigor and stability, in value in the sight of God, in benefits to our soul, even in honor before the heavenly court, every outward deed of splendor and magnificent display. Oh, the fulness of the riches, the sublimity of the inexhaustible divine abundance of the inner life! "*Regnum Dei intra nos.*" The kingdom of God is within us.

Even if we should not always be so vividly aware of it, feel it, or taste of it, what does it matter? Does it therefore cease to be a reality? "The just man lives by faith. *Justus meus ex fide vivit.*" Temporary aridity, disconsolation, temptations, difficulties, sadness or dejection, do not in the least alter the truth, the actuality, the worth of the supernatural entities, nor can they in the least minimize the wonderful treasures offered us by the inner life.

These have a splendid growth if we persevere in genuine recollection of spirit, and do not allow ourselves to be led astray by the false and deceptive earthly enticements, pleasures, and sensual gratifications. No matter how recalcitrant sentiment and imagination show themselves and cater to what sparkles and flatters, what pleases and delights, let us not be led astray. In prudent reserve let us hold back and at any cost, with the will at least, remain united with Jesus our God, our One and our All. "*Regnum Dei intra vos est.*" Outside of ourselves, in sensuous gratifications and the lust for pleasure, in satisfying curiosity and self-love, the kingdom of God simply cannot be found, but only dissipated and lost.

"Nowhere," says Father Faber, "may we seek the kingdom of God except in ourselves and in heaven." What a man of recollection, of the profound interior life, this worthy servant of God was, is well known. And yet, after having for years achieved heroic heights in this Christlike living, he was not satisfied, but aimed at still greater perfection. Grace came to his assistance and, through special divine lights aided him to scale newer heights.

One day he was assailed by grave temptations. It was a difficult struggle not to yield to dissipation and be overcome, and, as he expressed himself, to return within himself, "*redeundi ad se.*" Suddenly he thought of the Most Blessed Sacrament. While considering that through this Sacrament Jesus offers us ways and means for entering into our hearts, he experienced great comfort and new courage in the thought of his nearness to the God of Love. As if by the gentlest touch of grace, he understood that Jesus wishes to dwell in our hearts in order to show us whither we should go and even radiate light and strength to our companions. It must be a turning away from the outer world. In our effort for complete detachment, we must follow Jesus whither He leads us through Holy Communion, and daily learn more and more how to enter wholeheartedly into ourselves in fostering the inner life.[10]

Oh, we will follow Jesus! In us, He has in a certain sense become incarnate; in our hearts He is bedded like a child. In our hearts, too, He wills to grow and wax strong in wisdom and grace before God and men. In our hearts and from that vantage point, He desires to promote the true honor of God, to work for the salvation of souls—our own and the souls of others—by disseminating and increasing the knowledge and love of God. We will, therefore resolutely banish all distractions and everything that has no part with the Divine Infant. We need all our energy, all our attention to care for the Child in us, to protect Him and to rear Him to manhood. There is truly not a moment at our disposal to bother about the trivialities and the nothingness of worldlings. A life of recollection, a solidly disposed interior life, is absolutely essential for us. *"Intrans in domum meam conquiescam cum illa."* I will enter into my house and dwell there, abide there and seek repose with Eternal Wisdom.

---

10 Blessed Peter Faber: *Memoriale,* August, 1542, p. 105.

3. MORTIFICATION EFFICIENT MEANS FOR CULTIVATING THE INTERIOR LIFE

It is self-evident that here we speak only of a solidly integrated interior life. There are erroneous ways and serious disillusionments from the part of the enemy—our own nature. There is really no thought of recollection and a substantial interior life if we are wholly absorbed in our miseries, bodily or spiritual; if we make much of our difficulties, as it were, bury heart and mind therein, and thus be more concerned with ourselves than with God and the "Father's business." This would be like going into the stable at Bethlehem and staying there awhile, but occupying ourselves only with the bare walls, the filthy pavement, the hard crib, the wretched bed of straw. The Child Himself we would hardly notice.

We do not know how to bestow our whole attention upon Jesus, nor to give all for His love. No matter how poor and empty our heart, He still desires to dwell there, because of its poverty. Little wonder that because of our mistaken notion of the inner life and recollection, we enjoy so little of the peace and the cheerfulness which are the fruits and the richest sources of true inward living. "*Si quaeris te ipsum invenies te ipsum.*" He who seeks only himself, finds himself only, full of wretchedness, and misery, and poverty.

Naturally, we are to be occupied with ourselves, to heed what happens in our interior, to be watchful over our thoughts and desires, our speech and actions, for they are essentially part of the inner life; everything, however, must be done at the right time and place and in the proper manner. Self-knowledge is necessary, yet we may not yield to cowardice and self-pity, but rather, despising self thoroughly, crush exaggerated self-love. In the consciousness of our total insufficiency, we must aim to seek Jesus alone, live for Him, and devote ourselves wholly and unreservedly to Him.

It is good to know our inherent weakness and instability, to recognize our difficulties and our misery. Though we feel the pressure of our insufficiency, we must guard against letting this burden and the realization of our disabilities overwhelm us with discouragement and ill humor. Such awareness ought rather help us regard them as so many precious opportunities for the exercise of patience, humility, and love, and bring us closer to Christ, who alone is our consolation, our strength, and our support.

In short, only interior living in union with God, only the concern with our ego that ultimately leads us to Christ, helps us find Him and His treasures and aids us in dispensing them to others is genuine; only this is an essential part of the inner life. You will find a Child wrapped in swaddling clothes and laid in a manger. The manger and the swaddling clothes, no matter how poor, were for the shepherds the sure signs of the presence of Jesus, the object of their quest. "*Invenietis infantem pannis involutum et positum in praesepio.* And this shall be a sign unto you: You shall find the Infant wrapped in swaddling clothes, and laid in a manger."[11]

There is another false concept of the inner life and of the practice of recollection. It would require us to engage in formal prayer all the time, always to busy ourselves with the things of God, and be occupied solely with spirit-

---

11 Luke 2:12.

ual matters. This is naturally a gross misunderstanding. The inner life is nothing forced or unduly severe. It is simply the overflowing of inner richness and profound adoration.

It stands to reason that when we pray we should summon our best efforts to make our spiritual exercises wholly worthy of God. We need not crowd out mundane concerns, for in all these there is still a faint glimmer of vocational obligations performed conscientiously with total dedication. If our religion is a nearness to God, living with God, we shall rejoice in acquitting ourselves of every duty because it is God's Will. This is living an interior life in closest union with God, and it is, in truth, a reflection of Him.

If we neglected the custody of the heart, we should try in vain to control our imagination or the inevitable struggle in the daily round. The secret of the interior life, its core, resides in the diligent custody of the heart. Its demands are absolute: self-control, the curbing of our wishes and desires, where they transgress what is reasonable, our evil inclinations through interior mortification and denial, refusing them all they demand outside of God. It calls for liberating the heart more and more of inordinate attachment to creatures, giving it a strong impulse toward loving Him who is alone worthy of our affection, and surrendering to Him a recollected, reverent heart.

Why are we so often dissipated, so much a creature of our imagination, so arid, dry and listless in the spirtual exercises? Really these ought to be our soul's delight, the best that it is ours to give to the Lord. We often yield to our sensuality, our curiosity inducing us to cater to creatures, and often attach ourselves to the trivialities and worldly joys which are permitted us even in religious life for worthy reasons. Yet the Apostle tells us to use them as if we used them not. Our heart and its affections should remain within, looking to the permanent values of our work in the service of God through our vocational duties. Vanity and pride frequently take us out into the market place to be seen by men. To be recognized, to gain influence or curry favor, all these are a pleasant sensation, something which the blind heart seems unable to relinquish.

Good God, while we are frittering away our precious time and aspirations for fleeting honor with men, the Triune God with the whole heavenly court awaits us. He would proffer us His infinite pleasure, His divine satisfaction and recognition, if we would be hidden, forgotten by men, remain unknown, and in our hearts desired at least to be alone with Jesus, to learn the secrets of His divine love and infinite gifts. How foolish we are to seek on the outside what we could find in overwhelming measure in our own heart. Such is the condition of our spiritual weakness and inertia. It takes more than a day to achieve this victory; it calls for great patience and the frequent renewal of effort on our part, without stint.

Where shall we find the Holy Child, we ask once more. In a place where there is a total lack of everything that in the least flatters sensuality and pride. Our hearts must reach this stage of emptiness, which delights to be alone with God. All worldliness and a mind for what the world loves, admires, and values, must disappear. Human situations and worldly adjustments must be made to fit into our program of spirituality and renouncement. Then we may hope to behold the Child.

"*Apparebit benignitas et humanitas Salvatoris nostri.*" In His whole benignity and lovableness He will manifest Himself."*Frequens illi visitatio cum homine interno.*" Jesus loves to visit with the truly interior man; His converse with him is sweet; consolation and the fulness of peace are His gift and His friendship surpasses all understanding. So it is in truth. "*Regnum Dei intra vos.*" An entire kingdom of God will unfold itself to our interior, and qualify us to help others toward a similar happiness.

CHAPTER VI

THE CONSOLATIONS OF THE HOLY SPIRIT

> *"The spirit of the Lord shall rest upon him . . . and his delight shall be the fear of the Lord. Not by appearance shall he judge, nor by hearsay shall he decide. But he shall judge the poor with justice."*[1]

What glorious and sweet names Holy Church in the liturgy of the Pentecost Mass gives the Holy Spirit! She styles Him "of Comforters the Best, (*Consolator optime*)"; she speaks of Him as "the soul's delightful Guest (*dulcis hospes animae*)"; again, as "the pilgrim's sweet relief (*Dulce refrigerium*)." These epithets chime like sweet bells in the depths of our soul. The Church directs us to beg the Holy Spirit to visit our soul, take up His abode therein, and wholly fill it. Indeed, we should plead with Him:

"Rest art Thou in our toil, most sweet, Refreshment in the Noonday heat, and solace in our grief.
O Blessed Light of Life Thou art, Fill with Thy Light the Inmost hearts of those that hope in Thee!"

We ask ourselves to consider well and be deeply penetrated with the idea that the rich content of these words has become an inexpressible reality. In very truth, the

---

1 Isa. 11:2-4.

Holy Spirit dwells in our soul richly dowered with grace, and He, the great God, works in us what all these sweet names signify, in a far greater degree than these epithets are able to express.

At one time God made the promise through the prophet Isaias: "For thus saith the Lord: Behold I will bring upon her as it were a river of peace, and as an overflowing torrent the glory of the Gentiles . . . As one whom the mother caresseth, so will I comfort you, and you shall be comforted in Jerusalem."[2]

All this has long since been fulfilled. When Jesus, Our Saviour and Redeemer, left the earth, He did not leave us behind as orphans. Oh, no. He sent us the Comforter, the Holy Spirit. With Him peace has spread out over the Church like a river; through Him the faithful children of this Church will be caressed more tenderly than a beloved child, which the mother caresseth on her knees. The Holy Spirit "is" the best of Comforters; He "is" the intimate, beloved Guest of our soul; He "is" our sweet relief, the Father of the poor and the light of hearts; for He is the "Father of mercies, and the God of all comfort."[3]

How the Holy Spirit acts as Comforter, we shall now ponder. He Himself, however, "the Blessed Light of Life (O Lux beatissima)" may show us what a sweet Comforter He is in reality. May He strengthen us to apply faithfully the means of participating in His comforts all the time, and thus become capable of consoling and strengthening others at the opportune moment.

---

2 Isa. 66:12, 13.
3 2 Cor. 1:3.

1. THE BEST OF COMFORTERS

a) *Faith the foundation of all consolation*

There is no dignity *more sublime,* or honorable, than to be a *child of God.* Can there be a more splendid, *more remunerative position* than to be friend, brother of Jesus Christ, and therefore co-heir of His glory? No millionaire on earth possesses a more precious and valuable treasure than is ours in sanctifying grace, with the virtues and gifts which adorn it as with so many pearls and priceless gems.

The human heart cannot conceive of a *greater happiness* than to taste the good pleasure of the Heavenly Father, the Infinite God, the Lord of heaven and earth, and to be loved as a friend and brother of Our Lord, enthroned as King of Glory at the Father's right. No greater happiness can be imagined.

What follows naturally? One who finds himself in such a situation will necessarily enjoy lasting peace and contentment, and often feel an indescribable consolation when he becomes conscious of his overwhelming bliss and peace. Well for us, for we enjoy such a sublime, incomparably exalted relation to God and to His Incarnate Son, Jesus Christ. What joy! Let us ponder it briefly.

A child of the Heavenly Father

"I will receive you: and I will be a Father to you; and you shall be my sons and daughters, saith the Lord Almighty."[4] And He kept His word, for He is faithful to His

---

4 2 Cor. 6:18; Jer. 31:9.

promise. As He has "predestined us unto the adoption of children through Jesus Christ, according to the purpose of His Will," "unto the praise of the glory of His grace, He hath graced us in His beloved Son."[5] We are, therefore, no longer servants, but children. Everyone can now say in the sublimest sense of the word, *I am a child of God the Heavenly Father.* Regenerated in God through sanctifying grace, we are much closer to the Heavenly Father than the earthly son to his father. Since we participate in the divine nature, as far as this is possible for a creature, the bonds that unite us with God and the relation of intimacy with Him are inexpressibly more tender than between parents and children.

This is a reality, but a reality so sublime that St. Peter Chrysologus applies thereto the words of the Apostle of the Gentiles: "Neither eye hath seen, nor ear heard, and in no human heart has it entered what God prepares for those who love Him."[6] At an earlier period, the Disciple of Love, full of astonishment and admiration for such an unprecedented dignity, cried out: "Behold what manner of charity the Father hath bestowed upon us, that we should be called, and should be the sons of God!"[7] We may not only call ourselves His children, but are such in truth.

Brother of Jesus

From these reflections there follows also our relation to Jesus Christ. St. Paul styles Him the firstborn among many

---

5 Eph. 1:5, 6.
6 72d. Hom.
7 1 John 3:1.

Brethren. We are of the number of these brethren. When the Risen Christ appeared to Magdalen, He commissioned her: "Go to My brethren, and say to them: I ascend to My Father and to your Father, to My God and to your God."[8] Go to My brethren! Jesus applies also to me the sweet name, brother. Each of us can truly say: I am not only called the brother of Jesus, but am it in reality, since, according to St. Paul, the Father through sanctifying grace "made me conformable to the image of His Son."[9]

What prospects open out before us on this account? What sort of a future may we anticipate? It is of such brilliance that St. Peter jubilantly cries out: "Blessed be the God and Father of our Lord Jesus Christ, who according to His great mercy hath regenerated us into a lively hope by the resurrection of Jesus Christ from the dead. Unto an inheritance incorruptible, and undefiled, and that cannot fade, reserved in heaven for you."[10]

I, a child of God the Heavenly Father, a brother of Jesus Christ, co-heir of the heavenly kingdom, even now holding a right to immeasurable riches and eternal glory! What dignity, what happiness! Truly, I need only become deeply conscious of this privilege; I need only rightly recognize and understand what are the goods I already possess, and I will be filled with consolation. With my happiness and deep peace of soul, no worldling's can compare.

---

8 John 20:17.
9 Rom. 8:29.
10 1 Peter 1:3, 4.

b) *The Holy Spirit our Comforter—*
our relation to Him

Who is it that furnishes this consciousness? Who imparts this interior knowledge and thereby opens a fountainhead of unspeakable comfort?

It is the only true Consoler, the Holy Spirit, who speaks these words of peace to my soul, and in His blissful light lets me realze them fully. "*O lux beatissima, reple cordis intima tuorum fidelium.*" "We have received," St. Paul tells us, "not the spirit of this world, but the spirit that is of God; that we may know (understand) the things that are given us from God."[11]

His most holy Person has created these marvellous relations. The Eternal Father conceived the resolve to adopt us as children. Jesus Christ has by His Most Precious Blood earned for us the grace of participating in the Divine nature. The Holy Spirit carried out the divine decree, by adorning our soul with sanctifying grace. St. Paul testifies to this when he declares: "The charity of God is poured forth in our hearts by the Holy Spirit, who is given to us."[12]

We are also in a particular manner near to the Holy Spirit. He has not only given us sanctifying grace with all the gifts that accompany it. In and through it He has given us Himself, in such a manner that His most holy Person dwells in us in incomprehensible intimacy. He cannot be closer to any other creature; so near is God to us. Who could better converse with us about our relations to God than He, the source and end of it all! Who would more easily make known to us the ineffable treasures that are

11 1 Cor. 2:12.
12 Rom. 5:5.

ours! Or more effectively console us by manifesting to us the happiness that we enjoy in the possession of such unfathomable riches than again the Holy Spirit, the sweet Guest of our souls, whose presence is the most excellent of all gifts.

The Holy Spirit Himself avers that He is the author of all these blessings, that His most holy Person dispenses His consolations. He tells us by the mouth of the Apostle in Galatians: "And because you are sons, God hath sent the Spirit of His Son into your hearts crying: 'Abba, Father.' Therefore now he is not a servant, but a son. And if a son, an heir also through God."[13] A marvellous, consoling testimony! All imaginable ideas of genuine consolation are inherent in it, as all true benefits are comprised in the sonship of God.

c) *The threefold manner of dispensing consolation through the Holy Spirit*

The *first and ordinary manner* consists in this that the Spirit of God dwells in us, keeps aloof all doubt as to the sonship of God, the state of grace and similar things; that He relieves souls of all inquietude, restlessness, and worry, or at least does not allow them to interpenetrate the soul and work havoc, but affords us easy relief in surmounting these obstacles. The Holy Spirit grants us His peace; the soul may feel at home in the service of God like a child in the father's house. "*Reddit animam quietam,*" St. Ignatius said, "*et pacificat illam in suo Creatore ac Domino.*" He quiets and calms our hearts and grants us security in the

---

13 Gal. 4:6, 7.

4

love of our Lord and Creator, who is at the same time our Father.

The second more excellent manner consists in this that the Holy Spirit grants us glimpses of the treasures hidden in the sonship of God. But they are glimpses, inner recognition, as no amount of study can achieve, nor scientific formula lay bare, as only the Spirit of God can pour them out over our willing hearts. As often as He grants them, we not only comprehend that we are children of God, not only attain certainty about our intimate closeness to God, but we also taste the happiness of realizing these exquisite gifts, which adorn our soul in the splendor of grace.

In pondering the riches we already possess, as well as those we anticipate, our hearts are transported with intense joy. Love waxes strong as we become aware of the magnitude of God, whose sons we are not only called but are such in reality. His infinite lovableness is opened to us, we taste it fully and our heart is overwhelmed with love. Our hearts are so charged with the fire of that love that, according to St. Ignatius again, "We are unable to love any created thing further in itself, but solely and alone in the Creator of all things." What truly heavenly comfort! Here the Holy Spirit reveals Himself in truth as the Sweet Guest of souls, as the source of holy delights and the purest joys. He leads us to the Heart of the Father that we may feel the immense ocean of goodness and love of this Heart, now wholly ours, as we are His. *"Dilectus meus mihi et ego illi."*

There is still a *more excellent manner* of our receiving the comforts of the Holy Spirit. He imparts to the soul not only the ordinary moral certitude about her relations to God and the blessings inherent in the sonship of God.

He deigns to assure her that she numbers among the chosen ones and is a child of God in the state of sanctifying grace, not merely now, but that it will be her portion forever in the glory of heaven. Oh, this testimony must be a foretaste of heaven on earth. Yet it remains an exceptional grace; it is a gift which the Holy Spirit vouchsafes only to certain individuals wholly at His divine pleasure. We may, therefore, neither desire nor demand it. The two manners, treated earlier not only allow us to ask for this gift, but make it imperative, in accord with the requirements of our Rule. They belong essentially to intimacy with God, which St. Ignatius solicitously commends. In fact, they constitute this trustful relationship in its different steps. This intimacy must be the object of our earnest desire and our constant striving. It is our business to apply the means faithfully to dispose our hearts for the manifestations of the Holy Spirit, who dwells in us, ready to impart those consolations to us and thus grant us peace and joy in the service of God.

2. WAYS AND MEANS OF ACQUIRING CONSOLATION

The spiritual exercises may safely be recommended as capital means. It is true, the spiritual exercises are necessary means. Unless he is solicitously concerned in God and things divine, no one may expect the Holy Spirit to visit the soul with His inner comforts in the manner touched upon. But the chief means are two others.

a) *The faithful accomplishment of the Will of God*

"When Jesus," we read in Mark, "had been baptized by John, coming up out of the water, He saw the heavens opened, and the Spirit as a dove descending and remaining on Him. And there came a voice from heaven: 'Thou art My beloved Son: in Thee I am well pleased!' "[14]

Why was Jesus vouchsafed to hear this blissful testimonial? Why was there an incessant repetition in His innermost Heart of what took place openly for His glorification? Because the Will of the Heavenly Father took precedence over all else. It was His sustenance, His consolation, His honor, His life. Because He fulfilled this most holy Will as it manifested itself in the orders of His parents, in the precepts of the Law, in the prophecies, for the term of His life most perfectly, to the little word "*Sitio,*" I thirst. "*Quae placita sunt ei, facio semper.*" "What is pleasing to Him, I always do," is the basic impulse of His Most Sacred Heart.

How well we know what pleases the Heavenly Father! He deigns to make His holy Will known in the smallest details, in the dictates of our superiors, and in the precepts of the Holy Rule. Well, then, if we desire to taste similar consolations, to feel assured of being God's children, to know how He loves us, and how truly His divine pleasure rests on us, let us imitate our firstborn Brother, Jesus Christ.

"What is pleasing to Him, I always do." This will have its own reward. If, for example, I rise promptly in the morning at the first signal, and show by this cheerful readiness that to serve the Father is my life, His Holy Spirit will not seldom allow me to feel the satisfaction of being dear to the Father and worthy of His love.

If through the day I heed every summons of the bell, every known will of my superiors, no matter in what con-

14 Mark 1:10.

cerns, with readiness and loving response, I may rest assured that my heart will many a time break forth in the jubilant cry of "Father!" I will then taste of the manna hidden therein, for it is the Holy Spirit that motivates this heart's cry. It is He in whom we cry "Father!"

To cite one more example. If I observe the rule of silence conscientiously, and not suffer trivialities to deter me from keeping it faithfully, I may be convinced that the Holy Spirit will teach me more perfectly how to win the Heart of my Heavenly Father and obtain precious gifts for me as well as for others. In my prayers I will frequently experience how this ineffable Spirit comes to the aid of my weakness. How He Himself in me asks with inexpressible sighings and how He entreats not only for me, but for my religious associates, for others with whom we labor, and for all men in the Mystical Body: *"ipse Spiritus postulat pro nobis gemitibus inenarrabilibus."*[15] "The Spirit Himself asketh for us with unspeakable groanings." Let us, therefore, be prudent children and faithfully, perseveringly observe all the injunctions of our Rules and precepts, and the word of lawfully constituted authority, manifesting to us the Father's Will. He who observes the law is a prudent son. *"Qui custodit legem, filius sapiens est"*:[16] "He that keepeth the law is a wise son."

b) *Purity of heart and mind*

The persevering cleansing of the heart through untiring mortification of our perverse inclinations is another

---

15 Rom. 8:26.
16 Prov. 28:7.

approved means of enjoying the support of the Holy Spirit in our striving for the inner life. It may seem harsh, but it is the means of all means; like none other it affords the activity of the Holy Spirit free access to our interior, where He loves to be at home.

The more insistently we curb the tendency to satisfy external cravings, for dissipation and curiosity, the more will our inner auditory channels be perfected and attuned to the reception of the wonderful things which the Eternal Wisdom longs to impart. The more faithfully we mortify our sensuality, our love of convenience, and curb our sensual appetite, the purer, the more wholesome and refined will be our spiritual tastes. We will enjoy the sweetness of the paternal Heart of God, His tender manifestations of love, together with the delightful repose and peace we find in Him.

The more determined we are in opposing our self-will and pride in its varied manifestations and demands, the more will the hardness and instability of our heart disappear. *"Auferam cor lapideum et dabo eis cor carneum."* "I will take away the stony heart out of their flesh, and will give them a heart of flesh."[17] It will be meek and mild, beneficent and benign. Love will more and more kindle within it; a love that will love God above all things, all without exception, most tenderly in God. Therefore, it will submit willingly to every labor and fatigue, sacrificing self completely in order to lead others to God the Father.

May the Holy Spirit impart this love to us ever more

---

17 Ez. 11:19.

generously. The Father has sent Him into our hearts that we may be His children, like unto the image of His Son, Jesus Christ. "Now we have received the Spirit that is of God; that we may know the things that are given us from God."[18]

---

18 1 Cor. 2:12.

CHAPTER VII

THE SIGNIFICANCE OF CONSOLATION
IN THE SPIRITUAL LIFE

> *"But if I go, I will send Him to*
> *you.... He will receive of what*
> *is mine and declare it to you."*[1]
> *"The disciples were glad, when*
> *they saw the Lord."*[2]

What the gospel here tells us of the apostles and
disciples has been repeated countless times since the
resurrection of Christ; it will be repeated again and again
for all who are close to the Saviour. He, the Lord of life
and death, of sorrow and contempt, He, the glorified,
transfigured Saviour, shows Himself to them and they
rejoice exceedingly on seeing Him.

In reality it occurs but rarely that Jesus reveals Himself
visibly, as He showed Himself to the disciples, but He
manifests Himself in many joyous encounters, through
inner visitations, through the *visitationes spirituales,* the
spiritual visits, as we style them, and as St. Ignatius
frequently spoke of them. Our Lord makes these visits for
our consolation and fortitude in the daily struggles of our

---

1 John 16:7, 15.
2 John 20:20.

spiritual life. Of these it may always be said as of the disciples, we rejoice, our heart tastes something of the inexpressible delight which fills the Divine Heart of Jesus entirely and makes It an inexhaustible source of spiritual strength and consolation. We should try to become deeply aware of the importance of this spiritual visitation, of the worth of consolation, and renew ourselves in using the means to render us worthy of participating frequently in so precious a good.

We all know from experience how Jesus manifests Himself and His nearness to us. We may distinguish two sorts of consolation: first, the extraordinary, in which, according to St. Ignatius, the soul glows with a higher degree of love of God, her Creator and Lord, in a manner to be more deeply felt than expressed. In such moments, the soul tastes the sweetness of all that appertains to God, what is supernatural, what is heavenly.

There is also the ordinary consolation, often spoken of as the basic consolation. In this is included all that imparts to the soul peace and quietude in God, in the Blessed Trinity. It is the constant, submissive, cheerful surrender to God and His service. The former is easily discerned, but the latter is sometimes hard to detect; it may be easily mistaken for a natural peace and temperamental satisfaction. There is, however, an infallible test. It is surely genuine, if we take self-denial seriously and not pass it off lightly as of no concern; it is genuine, also, if we feel at home in our spiritual communings with the God of our heart. In general, our prayerlife must constitute our dearest occupaion in God's service, regardless of the state of our inner advancement, or our external occupation with material charges and commitments. So much for the essence of consolation.

1. CONSOLATION A MARK OF DIVINE TENDERNESS

Spiritual consolation is without doubt something valuable and of importance for the life of perfection. In a certain sense, it is something necessary for the pursuit of our inner striving. There is to be no compromise with worldly desires and aims. Implicit consecration to our God and Lord, fidelity and unquestioned surrender, must be our aim, with a heart at peace and the hope of eternal light in the Father's Bosom. "In His Light we see light." Interiorness is the atmosphere of the Holy Spirit. In Him we find joy of spirit and abandon. "And they were filled with the Holy Ghost . . ."—with the spirit of Christ and His consolations.

In judging consolation and, therefore, also in its practice, there are two extremes to be watched. We may esteem it highly and be too seriously attached to it, or the reverse may hold; we may lay too little stress upon it. The first error occurs more frequently in the beginning of the spiritual life. The novice easily forgets that consolation is but a means. He confuses the gift with the giver; when he misses consolation he thinks he is losing God, that nothing remains and that all is lost. This deception, the over-estimation of spiritual comfort, is one of the chief sources of pusillanimity and cowardice among beginners in the religious life. It is the business of those that guide and direct them to make clear just wherein lies the truth, and to remind them that the consolations God grants His servants do not constitute the essence of sanctity.

The contrary misconception appears rather late in life; it is much more frequent than it seems. We no longer find joy and delight in the spiritual exercises as we should. They leave us cold and indifferent. It seems that God, with whom we have perhaps enjoyed delightful intimacies in the past, withdraws from us. At such a time, instead of ascribing this lack of joy to negligence and lassitude, St. Ignatius remarks, we easily seek cover in the cowardly thought that, after all, such comfort is non-essential. Since we neither value nor esteem it, we no longer seek to recapture it. Our spiritual life lacks vigor and initiative. In short, we gravitate towards a listless, matter-of-fact daily life, and the interior spirit may die and gradually disappear.

It is our serious duty to guard against this pernicious error. It is beyond question that virtue and sanctity do not consist in consolation, but it will always be a significant means of advancement on the way of perfection. With Christ we can then say, "I do always the things that please Him."[3] Nor should we grieve for lack of consolation or yield to discouragement. To grow indifferent, however, towards this great means of spiritual power and to neglect the striving for a return of such moments of grace would be culpable, indeed, and dangerous in the extreme. It would expose us to the vicious net of the Evil One, and we would gradually sleep away in pernicious lukewarmness.

---

3 John 8:29.

2. ORIGIN AND SOURCES OF CONSOLATION

a) *Consolation is a special gift of God, a gift through
which He wills to manifest His love for us*

It is a mark of divine tenderness. Who would dare place
small value on such a gift? Who could be indifferent to it?
We are so receptive and appreciative of human kindness,
and therefore we avoid all that might eventually deprive
us of this great good. How much is done to win human
hearts and to obtain marks of affection! O Great God! For
Thy good will and affection, O Infinite Majesty, for the
external marks of Thy friendship—for consolations in the
truest sense are just these—for all this we care so little in
utter neglect.

b) *Consolation is in a certain sense a sort of apparition
of the Saviour. A visitatio spiritualis, a visit from
the soul's best Friend*

It is a manifestation of His nearness through the light,
which He, the Sun of Justice, radiates, and through the
joy which He allows to overflow into our hearts from His
glorious Heart, the Ocean of delights. He, Himself, the
most delicate lover of our soul, allows us to realize in
moments of consolation that He fulfills the promises He
gave us in the words: *"Et veniemus ad eum et mansionem
apud eum faciemus."* We will come to him and take up
our abode with him. His consolation, indeed, shows us
that with the Father and the Holy Spirit He has entered in
and taken up His lasting abode with us. Therefore, indifference toward such manifestations, prescinding from
other evil results, is, to say the least, a mark of gross

discourtesy and lack of reverence and respect toward our Divine Saviour.

c) *What is consolation, finally, we ask according to its origins?*

It is a *motio spiritus sancti,* an incentive of the Holy Spirit. It is a wholly supernatural effect coming to us either directly from Him or from an angel. The Holy Spirit is positively acting in us; we are aware of His presence. Is that something slight? The Spirit of God seizes upon our soul and lifts it to heavenly knowledge and to the purest, holiest feelings of delight. Thus it makes our heart capable of desiring, petitioning, and entreating for all blessings on the interests of God and of immortal souls, as we could not achieve it otherwise.

If the Holy Spirit Himself deigns to work in our hearts, who would dare think and speak depreciatingly of such manifestations of divine grace? *"Spiritus sanctus postulat pro nobis gemitibus inenarrabilibus."* "The Spirit Himself asketh for us with unspeakable groanings."[4] Without doubt we have sometimes experienced the truth of this pronouncement of St. Paul. It is easier to feel at heart than to put into words how consoling the visitations of the Triune God are in the soul. St. Ignatius holds that consolation is essentially a gift, a special manifestation of grace on the part of our Divine Saviour.

---

4 Rom. 8:26.

2. FRUITS OF CONSOLATION

The effects correspond to the origins. These also show that it is a treasure, a gift that we must esteem, a means of progress in the spiritual life towards which we may not be indifferent or listless. "*Gustate et videte, quam suavis est Dominus.*" "Taste and see how sweet the Lord is."[5] This is the first and most excellent fruit of consolation. We should become consciously aware of God, should note that in Himself He has infinitely more delight and sweetness than all creatures together could offer us. What is the reason for this happy note? God desires our heart, our whole love.

a) *We cannot love what we do not know*

We must, first of all, learn to know Him thoroughly, with a knowledge that fascinates the heart and even carries it away, as it were. No knowledge can achieve this goal in the measure of the knowledge we gain from the inner visitations of consolation. Years of study will never achieve what a few enlightenments will accomplish when God Himself comes close to us.

Oh, between the knowledge which science affords and that which comes to us through inner lights and consolations, there is a tremendous difference. This accounts for the ardent love of God that burns in the hearts of men of prayer, or better still in the hearts of those who dispose themselves by zealous preparation for divine consolations. They taste, observe, become inwardly aware of the reality

---

5 Ps. 33:9.

of God and, in general, of supernatural things. *Gustate et videte!* Taste and see! Therefore the heart is always pliant and allows itself to be fettered to God with indissoluble bonds and chains.

> b) *A second effect of consolation certainly not to be underestimated is that it makes all things light*

We walk resolutely, we even run, as the Psalmist confesses of himself, on the ways of God, of the Counsels, of the Religious Rule, as often as God through His nearness expands our hearts. Would we not be fools if we neglected on our part everything that such a visible, palpable divine help so often makes possible for us? One who does not apply the means that prepare us for consolations is not aware of what he is doing; he is squandering priceless opportunities for everlasting good. When difficulties break in upon us, when trials and disconsolation assail us, we shall draw strength and support and vigorous initiative from all that we have learned from our moments of spiritual consolation.

With St. Paul we cry out: "I know in whom I have believed." We shall not let ourselves be so easily deceived. For *vidimus gloriam ejus,* we have seen His glory, our heart belongs to Him in joy and in sorrow. God is ready not only to lead us by the hand along the path of virtue, but if we really wish it, He will often, very often, carry us on His arms, press us to His Heart, and go forward with us to meet any encounter. We, alas, prefer to go on laboriously, and do not allow Him to act. Oh, that we would let the world with all its blandishments and trivialities go its own way and afford more room in our hearts to the divine manifestations of consolation and love! It would please the Lord and draw blessings and graces upon any apostolic labor we undertake. Through them the words of the Saviour find fulfilment: "My yoke is sweet and My burden light."[6]

c) Light and Consolation—Requistites for Apostolic Labor

Consolation is absolutely necessary. This, of course, does not apply to the ordinary Christian in the same degree. Those who concentrate only on avoiding sin, on observing the Commandments, can more readily dispense with supernatural consolation. There remain to them so many natural pleasures and delights, which they may lawfully enjoy without sin or disadvantage to their soul. It is different with those who have professed the Vows of religion, and who desire to attain to a higher degree of the friendship of God and His Blessed Vision in heaven, and with it taste the hundredfold of consolation in the glorious life. Through their holy Vows, religious have closed to some extent the main sources of earthly pleasures and enjoyments. What is still permitted to us, and what may be indulged without sin, is relatively but a small matter. Even in this regard we should retrench ourselves magnanimously, in as far as possible. If we wish to attain the perfection that our vocation marks out for us, we must detach our heart from earthly vanities.

I do not exaggerate when I say that we must seek the

6 Matt. 11:30.

opposite of earthly consolations—privations, humiliations, and what is more disagreeable to human nature. If the choice is ours, we must reach out for the less good, the poorer and the inferior, for what is repugnant to nature, as if all this were our best portion, because Jesus Himself has chosen it. We should try to do this with the same zeal, the same perseverance in daily practice as the worldly-minded allot to the agreeable diversions of their day.

But let me ask, who will be able to endure this in the long run, this isolation from inner delights? Our heart is created for blessedness. Even here on earth it needs something to give it joy and delight. We, therefore, see the necessity of supernatural consolation, where earthly comfort is cut off. Those who have wholly renounced all joys purely of earth, who have sacrificed what one loves and esteems here below, have more need of consolation, lest aridity and dryness mar their spiritual striving. They need much of the consolation that elevates, inspires, and warms the heart to interior joy and love.

Consolation is specially useful and even necessary for the apostle, who goes out to demonstrate the vanity and insignificance of earthly things, the beauty and lovableness of God, His infinite love in our regard. Would we extol the charm of devotion to Mary, the intercessory power of the saints and angels of heaven and all that it contains, we must ourselves have become aware of it in our own soul, must have tasted and envisioned the indescribable beauty and sweetness of the Lord. Interior consolations and light must often be with the apostle of souls, as a foretaste of the spiritual delights, of that inner joy that draws us to heavenly things. Only then can we hope to make others feel a distaste for earthly joys, to lift hearts and win them for espousing the joys that speak of everlasting bliss beyond.

An apostle needs faith, hope, and love to buoy up his enthusiasm and courage. For this reason consolation is imparted generously to those who are true apostles, with sacrifice of personal preference and resolute bearing of inconveniences and disappointments. What did St. Paul confess? *"Superabundo gaudio in omni tribulatione."* "I exceedingly abound with joy in all our tribulations."[7] And St. Francis Xavier must even beg God to halt the excessive flow of consolations. They all experienced them, all who were in any way filled with the same spirit. The Spirit of God was operative through inner visitations and intimate converse with every individual saint, conferring on them deep peace of soul and trust in the Lord.

What must we do to maintain ourselves in such a soul-state of inner joy that God may often vouchsafe us the gift of His consolations? Fidelity in little things is necessary, above all. Every negligence in this regard entails its own punishment through a lessening or the complete withdrawal of consolation.

3. MEANS OF ACHIEVING CONSOLATION

Two other means, however, are indispensable. They prove that genuine consolation is something solid, and that the light it sheds into the soul is of inestimable worth.

---

7 2 Cor. 7:4.

These means are *purity of heart, and humility and submission.*

a) *Blessed are the pure of heart, for they shall see God*

Our Lord in promising this does not refer only to the Beatific Vision in heaven, but to its fulfilment here in spiritual consolations. It stands to reason that the purer our heart is, the more frequently shall we partake of these tokens of love on the part of the Saviour. But the reverse, likewise, holds. This is preeminently the case in all that pertains to the virtue and the vow of chastity. The opposite vice, says St. Thomas Aquinas, renders the heart wholly unfit for spiritual consolations. A pure heart, however, attracts God and draws Him irresistibly into hearts that are well prepared and fortified with humility.

b) *God loves the humble man, bows down to him and grants him copious gifts and graces*

If occasionally, He allows the humble man to suffer, He very quickly raises him up to peace and quiet in the Lord. He reveals His mysteries to the humble man, for he rests in God, and nothing disturbs his peace of soul, even when tempted and oppressed. God is unchangeable; under all circumstances He is the same God of consolation, who draws the pure and humble man to His Heart there to taste indescribable delights.

Let us then faithfully cooperate with divine grace, keep our hearts pure, be submissive in the spirit of living faith, and inner bliss and comfort will be ours. We shall often taste and see how sweet the Lord is, and be the better able to lift others to a love of heavenly things and win them for God.

"Thou has girded me with strength unto battle: and hast subdued under me them that rose up against me."[8]

---

8 Ps. 17:40.

PART TWO

THE PRACTICE OF THE INTERIOR LIFE

"To know also the charity of Christ, which surpasses all knowledge, that you may be filled unto all the fulness of God."

Eph. 3:19.

CHAPTER VIII

GREAT ACCOMPLISHMENTS

*"Then said I, 'Behold, I come . . .
to do Thy Will, O God!"*[1]

I. Fulfilling the Holy Will of God

We should all like to accomplish great things; it is,
therefore, of the utmost importance to have the correct
norm for true greatness. The correct norm is simply the
Will of God. Only what is done for Him is truly great. It
may be materially of little significance, but it is great in
the sight of God. A glance at the life of Jesus clarifies this
important truth. He is the very source of our growth in
the inner life.

We are all eager to achieve perfection; we desire to
do great things in the service of God. It is of the greatest
importance, therefore, for us to know what is really great
in the sight of God, according to eternal, immutable
standards, that we may judge impartially what matters in
the divine appraisal. With defective scales everything is
weighed incorrectly; false measurements yield only false
value. This may happen to us in the spiritual life, if we
do not apply the correct basis for our judgments, our

---

1 Heb. 10:7.

evaluation. Great achievements, to be sure! But what is really great?

It is necessary for us to distinguish between true and false values, for the enemy, in league with our lower nature, utilizes our natural desire for great and conspicuous achievement surreptitiously to lead us astray. Again and again he tries to induce us by his cunning to regard sham greatness as of genuine worth. There is hardly another beautiful idea behind which the Evil Spirit hides from souls with lofty aspirations; there is hardly another which he utilizes so deftly for his purposes, hardly another through which he stealthily generates so much dejection, sadness, dissatisfaction, murmurings, bitter criticisms and complaints, as this one. He succeeds whenever the correct measuring rod is not faithfully applied. Let us examine this norm again very carefully, in order to draw upon it with new zeal, for the specific purpose of bringing our life and all individual actions to harmonize with it.

True greatness as it affects our whole life, is in the last analysis only what conforms with the Will of God and is performed with due regard and reverent homage to the Divine Majesty. It is truly noble, worthy of God, even if to the natural eye it seems almost insignificant and worthless.

1. CHRIST ALWAYS LEADS, AND IT IS OURS TO FOLLOW

A glance at the life of Christ clarifies this important truth, so vital for apostolic labors. Our Divine Saviour willed most assuredly to achieve great things, to live a life on earth in which there would not be a single wasted moment. There was question of making atonement to an Infinite Justice, to glorify the Name of the Infinite Majesty with brilliance and splendor. There was question of redeeming a whole world; of showing to countless noble and magnanimous souls the ideal of true greatness; of setting the example of a life pleasing to God filled with good and meritorious works. Let us note how the Lord achieves this surpassing end.

He embraces the Will of the Father: "Behold I come to do Thy Will, O God."[2] To the Father's Will are directed all His thoughts and intentions, His wishes and desires; He touches nothing, nothing pleases Him if it does not bear the impress of the sweet Will of the Father; nothing, no matter what it be, attracts Him if it lies outside the Divine Will. With complete renunciation of personal plans and desires, and volitions, He engages the whole piercing insight and the depth of divine intelligence, the whole elasticity and breadth of His Heart, the whole energy and strength of His Will, to devote it to the things that are of the Father, to what His holy Will designs for Him.

"Descendi de coelo, non ut faciam voluntatem meam, sed voluntatem ejus, qui misit me." "I came down from Heaven, not to do My own Will, but the Will of Him that sent Me."[3]

Day by day this remains His endeavor. His ear is open to hear what the Father wills. "In the morning He wakeneth my ear, that I may hear Him as a master."[4] No matter how hard or disagreeable it may be what he hears,

2 Heb. 10:7.
3 John 6:38.
4 Isa. 50:4.

or how contradictory to the opinions, wishes and cogitations that nature would suggest, He rejects nothing. "The Lord God hath opened my ear, and I do not resist: I have not gone back."[5] With a holy vehemence as one hungry for food, His Heart desire this Will, and to fulfill it is His daily bread: *"Meus cibus est, ut faciam voluntatem ejus, qui misit me."*[6] "My meat is to do the Will of Him that sent Me." And yet, for the whole period of His life, this Will proposed to Him, for the most part, what from a merely natural point of view was distasteful, and often seemingly unpalatable; it could arouse no interest or enthusiasm, and was contradictory to every natural impluse, as being wholly impracticable and useless.

2. THE PERFECT FOLLOWING OF CHRIST CALLS FOR COMPLETE SURRENDER

We further ponder the life of Christ in this regard. Spiritually mature, also according to His human nature, in the womb of the Virgin Mother a man—*"femina circumdabit virum"* - "A woman shall compass a man."[7] He is to be minor, a child, for years subject to the guidance of others, whom He infinitely surpassed in judgment and in every accomplishment. *"Ecce venio!"* "Behold I come: to do Thy Will, O God!"[8] I seek naught else on earth.

He was subject to human beings. *"Et erat subditus illis."* Gifted, qualified, talented, as none of His contemporaries, He possessed consummate wisdom, even according to His

---

5 Isa. 50:5.
6 John 4:34.
7 Jer. 31:22.
8 Heb. 10:7.

human nature. He was magnificently conversant with the intricacies of the scientific achievements, with unlimited capacity for teaching, with a facility for associating with others apprehending the hidden power of personalities, inundated with grace, that seeks its equal.

All this magnificence and splendor He is to bury in the corner of a dusty workshop. Not for one, two, or even three years, but for decades He is to ply the lowly trade of a carpenter. *"Ecce venio!"* "Behold I come: to do Thy Will, O God!" He remains in seclusion in a hidden life for thirty years. *"Nonne hic est faber?"* "Is He not a carpenter?" Indeed, He was, and remained such to the hour the Father had ordained.

Finally the time had come for Him to step out, to begin a work which benighted human eyes regarded only as such, but which was nothing less than the continuation of the magnificent work which for thirty years He had wrought day by day, and carried it out to the greater glory of the Father —the fulfilling of the Divine Will. He seeks after nothing else now. *"Ecce venio!"* "Behold I come: to do Thy Will!" Therefore, He disposes His whole public life not according to the dictates of personal judgment and will, not in accord with personal tastes and plans, but perfect conformity with the dispensations of the Father, exactly as He ordains it.

His words, conversations, and discourses are wholly in accord with the Father's Will. He, Himself tells us clearly: "For I have not spoken of myself; but the Father who sent me, He gave me commandment what I should say, and what I should speak . . . The things, therefore, that I speak, even as the Father said unto me, so do I speak."[9] What of His miracles, His works, and His whole mode of action? They are what the Father enjoins. He takes not a single step nor moves His hand to anything outside the Father's Will. "*Me oportet operari opera ejus, qui misit me.*" "I must work the works of Him that sent Me."[10] How sublime a word!

And what are the limits of the scope of His activity? How is it circumscribed? How far could He have reached with His inexhaustible command of persuasive eloquence, which He exercised with the greatest facility, possessed of the power of miracles, of the universal gift of tongues, in the very flower of manhood. He is surrounded on all sides by the direst need and poverty; the relatively small strip of land where He lives is enveloped by the darkest night of error and crassest heathenism.

From a natural point of view, according to the standards of human wisdom, should He not have fared forth into all the world and let His voice ring out across the plains to the very ends of the earth? But, no; "*Non sum missus nisi ad oves, quae perierunt domus Israel.*" "I was not sent but to the sheep that are lost of the house of Israel."[11] It is not the Father's Will, therefore it is not His, He is not come to work according to human plans and cogitations, but to fulfill the Will of Him who sent Him.

Only the accomplishment of the Father's Will, no matter under what conditions, has worth in His sight. This alone He considers truly great, a perfect offering to the

---

9 John 12:49, 50.
10 John 9:4.
11 Matt. 15:24.

Infinite Majesty of the Triune God. From this disposition alone will proceed the salvation of the world, which turned from God through disobedience. Only through it is God glorified, whose Will must "be done on earth as it is in heaven."

Jesus, therefore, never hesitates to break off His career in the midst of a most glorious outward activity. Not for a single moment would He prolong it beyond the hour ordained by the Father. As soon as the Father no longer wills external works, nothing has any further fascination for the Eternal Word, nor is great in His esteem, nor worthy of God. It is in His eyes no activity at all, merely a shell from which the kernel has been taken, a ring without the sparkling diamond. He no longer finds there what His whole being craved, the Father's Will. There He can no longer accomplish what in His eyes alone is a genuine achievement, namely, the fulfilling of this adorable Will.

Without hesitation, therefore, He abandons the scene of His labors, which human calculation would have selected as the most appropriate for a personality with the surpassing talents, gifts, and exquisite distinctions and attainments that adorned Him for the exercise of the most fruitful, astounding activity, not for two or three years, but for the long stretch of a lifetime.

What does He now undertake? It is simply told. "*Ecce venio! ut faciam Deus voluntatem tuam.*" "Behold, I come, O God, to do Thy Will!"

And what does this Will suggest to Him? Something so unreasonable and impracticable in the sight of men, that since the creation of the world nothing similar has ever been ordained; something that viewed in a purely natural light would tend toward the frustration of His entire activity, a useless squandering of the most glorious talents and capabilities, the ruination of His magnificent personality. Jesus is confronted with the *scandalum crucis,* the most shameful suffering, the cross, wherein pure common sense, even with the aid of all its keenest insight and wisdom, sees naught but scandal, pure folly.

"Ecce venio!" "Behold I come!" the Heart of Jesus cries to the Father. He embraces the cross wholeheartedly; He loves the cross, because therein He finds the Father's Will. He loves it because He can show clearly why He came down from heaven, what He sought on earth, and to what extent He was resolved to be true to His ideal, the perfect accomplishment of the Father's Will. *"Sed ut cognoscat mundus, quia diligo Patrem, et sicut mandatum dedit mihi Pater sic facio. Surgite, eamus!"* "That the world may know that I love the Father: and as the Father has given me commandment, so do I: Arise, let us go hence!"[12] And He goes forth and continues to do what He had done for the whole span of His life. He stands fast in obedience, and now unto death, even to the death of the cross.

How truly He can now say to the Father: "I have finished the work which Thou gavest Me to do."[13] It is the work which the Father had commanded Him, and only that. No desire, no word, no step, has taken place beyond the pale of the intentions of the Father, of the eternal plan, as the Father cherished and manifested it to Him. "The work which Thou gavest Me to do," but it shall be the whole work. The mind with all its faculties and capabilities, the will with all its strength and plenitude of

12 John 14:31.
13 John 17:4.

virtue, the heart with all its yearnings and love, the body with all its members and senses—here they were fittingly employed, here they were pressed into sublimest service. *"Opus consummavi, quod dedisti mihi, ut faciam."* Everything has been accomplished as the Father willed it. For this very reason it is full of the glory of God the Father: *". . . gloria Domini plenum est opus ejus,"* full of the glory of the Lord is His work."[14] So plentiful are the merits and the successes that they suffice for the salvation of millions upon millions of souls; that from the abundance of this plenitude we may all receive grace upon grace. It is filled with honor and renown for Himself, for the Father has given Him a name that is above all names, so that in the Name of Jesus all knees bow of those who are in heaven, on earth, and under the earth.

The life of Our Divine Saviour shows us more clearly, more reliably than all other things could, what it means to accomplish outstanding deeds. Let us consider what it means for us always to do what the Father wills. What does God ask of us?

3. "LET US NEVER FORGET OF WHAT HEAD WE ARE THE BODY"[15]

How happy are all those who live under obedience and particularly religious. Can they not cry out with the Prophet: *"Beati sumus, Israel, quia, quae Deo placent, manifesta sunt nobis"*? "Happy are we, O Israel, since it was made manifest to us what pleases God."[16] Through

---

14 Ecclus. 42:16.
15 St. John Chrysostom.
16 Bar. 4:4.

the Rules, the daily horarium, the injunctions of superiors, everything has been made known to us, to the smallest details. If we are in earnest about an enterprise to redound to God's greater honor, a venture that is significant in the sight of the Most High, very well, here is the field of labor. No matter what seems to me of great importance, or in keeping with my competence and tastes, or my own choosing, since it is not in the pattern of God's loving designs, it ceases to be of any value. I can be happy only when I do what God wills, in conformity with His paternal pleasure. There must be a change in spiritual perspective, if I would elude the machinations of the wily tempter and live contentedly in the peace of absolute submission in the spirit of faith. If the Will of God is the sole object of my desire, I shall accomplish what is pleasing to the Most High.

In this inner light of the significance of the Will of God and its power in helping us fashion our sanctity on the anvil of self-denial and humble submission to those who hold His place in our regard, we have a powerful weapon. "Do not be deceived," says St. Francis Xavier, "by the insinuations of the Evil One, who tries to convince you that in another obedience or occupation you would acquit yourself with great splendor for God and your special interests. His intention is to bring you to perform badly what obedience has enjoined."

More and more realizing the eternal warfare between Christ and the Tempter, we must stand victoriously at the post assigned us by God's Will. Especially at the outset in the spiritual life, we must study diligently to banish what in the least tends to diminish our love of the word of obedience, welcoming all the hardships that are inseparable from a life of consummate surrender and inner aspirations for holiness. With a vigorous gesture of determination we must brush aside all allurements that lack the genuine note of God's Will, even should they present themselves in the brilliant garb of the greater glory of God. We reject the sinister approach: "*Vade, retro, Satana!*" "Begone, Satan!" I have come not to do this or that, but to fulfill the Will of Him who has led me into the communion of His Son Jesus Christ Our Lord.

"God is faithful: by whom you are called to the fellowship of His Son Jesus Christ Our Lord."[17] This most adorable Will is now presented to me, and therefore I neither have nor will have any other solicitude than to perform with the utmost exactness for the love of God, what is mine to do at the present moment. This is something truly great and worthy of offering to the Triune God. Even if it be a trifling matter, small in its reach, in the sight of God it is great and pleasing to Him. Let us therefore have on our lips the words of Jesus: "That the world may know that I love the Father, and as the Father hath given me commandment, so do I."[18]

II. DO EVERYTHING AS GOD WILLS IT

We are all eager to achieve great things in virtue and holiness. For this purpose, God imparts to us an overwhelming measure of graces. We are eager to do much for the salvation of souls in divers ways, for it is the special mark of our vocation. We wish to be competent laborers in the Lord's Vineyard, stalwart oarsmen in the bark of

---

17 1 Cor. 1:9.
18 John 14:31.

Peter, pillars of Holy Church, and steadily perfect ourselves. Over and above all this, we wish to promote first and foremost the honor of God, who enriches us from an inexhaustible store. To distinguish ourselves in the service of our Eternal King is our inmost desire. How easy it is for us to render this homage in the simplest act of holy obedience, doing what God wills, as He wills it, and finally from the highest motives, because He wills it.

1. GOD IS GLORIFIED BY OUR COMPLETE SURRENDER

We have seen that this is the supreme norm by which our actions are to be judged, and it is the only one reliable and sure. What does not correspond to it, no matter how significant in itself in the eyes of the world, is nothing, it is useless, a loss of time and effort. The eye of faith must be operative here in full splendor. Whatever obedience or our duties of office enjoin is resplendent with the mark of the Divine Will. We must discharge our duties in the best manner possible. In the work entrusted to me there inheres the request that I carry it out according to its nature, be it meditation, study, instruction, recreation, prayer, or whatever else it be. It is not simply a matter of passing time. The goal of my commission must be attained.

Unless I bestow upon my work the attention it deserves, I will very likely perform it superficially, and the word of the prophet will more or less apply to me: "Cursed be he that doth the work of the Lord deceitfully."[19] If I lack the interest requisite for its discharge, it is my business to pro-

19 Jer. 48:10.

vide it. A rational being, able to contemplate things on all sides, above all priests and religious, will easily find what is enjoined by the Will of God lifted into a higher category. They will see it resplendent in a marvellous new light, with many attractive aspects. Not everything that is opposed to nature is thus removed, but it may be passed over more lightly.

I will be solicitous about something I desire ardently. For this purpose we have received physical and spiritual faculties from God, namely, to use them well in the specific job we have in hand. The means must be employed, the faculties drafted into service wisely and to the purpose, but earnestly and not by halves. "Be not slack and remiss in thy works."[20] God expects a perfect performance of us, to the best of our ability.

On the other hand, however, He does not expect more. It is well to take this to heart, lest we dissipate our energies in disordered, extravagant expenditure of strength, and yield to useless worries, cowardice, discontent, and dejection. Nor does God exact the same degree of achievement from everyone. He does not apply the same measuring lines in all cases, so that He would regard as great only what appeals to Him. He desires five talents as the fruit only from him who has received five. He is therefore satisfied with two talents from him who has received but two. He who has received only one, but works with it as best he may and puts it to profitable use, will on appearing with only one talent newly gained hear the words: "Come, thou good and faithful servant!" as well as the others. God has no need of our goods, looks not so much at the results

---

20 Ecclus. 4:34.

achieved as upon our good will, the readiness to serve Him, our surrender to His least inspiration and the love that enlisted our best resolves and carried them through.

We pay so little heed to this consoling truth and, consequently, we too often yield to merely natural considerations; we forget that in all our works we are servants of God, also in those that are more exterior, more exposed to the human eye, and subject to the judgment of men. Even these works, no matter how they succeed, are worth exactly as much as they have value in the sight of God. He desires us, indeed, to take cognizance of men and strive to meet their just demands: *"Providemus enim bona non solum coram Deo, sed etiam coram hominibus."* "For we forecast what may be good not only before God, but also before men,"[21] St. Paul counsels us.

We discharge our duty because God wills it, and just as He wills it. Our peace and satisfaction, our interior happiness and freedom of spirit should by no means be determined by the measure of outward success and the opinion of men. We are servants of God in everything we undertake. "Whatsoever you do, do it from the heart, as to the Lord, and not to men."[22] Our great concern, therefore, may not be the opinion of men, but the judgment of God Himself. One thing alone is decisive for us: How is the matter constituted before the all-seeing eye of God? What does He will and expect? If I have done all in my power, I have corresponded with the designs of God regarding the exterior aspect of the work perfectly. Beyond this exterior phase, there is another aspect of great

21 2 Cor. 8:21.
22 Col. 3:23.

importance, since we are serving the Most High. The work must not only be done well, but with prudent regard for accompanying circumstances.

2. "PROVIDED ONLY THAT CHRIST IS BEING PROCLAIMED"[23]

An earthly lord or master looks only to see whether and in how far his commands have been discharged. He asks for no more than exterior performance. With God these matters take a different turn. The slightest negligence must be avoided. To Him these things are by no means indifferent. Our filial attitude and interior disposition of humble docility in carrying out His loving designs is in some instances the principal part. The work may be marred by remissness and neglect, or it may be something pure, sparkling, and adorned with precious stones. No one is empowered to free me from the obligation of seeking God in all things. He is displeased with our infidelities and deliberate infractions of cloistral discipline, or Christian charity, or lack of submission to authority ordained of God. If I find things agreeable, fascinating, I must be watchful lest I yield too much to personal satisfaction. Many acts of interior mortification are indispensable.

If, on the contrary, the matter is disagreeable, annoying, colorless or repulsive, I must exercise sufficient self-control to make the best of it in a delightful act of homage of the love of God. "*Servite Domino in laetitia.*" "Serve God joyfully," is a splendid exhortation here. If one is gifted and can function with ease in difficult matters, vanity may creep in to vitiate the work. Subtle self-complacency

---

23 Phil. 1:18.

may tempt him to make light of others, who in spite of honest effort, still achieve but little. The omniscient eye of God is sure to detect my unlovely sentiments. He knows in how far I obey the injunction of the Holy Spirit: *"Noli extollere te in faciendo opere tuo."* "Extol not thyself in doing thy work."[24]

If my faculties are limited, and I achieve nothing but mediocrity or even less, then I am easily discouraged and depressed. God expects me to rise superior to these moods and to conform with perfect suavity to His holy Will. This is an excellent opportunity for the practice of virtue, and putting to the best use the talents God has given us, be they only one or two. Love supplies whatever might be lacking in our deeds. God would have us remember that we are to work for Him alone in His Divine Presence, detached and full of joy. We should carefully avoid faults and imperfections and aim towards sharing Christ's love of us in all we do. Only when adorned with these virtues, as with sparkling gems, can we hope to merit the pleasure of God in our work. *"Et omne opus electum justificabitur, et qui operatur illud, honorabitur in illo."* "And every excellent work shall be justified: and the worker thereof shall be honored therein."[25] Words full of unction, if pondered in silent prayer.

We all know very well how many circumstances may enter into the daily performance of our assigned obedience. Yet the means of sanctifying them all is our present concern. Weather conditions, dwelling, the place, the distribution of time, the fixed horarium, frequent interruptions,

---

24 Ecclus. 10:29.
25 Ecclus. 14:21.

all are paramount in creating a favorable atmosphere for successful and agreeable work. My attitude in these circumstances is by no means negligible; it is as noteworthy as the charge itself. God observes the sentiments, the judgments, and the attitudes that sway my heart. All these circumstances cumulatively are willed by Him in every contingency, regulated and permitted by His loving Heart. He desires me to conform; He looks for my willing surrender to His merciful designs, and proffers sufficient and abundant grace and spiritual strength. Let me ponder the words of Holy Writ, the Saviour's own in the Apocalypse: *"Non invenio opera tua plena coram Deo meo."* "I find not thy works full before my God."[26] Alas, to my shame I must admit that my works are not full. I have used the gold that my Lord gave me to fashion a beautiful crown, but the many precious stones He offered me in the process of the work I failed to set in the crown, and let them be lost. On the very spots where they should be sparkling, the gold itself has lost its lustre, is mixed with ignoble metals, sometimes wholly replaced by them.

Is not attention to this multitude of details a positive hindrance to free and spontaneous execution of the Divine Will? This contention holds only for those who would seek virtue outside the special areas of assigned work. Otherwise it is worthless as a fictitious cover for lukewarmness. Let me ask, what is more conducive to the progress of my work, impatience, moodiness and disgust, or resignation, equanimity and cheerfulness in the Lord? Cheerfulness in our duties is of inestimable value in maintaining a fitting balance for the wholehearted performance

---

26 Apoc. 3:2.

of our God-given tasks. An occasional glance Godward, the good intention, recalling supernatural motives, making a brief visit to the Blessed Sacrament—these work wonders in the soul tried in the effort to acquit himself valiantly and unselfishly. The least act of mine will be greatly enhanced in this manner, and the sweet odor of the sacrifice and oblation of our cherished plans and ambitions for God's love and honor will rise as a powerful intercessor to the throne of the Triune God.

Let us repeat that to cultitvate the indispensable peace and equanimity for any activity pleasing to God, I must surrender myself unconditionally with the utmost trust of a loyal son to the dispositions of my heavenly Father, fully convinced that His loving Providence guides me unfailingly through my superiors. It is the supernatural point of view that gives light to the willing soul. In this spirit of living faith, I must apply myself with all the circumspection and prudence in my power to discharge well the specific task assigned, overcoming myself and using the means to curb the passions. Holy obedience will be a mighty impetus to the most perfect performance of my charge, my seizing every occasion for acquiring the virtues that are so large a part of our ordinary work. Thus its performance will be greatly enhanced in the sight of God, as it registers a decided strengthening of the will for further victories.

Our daily meditation will charge our soul with the spirit of faith and every virtue; it will fructify with heavenly grace and light all that we encounter through the day. A momentary thought of the presence of God before beginning the work will suffice to dispose the heart to our best efforts. By a careful scrutiny of our conscience in the daily examen, we detect the forces that influence our actions one way or another. Thus we the more easily dispose ourselves, with a firm will, to proceed in the spirit of total abandonment to the Will of God in all things, losing ourselves in His divine immensity and all-loving Providence. In this spirit of pure intention our work will please God and draw down blessings upon ourselves and others. In our day where externalization in every line seems the hallmark of successful endeavor, it is especially important to stress the pure intention. Like a diamond among the other precious stones that embellish our work, the pure intention will shine out with distinctive lustre giving joy to the Heart of God. By faithfully utilizing the means just spoken of, we will be able to discharge our duties in union with the holy Will of God and overcome the inertia of natural dislike and ennui.

III. Do Everything For God Because He Wills It

We need hardly dwell further on the great role the inner spirit plays in all our actions and omissions. This spirit is absolutely necessary; supernatural motives must vivify our words and works and thus render them precious in the sight of God, deserving of merit for eternity. The words of Sacred Scripture will have a deeper meaning for us: *"Gloria Domini plenum est opus ejus."* "Full of the glory of the Lord is His work."[27]

---

27 Ecclus. 12:16.

1. LOVE OF THE FATHER WAS THE SOUL OF CHRIST'S LIFE

a) *Childlike trust and joyous hope are two levers
that raise our hearts heavenward and render
our actions meritorious for heaven*

Motives of love to encourage the inner life, strengthen us in the patient carrying of a cross, or any disagreeable happening, with joyous anticipation of a beautiful heavenly crown, are a positive asset in the spiritual life. The intense desire to be truly interior souls, with a deeper realization of transcendent values lifts the soul above earth's lowliness.

b) *Joyous hope*

The Psalmist must have been a man after the Heart of God. Yet he was not remiss in applying even these lesser motives to maintain his fidelity at a white heat. "I have inclined my heart to do thy justifications forever, for the reward."[28] He himself admits that the hope of the recompense moved his heart to yield to the demands of a just and merciful God.

Moses did likewise, and the Lord Himself gave him the testimony of being a most faithful servant. The joys, the honors, and the delights of the royal court were at his disposal, but he preferred to share the sufferings and the hardships of the people of God. Why? we ask. "He looked at the recompense." "*Aspiciebat enim in retributionem,*" says St. Paul. "Rather choosing to be afflicted with the people of God, than to have the pleasure of sin for a time."[29]

---

28 Ps. 118:112.
29 Heb. 11:25.

His eyes were fixed on the reward in the life to come. This was peculiar to the just of the Old Testament.

The efficacy of these incentives, however, and the value they put upon our acts and omissions, have not been abrogated by the New Dispensation. On the contrary! Who is more eloquent in depicting the reward that awaits the faithful servant in the life beyond than Jesus Christ Himself? How He aims to replenish our hearts with the hope of celestial rewards! How He aims to awaken in us a holy longing for the kingdom which His heavenly Father has prepared for us! He never wearies of announcing His "Beatitudes": Blessed are the poor, blessed the meek, the peacemakers, the pure of heart. An eightfold "Blessed" flows from His divine lips, and in conclusion He once more flings wide the portals of heaven: "Be glad and rejoice, for your reward is very great in heaven."[30]

There remains not the slightest doubt that through the motives of a wholesome fear of punishment and the hope of an eternal reward, we should intensify our zeal. St. Ignatius observes that though we should be primarily guided by love, yet we do well to make much of these lesser motives and inducements to virtue. They will aid us to lift our weak nature, to make it impervious to the enticements of earthly joys and delights, as well as encourage us to persevere faithfully on the way of the cross.

c) *The spirit of the love of the Father*
in the spirit of Christ

For us who desire to excel in the service of God and give Him joy, this will not yet suffice. Even if the fore-

---

30 Matt. 5:12.

going incentives are infinitely superior to all mere temporal motives, we must still aspire to higher things, and not fail to enhance the silver with gold, as St. Paul exhorts us: "But be zealous for the better gifts. And I show unto you yet a more excellent way."[31]

A far nobler spirit must animate us and pierce to the depths of every act. It is the spirit of love. This is necessary; the spirit of love is the spirit of Christ, and it must, therefore, be the spirit of those He has chosen. Attracted by His ineffable person and united to Him through the most tender and intimate bonds, they are, consequently, of one heart and soul with Him. The example of Jesus is the strongest motive for those who wish to follow Him closely. What was the soul of His actions and omissions? What beautiful intention prompted His every act?

2. "HOW HATH HE NOT WITH HIMSELF GIVEN US ALL THINGS"[32]

"Ecce venio!" "Behold I come," He says in the first moments of His life. "Behold I come! It is written of Me that I should do Thy Will." *"Deus meus voluit!"* Yes, my God, I will it. Do we understand these words? It suffices for the Lord to know that God wills it, and with His eyes fixed upon the Father's Will, He enters upon His giant course with irresistible power and strength. "Behold, I come. My God, I will it," because Thou willest it, in order to please Thee.

The same pure intention guides Him along the path He trod magnanimously. "Did you not know that I must be

---

31 1 Cor. 12:31.
32 Rom. 8:32.

about My Father's business?" we hear His reply to His Mother. It is easy to detect in these words again a ray of the fire of love that burns in the Heart of Jesus. It is the Father's house, the Father's Business, the Father's Will; more is not needed to rivet Him with His whole strength, His whole person to it. For Him it is self-evident that He be where His Father wills Him to be, that He should do what the Father wills Him to do, that He act as the Father expects it of Him.

"*Quae placita sunt Ei, facio semper.*" "I do always the things that please Him,"[33] again He tells us. God, My Father, His pleasure, His honor, these are thoughts which alone preoccupy His divine mind.

Love is the preeminent motive of all the actions and omissions of Our Lord. Even at the weakest moment of His life, if we be permitted to say it, in the hour in which He allowed His whole human nature to resist the pending passion, His love still retains the upper hand. "If it be possible!" He cries to the Father on Olivet. "If it be possible, let this chalice pass from Me. Nevertheless not as I will, but as Thou wilt!"[34] The Father, His Will, His pleasure are here again the mainstay of His implicit trust, consoling, encouraging, animating Him. They are the motive that fortifies Him, until He finally cries: "*Surgite, eamus!*" "Rise, let us go!" And with determination and resolve He goes forth to meet suffering and His bitter passion. With irresistible power the love that fills His Heart to overflowing urges Him on.

---

33 John 8:29.
34 Matt. 26:39.

Peter soon becomes aware of this when he would defend his Lord by means of the sword. Here again, His love breaks forth in the dreadful silence: "The chalice which My Father hath given Me, shall I not drink it?"[35] To Him it is incomprehensible that something which the Father wills should be left undone.

This is the spirit of Our Divine Saviour. He began, carried through, completed His work because the Father had laid it on His shoulders and willed it so. All other motives were subservient to this noblest and most sublime force. All the intentions He may cherish for the practice of virtue, of amassing merit, saving souls, to enter the glory of heaven, all these should finally have one purpose—the Father's glory, His honor: "I seek not My honor, but the honor of Him who sent Me."

Like the rays of the sun, when they gather in a focal point comprising all their splendor and fire, so all the activities of His Most Sacred Heart have one aim, to glorify the Father, to please Him, to accomplish His Will. *"Opus consummavi, quod dedisti mihi."* "I have accomplished the work that Thou hast given Me." With these words He approaches His Father at the end of His life. Thus we hear what characterized His activity all through life; the Father's pleasure by the perfect fulfilment of His most holy Will. How pure, how scintillating was the good intention with Our Divine Saviour! The spirit of love reigned supreme.

Dare we act differently, wishing as we do to follow Jesus most closely, to be of one heart and mind with Him, to strive to bear some resemblance to Him, in consequence

---

35 John 18:11.

of our sublime vocation? Surely not, for to please God, to act through love of Him, is the spirit of Christ, and it must also be ours.

3. "EACH STEP TAKEN IN LOVE IS A STEP IN HOLINESS, IN UNION WITH GOD"[36]

Let us briefly consider the value of the pure intention or loving sentiments in all our actions, from another angle. Its efficacy is threefold, aiding us to a more perfect discharge of our duties, imparting to them a higher, interior worth, and rendering them pleasing to God.

a) *The perfect discharge of our duties*

"In all thy works, keep the preeminence."[37] Who will most perfectly correspond with this injunction of the Holy Spirit? Most assuredly he who desires to please God in giving Him joy. If that is my aim in all I do, I will not be careless in the least. I will, as far as possible, devote the same solicitude to each task, because He for whom I labor is always at my side to aid and encourage me.

I am privileged to work for an omnipresent God and Father. Whether men observe me or not, or the surveillance of Superiors be operative, I am always under observation. If I wish to satisfy my Divine Master, I will never be guilty of lassitude in the least performance. I will perform all my work not only with meticulous care, but with loving regard for the pleasure of God. God knows of what I am capable; He knows my faculties and talents and the

---

36 Marmion.
37 Ecclus. 33:23.

graces that are allotted to me. When I work in the presence of the Omniscient One, therefore, for His love alone, to afford Him the pleasure of a child to his father, I will do everything as well as possible under the circumstances. Men may regard my work as far from excellent, it matters not, for in the sight of God it may have great merit. The pure intention aids me in achieving a more perfect work in every regard.

b) *The inner value of our work is greatly enhanced by the good intention*

This second advantage is of deep significance, if we would render our works pleasing to God. Two religious, for example, may bestow the same care and efficiency upon a piece of work, yet the one yields little more than worthless coin, whereas the other by reason of the oft renewed pure intention produces brilliant gems at every turn. The discrepancy may be easily explained. The first religious acts from habit and lower, earthly, human considerations, hardly from supernatural motives and love of God. The other religious seeks in all she does only God and His infinite pleasure. Obstacles only blunt the sharp edge of worldly suggestions and aid to an ideal performance in the sight of God. In this case the words of St. Anselm are verified: "Everything, even the lowliest, the most ordinary, performed through love, will be transmuted into gold; still more, it will be divinized."

This transformation comes to pass through the most intimate union with Christ in virtue of the love that prompts my act. In the strength of this consideration, we should feel ourselves impelled, as far as possible, to perform all our actions with the pure intention, for love of God, solely for His praise and glory.

c) *A third and most inestimable advantage of the pure intention is this that it augments God's greater glory and delight*

Our Lord Himself assured us that the good intention gives pleasure to God; it delights His eye as He told St. Gertrude on one occasion. Weary and fatigued, she had refreshed herself with delicious grapes. As was her wont, she did this with the pure intention, as if she were offering this refreshment to Jesus Himself.

Behold what a beautiful reward was hers. She was delighted to hear from the lips of the Lord these words: "I will admit that you have made a genuine compensation for the bitter draft I took on the cross for love of you, for I have just now tasted an inexpressible sweetness from your heart. Remember, my daughter, the purer your intention in the daily little acts even of service of the body, the more you desire lovingly to honor and praise Me thereby, the greater are the delights that your soul affords Me."

Let us, too, prepare such a delicious treat for Jesus. Through loving sentiments, let us inform all our actions with that heavenly sweetness for Him. May the spirit of the love of Jesus our God predominate in us and be the generous motive force of our whole life; then we shall be entirely dedicated to God in holy love.

CHAPTER IX

GROWTH IN THE LOVE OF GOD

"Full of the glory of the Lord is His Work."[1]
"And the fire on the altar shall always burn; and the priest shall feed it putting wood on it every day in the morning."[2]

I. "For the Sake of Christ The Lord"

We read in Holy Scripture how God charged Moses to keep the fire always burning on the altar of sacrifice. There is an altar for everyone, on which the fire may never die out, but always burn brightly. St. Gregory alludes to the beautiful Old Testament text just cited, when he says: "The altar of the Lord on which the fire must incessantly burn is our heart; from it the flame of love must rise uninterruptedly to God."

1. THE FIRE OF LOVE

a) *Your heart is in very truth an altar of fiery love*

But every fire—even this—must be nourished. How can this be done? How does the flame rise to the very throne

---

1 Ecclus. 42:16.
2 Lev. 6:12.

of God with a sweet fragrance from the depth of our hearts? It comes to pass through the pure intention, which is in reality nothing other than the spirit of the love of God, forgetting self, invigorating our every deed, large or small. It must become so much a part of ourselves as to penetrate all our actions, even the least, that we may be wholly immolated the Thee, O God. "My God and my All!" O Lord, let us feel the warmth of love's sacred fire that never dies. Support us with Thy divine munificence.

b) *In how far have I acquired these noble sentiments?*

To what extent is the spirit of love dominant in my heart? From the Heart of Christ burning with love for us the stream of supernatural life breaks forth. How far is its influence felt in my thoughts, my wishes, my actions and omissions? In the spirit of faith, do I detect my God dwelling in me? He will give me strength to leave myself and in simple love to cling to Him. Thomas a-Kempis says: "God regardeth more out of how much love a man doth a work, than how much he doth."[3]

2. THE DEMANDS OF LOVE

Every sacrifice made for love of God insures new grace and wholesome energy and strength for shaping the soul unto Christlikeness. We often think that we are acting through love of God, and yet our work is vitiated by an overwhelming measure of self-love and selfish plans and aspirations. "Natural inclination," a-Kempis again observes,

---

3 Imit. Bk. 1. ch. 15.

"self-will, hope of reward, study of our own interests will seldom be absent." The greater my love of God, the more intimately will I study His divine complacence. How can I be assured of acting from motives of pure love? A splendid sign is equanimity of soul in time of distress and seeming neglect, or under criticism and censure.

If on such occasions I am perturbed, resentful, vindictive, I may be certain that love alone does not live in me and control my desires and aspirations. I sought human applause and recognition of my work, and lost sight of the power of love and of God's holy Will. Otherwise lack of outward success would not be able to disrupt my peace of soul so thoroughly and leave it parched and lifeless. Coveting praise and esteem the soul slavishly clings to earth. The many faults and imperfections constitute a formidable barrier to divine grace and generous detachment.

a) *The strength of my soul*

His divine pleasure will be the strength of my soul. I must immolate myself to the Father's Will in the spirit of Christ Himself. St. Paul admonishes us: "Whatever you do in word or work," he says, "let all be done in the Name of Jesus Christ." St. Chrysostom observes "for the sake of Christ." St. Paul again: "Whatever you do, whether you eat or drink, do all for the glory of God." Considering this, how could those who are striving for the perfection of the spiritual life, justify themselves if in the course of the day they barely call to mind momentarily the presence of God to make a renewed offering of all they do?

Priests and religious, in virtue of their divine call, aspire to a higher life, to promote the honor of God and defend

His holy rights, His secret operations. The pure intention is of major importance. In the flame of His love, all defects and selfish tendencies must be controlled. God has a claim to our every thought, word, and work. We must be on our guard lest other motives intrude to vitiate our best efforts. Sensuality, carelessness, creature comforts, indolence and lassitude, seek to enter the inner sanctuary of our heart and work untold havoc. These detestable intruders would induce us to swerve from the path of the purest service of the Most High. The saints, well aware of these dangers in sinister design waylaying virtue, exercised the utmost caution to achieve the victory, no matter what the price. It was love's inestimable privilege.

b) *The example of the saints*

St. Ignatius, Father Lancicius relates, achieved extraordinary perfection in this matter. He was wholly permeated by love. It was the very soul of his being. Every thought, every word of his tended straight to the Heart of God. There was nothing in his life that did not bear the sparkling impress of the pure intention and intimate union with the God of love.

Let us imitate the saints. It requires only a little attention to raise our heart to God with an aspiration, a silent thought and prayer, "O my God, all for Thee!" "For love of Thee!" "For Thy honor!" Or, the simple, "*Ita, Pater,*" "Yes, Father, because it pleases Thee!" These momentary outbursts of fervent love aimed directly at the Heart of the most loving Heavenly Father, soothe the spirit and help subdue the passions, as we find safe refuge in the clefts of His loving Heart.

c) *Cleansing the heart of inordinate love*

The love of God is further enhanced by self-denial, a cleansing of the heart of all that savors of self-love; it gladly immolates itself to the Beloved. It permeates our whole life with the spirit of the love of the God who is *all love* and abandonment to His holy Will. Without this whole-burnt offering, our protestations of love and loyalty would lack sincerity. They would be empty and incur the Lord's reproach: "This people honors Me with their lips, but their hearts are far from Me!" It is not enough to protest our love of God in all we do by mere words. We must resolutely reject everything that would vitiate our immolation; movements of vanity, comfort, convenience from selfish motives, laziness and indifference must be abolished in the conviction of our own unworthiness. Trust in Divine Providence guiding and directing all things puts on our lips the beautiful words of Augustine: "He crowns His own gifts in us."

The sacrifices asked of us are for the most part mere trifles, yet through every denial and oblation our heart grows purer and our love of God, more intense. This love will gradually reign supreme in our hearts and, finally, like the sun at midday, shed its rays over all we do.

"*Sol illuminans per omnia respexit,*" and all our activity will be replete with the glory of God; "*et gloria Domini plenum est opus ejus.*"[4]

"The sun giving light hath looked upon all things, and full of the glory of the Lord is His work."

---

4 Ecclus. 42:16.

CHAPTER X

"THE STARS AT THEIR POSTS SHINE AND REJOICE"

"The stars at their posts shine and rejoice: When He calls them they answer. 'Here we are!' shining with joy for their Maker."[1]

What the prophet here says symbolically of the stars, may also be said of us, particularly of religious. The voice of God-given authority called us, and we answered: "Here we are!" Oh, that the further words of the prophet may likewise apply to us! Namely, that we discharge our duties cheerfully at the post assigned us, there to shine and distinguish ourselves in faithful, humble service. A fine sense of spiritual values enhances our actions in the sight of God. "Shining with joy for their Maker." *"Et luxerunt ei cum jucunditate, qui fecit illas."*

1. "THE STARS AT THEIR POSTS SHINE AND REJOICE"—FIDELITY TO DUTY

Like the stars, we must persevere at our post cheerfully, discharge our duties in obedience, doing God's Will and concerning ourselves in His work. His grace is not wanting to our perfect surrender. This must be our constant aim,

---

1 Bar. 3:34, 35.

and we have exceptional reasons for such striving, through the light of faith. We shall work with joyous hearts and submission as long as obedience allows us to continue in our present employment. Our cheerfulness in all our undertakings derives strength from our love of God.

a) *Our work in obedience is God's Will*

It is the feeling of certainty and clarity in knowing the Will of God. The question: "Lord, what wilt Thou have me do?" "*Domine, quid me vis facere?*"[2] is definitely solved for us. God wills to guide us through others, yet it is always the Lord who in His loving Providence disposes our actions and omissions, who guides and directs us, in accord with His infinite designs. "The stars shine and rejoice; when He calls them, they answer, 'Here we are!' shining with joy for their Maker." Let us be on our guard lest Satan try to destroy our joy and inner certainty and trust. He is diabolically clever in devising ways and means surreptitiously or openly to deceive us into believing that elsewhere they could find a more congenial and satisfactory field for apostolic labor for the good of souls.

Dissatisfaction, disillusionment, and kindred feelings harass the perturbed soul under his attacks. Hear what St. Ignatius advises us in this encounter. He exhorts us not to let the slightest doubt arise, but to obey in loving surrender. He would have us cultivate invulnerable confidence and trust in the benign goodness of the Heavenly Father, who assures us that through docility to those given

---

2 Acts 9:16.

us as His representatives He will inerrantly lead us to peace in Christian charity and happiness.

"The stars at their posts shine and rejoice." To give light where God has called us, in the place to which obedience assigns us is something great. It is our privilege through God's goodness and ineffable solicitude. It is for us the only way, and so it remains indisputably as long as the voice of obedience desires it. Such consoling certainty should bolster our spirits and help us surrender willingly to the call of duty with alacrity and happy abandon. Think of the stars. "They shine and rejoice." Joy dilates the heart, makes it capable of noble, even heroic, deeds while it radiates peace and sweet contentment to our environment.

b) *Our work blessed by obedience*

There is another more potent reason for our cheerful dedication at the post obedience has marked out for us. It is the fact that there where God desires us to serve Him, we may actually contribute more to His honor and glory. What a powerful source of interior peace and loving surrender! It is hard for a man to labor without realizing the fruitage for which he toiled, without seeing results; it bears him down, as if it shut out the light of day. How delightful, on the contrary, is the feeling of having even in a small way bestowed a service on another, benefited ourselves and others by a generous, unselfish token or aid. Religious are fortunate enough to achieve this delight in their daily tasks, provided they are alert, be the work burdensome or light.

To be vividly conscious of being occupied in the sight of God is the criterion of value in all our endeavors;

our work must conform to the Will of God, or it is wasted energy. No matter how insignificant may seem the charge, or how weak and indisposed for its demands our strength may seem, we can always rely on the special support of God's grace, even beyond what our own limited understanding is hesitant to ask. "God guided the just and gave him the knowledge of the holy things, made him honorable in his labours, and accomplished his labours."[3] *"Honestavit illum in laboribus, et complevit labores illius."* In every office or work entrusted to us, there springs the fountain of interior joy.

How beautifully the Saviour points the way of laboring effectively for the glory of the Father, thrusting aside all thoughts of self or selfish aims! "My meat is to do the Will of Him that sent Me, that I may perfect His work."[4] St. Ignatius counsels well when he says: "May everyone be convinced that he will make progress in spiritual things in the degree to which he forsakes self-love, self-will, and the thirst for personal satisfaction."

Should we not in things that are naturally unpleasant or uncongenial, preserve our spirit of joy and inner satisfaction and peace in the charity of Christ? Since the voice of obedience has enjoined the momentary duties upon us, we may be assured of the richest graces and supernatural aid for their accomplishment. The cheerful acceptance of the Will of God in things that go against the grain is heroic and meritorious, worthy of a soul dear to God and consecrated to His eternal pleasure. If we strive to acquire virtue and holiness in the face of difficulties, we must fix

---

3 Wis. 10:10.
4 John 4:34.

our gaze upon the Father's divine plan and Will. To glorify God, to cooperate in His beneficent designs must be the end and aim of our endeavors under all circumstances.

2. "SHINING WITH JOY FOR THEIR MAKER"

This is our second privilege, namely, to give light at the post assigned us in obedience, and there to shine forth. The light we give must be pure and complete, a shining light. In hours of darkness and drab obscurity of God's light, we can still adore the loving Hand of God in our momentary desolation. We must do all in our power in the activity that is ours. God has sent us into His vineyard that we may utilize to the best of our ability the gifts and talents entrusted to us.

a) *The light must be complete and shining*

It will not suffice for our service to be whole and entire, simply marking time, so far as each one understands it and is capable of discharging it. It must be fired with enthusiasm borne up by faith, hope, and love of God. God the Lord does not send us into His vineyard that we may squander time in sheer idleness. Our place in this field of labor, our employment, no matter what it be , is truly God's concern. What He enjoins exacts our best and finest efforts unto perfect achievement. Not in vain have we been so long in the school of perfection. With the grace of God we have become familiar with the intimate ways of virtuous living.

The light we shed, therefore, must be shining, to show forth the greatness of serving the Lord our God, whose loving Providence directs our every step. We should surrender ourselves into the hands of our legitimate superiors with great generosity; they represent the holiness and majesty of God to us. What the voice of obedience enjoins is for us undeniably the Will of God, than which we can do nothing more perfect in life.

To execute this divine command, therefore, deserves the noblest aspirations. The clever insinuations of the tempter enticing souls to forego the sanctions of obedience in the daily round of duties must be absolutely rejected. The light must be complete and shining, stirring profound soul-depths. We must strive to attain the degree of excellence justly required of us in our apostolic vocation. Like the stars, we must shine and give forth our light, for love, and St. John tells us, "God is love."

b) *It must be a pure light*

We must, indeed, shine, but with a light of incomparable purity, uncontaminated by earthly admixture. Our work and the virtues for which the occasion arises in its discharge, must be managed in a way that approximates perfection for love of God, not for personal satisfaction, nor for the vain honor of men shall it be made an oblation to the Most High. Such ignoble sentiments when they creep in vitiate what is good, dim the light of our good works, of even the best. Where they are overwhelmingly present, they transform the light into utter darkness. "If thy eye be evil," Jesus says, "thy body also will be full of darkness," that is, if our intention is impure and ignoble, our work will be the same. "Take care, therefore," He con-

tinues, "that the light that is in thee be not darkness."[5]
Never shall this come to pass. We will solicitously discountenance all motives that do not reach beyond the
dark areas of the purely natural and human.

In all our endeavors, higher, supernatural motives
should radiate light and clarity to pierce the darkness, "as when a bright lamp illumines thee".[6] It is
salutary for us to consider the punishment God reserves
for the careless and negligent servant. A reinforcement
of our spiritual fortifications must be the determined
way of routing evil insinuations. Still more should we cling
to the hope of an everlasting recompense, which God in
His condescending goodness holds out to us. Thoughts
such as these are well calculated to rouse us to a realization
of the spiritual strength that resides in the love of Christ
and lifts us above the merely natural in our apostolic labors.
A self-sacrificing soul will eagerly respond to divine inspiration, instead of studying to satisfy selfish whims, in
cowardly flight. Through closest union with Christ and by
wholehearted denial, we enhance our inner life, grow
stronger, and participate more generously in the full measures of His grace.

The final object of our labors and all activity, aside
from any personal supernatural advantage, must be the
greater glory of God. In the spiritual life there can be no
deviation from this supreme and steadfast relation of
homage and adoration of the Most High. The entire performance must be resplendent in the purest light, scintillating and bright, to extol God's grandeur and magnifi-

---

5 Luke 11:34, 35.
6 Ibid.

6

cence, in thanksgiving for His ineffable goodness. This must be the one ambition of our life. Though lofty and geared to high perfection, it is nothing burdensome. Nor do we stand alone.

In our midst there is the Sun of Justice, Jesus in the Most Blessed Sacrament of the Altar. What an ocean of divine light streams from His Sacred Heart on all sides! Jesus wishes to rejoice in our love. "These things I have spoken to you, that my joy may be in you, and that your joy may be filled."[7] Let us have recourse to Him with our whole heart, with perseverance and strength, with profound exertion, thirsting for God and desiring to be wholly His. Then out of the fulness of our love we shall certainly radiate splendor and light in our assigned field of apostolic activity, in the purest light, in joy and exultation, like the stars shining for the glory of their Creator, our God and Father. *"Et luxerunt ei cum jucunditate, qui fecit illas."* "Shining with joy for their Maker." Our entire family, faithfully gathered about the Eucharistic Throne of Jesus in the Blessed Sacrament, will be, indeed, a heaven declaring the glory of God. Lord, that we may see! Enlighten us and let us see the beauty of Thy Face!

---

7 John 15:11.

CHAPTER XI

LOVE OF THE CROSS

> *"Greater love than this no one has, that one lay down his life for his friends."*[1]
> *"This is My Blood of the new covenant, which is being shed for many unto the forgiveness of sins."*[2]

I. The Victory of the Cross

"Ought not Christ to have suffered these things, and so to enter into his glory?"[3]

These words from the lips of the glorified Christ were addressed to the two disciples as they walked along slowly, perplexed, toward Emmaus. We Christians in this vale of tears, like the Emmaus wanderers, meet the Divine Traveler at life's crossroads. It is ours to believe in the power of His hand guiding us, and to be alive even to the faintest pressure from the Blessed Companion. Though we may not recognize Him, He walks along with us, solving our doubts and expounding to us the mystery of the cross.

---

1 John 15:13.
2 Matt. 26:28.
3 Luke 24:26.

1. FRUITFULNESS OF THE CROSS

"I will take the chalice of salvation, and I will call upon the name of the Lord."[4] From His cross on our altars He wills to draw our hearts to Himself. He would teach us how to carry our own cross, for it is laid on by the infinite goodness of a loving Father. In the strength of the Blood of Christ, let us be docile hearers of His divine teaching on this admirable mystery. Jesus, the Great Loving One, would be the unseen companion of our way. He stands there waiting, for He wills to be our Companion and Consoler on our journey to the heavenly Emmaus, where we shall behold Him face to face and sing His glory forevermore.

For this purpose He continues to dwell among us in our tabernacles, in the Most Blessed Sacrament. He nourishes us "with wine and quenches our thirst with water out of the rock." Daily we are privileged to partake of the supreme happiness of communicating under the species of bread with the hidden God in the tabernacle. Day by day we are free to converse with Him in intimate communion, in complete immolation of ourselves to His holy Will in all that concerns us. Though called to share His glory with Him in eternal bliss, we are still in a state of trial, subject to suffering and all manner of reverses, for we must follow the road to its final end, to extreme hardships and loneliness, should we lose sight of His gentle guidance. Alas, how often like the two disheartened disciples, we go sorrowingly along our way, burdened and fatigued! We are, therefore, truly in need of a Comforter, who will instruct us in the mystery of the cross, transmute

---

4 Ps. 115:4.

it, and drop deep into our hearts the glowing love of the cross. This Comforter is Jesus in the Most Blessed Sacrament of the Altar, the transfigured Son of God present in the tabernacle.

This may seem peculiar, for the willingness to carry the cross is taught us above all by the crucified, suffering Saviour. But the fruit of loving the cross does not thrive alone and not in its complete fulness and maturity in the contemplation of the bitter passion of Christ. It is true, the seed of love of the cross is there sunk deep into our hearts, again and again, fructified by the Blood of Christ. It develops there and reaches a vigorous growth, yet the full maturity and fruitfulness of love of the cross is tested only in the sunlight of the Risen Saviour. Companionship with Jesus glorified generates new courage and cheerful determination to follow the road marked out by Christ Himself, leading onward to such glory. The last remnants of the folly and hardness of heart, principally concerning the mystery of the cross that clings to us all, as it did to the two Emmaus disciples, must disappear in the surpassing splendor and glory to which the cross leads.

II. Glory and Splendor of the Cross

"The words that I have spoken to you, are spirit and life"[5]
"In your patience you shall possess your souls"[6]

2. our companionship with the glorified saviour fills us with the conviction that this holds also for us

From His comforting presence we steadily go to our lifework with an increased love of Jesus Himself and of

---

5 John 6:64.
6 Luke 21:19.

His cross. We leave Him with the intense desire to walk His way of the cross and ours, that leads to it, but not as yet to enjoy the glory that we beheld. How beautiful it must be to be assured of divine guidance at the Hand of God. We will renew ourselves in the love of the cross and accept disagreeable happenings, no matter whence they spring, with a deep sense of security. To bear them without yielding to the demands of self-love, may require a real sacrifice of us, but it shall not find us unprepared. This is the essence of our personal cross.

St. Bernard distinguishes three ways of bearing the cross meritoriously. We should bear it willingly, patiently, and cheerfully. He would have us bear what is disagreeable patiently, with complete surrender and with a holy, fiery zeal that is tenderly devoted to the thought of walking with Christ on the road leading up and around the Mount of Crucifixion. He would have us bear disagreeable things patiently, without consulting the dictates of nature. We shall naturally continue to feel the hard, bitter rind, but our will must remain firm, determined, joyous in this intrinsic test of our love for Him who loves us to excess, to His death on the cross. With the help of God's grace, we hope to achieve this purpose of our striving, and having attained it, cherish it perseveringly, not alone in desire, but in actual deed on every occasion.

a) *The patient endurance of what seems inexplicable to us, or what goes against the grain*

It is the ability to control ourselves under hardships and disappointments to such an extent that voluntary movements of disgust or discontent in word or action rarely occur. Our intellect will no longer be confused, nor our will weakened by these unforeseen and wholly uncongenial events to such an extent that we allow ourselves to be tempted to sin and to lose sight of God, who is still willing to be our guide and comforter on our apostolic journey.

The cross in one form or other is once for all unavoidable. To experience no reverses, to suffer no hardships, no severe trials of soul or body, is not the happy lot of the present life, but only of the life to come. But what joy to be loyally attached to our Great Leader. His intrepidity in the face of the gravest sufferings that human ingenuity can devise, must fire us with a like enthusiasm to conform to the cross, bold, fearless, intrepid, avid for even greater trials. God drove man from paradise not that he should find joys and delights, but that in labor, fatigue, and pain, he might do penance. Every reasonable human being, however, yields to sheer necessity and to the inevitable. To fight against the inevitable is foolish, indeed.

The folly is even greater if we are so strongly opposed to an evil that our attitude actually intensifies it. This occurs beyond doubt through impatience, rebellion, sadness and disgust. To the cross which in no way is lifted, the impatient bearer also adds sin and guilt, and the penance to be visited upon his sin. There remains nothing for us to do save to bow our heads in humble acceptance. *"Humiliate capita vestra Deo."* Bow your head before the Lord your God, who sends it, the Apostle admonishes us. It is necessary, all the more since our first duty is not to offend the Omnipotent God.

Let us, therefore, accept what is disagreeable with equanimity and calm content, as a token from the hand that once embraced the cross for us. This is naturally more easily said than done. Many a time impatience takes us by surprise; pride unwilling to be curbed raises its haughty head before we are even aware of it. We must, therefore, constantly be on our guard and fortify our hearts by eternal vigilance."*Patienter igitur estote.*" "Be you, therefore, also patient," St. James admonishes us; "*et confirmate corda vestra,*" "and strengthen your hearts."[7]

How shall this be done? What is the most substantial foundation for this first degree of the love of the cross? It is none other than solid self-knowledge and the unassuming disinterestedness that springs from it. Why do we grow impatient and fretful under reverses, disgruntled and depressed? Why not accept with good grace and resignation the daily weaknesses and pains? Why refuse the demands of love and even hesitate to empty to the dregs the chalice the Father lovingly offers us? We are all crossbearers, in one sense or another, for our vocation exacts willing and persevering effort to mould ourselves on the superb model of the Adorable Heart of Jesus.

In the face of such a truth all personal demands dissolve into nothingness. If we ceased to assert ourselves immoderately, we would not find things so easily burdensome, an almost unbearable yoke. We would humbly and patiently reach out for all that comes to us, no matter from what source. No longer would we then distinguish between persons who are inimical to us, or cross our path, nor so easily grow restive under trials and reverses. The art and manner in which they accost us finds us differently disposed, wholly resigned. To lay bare our meager virtue

---

7 James 5:8.

in thrusting aside this or that rebuff, real or imaginary, from whatever quarter it hails is proof of our slight confidence and trust in Him who is our strength, whose Heart is the font of humility and meekness.

Fundamentally to forfeit all claims at thought of our sinfulness is, in the eyes of the world, absolutely foolish and unreasonable, yet before God it is profound wisdom. In the higher light vouchsafed us, we find therein the surest means of patience in all occurrences, no matter how uncongenial or unexpected. All are God's messengers come down to seek admittance. Love will receive them most graciously with joyous resignation. It should be our earnest endeavor to get the better of pain, of sorrow or mishap, and of steeling ourselves to the heroic endurance of the overwhelming cross we deemed insupportable. On this firm foundation the unshakable structure of love of the cross rears itself. Let us, therefore, cherish and maintain this sentiment, which is not foreign to our soul.

Not in vain do we devote our spiritual exercises, days of recollection and prayer to the nourishment and building up of this fundamental principle in the spiritual life. It should be the chief fruit of these exercises to find sufficient vitality in moments of emergency to be patient and equably silent and understanding. In nothing that touches my person will I find an injustice; a gross misunderstanding, I will heroically brush aside and offer the opportunity to the dear Saviour for growth in virtue and likeness to His Sacred Heart. "Jesus, meek and humble of Heart, make my heart like unto Thine!" At the foot of the tabernacle, recalling my own sins and imperfections, I will bolster inner peace and soul-balance for hours of severer trials.

This is, indeed, no trifle, yet this first step is not to be our permanent resting place; it is merely the utmost a religious may allow himself when crosses press heavily. Beyond this frontier we dare not venture. Beginners as well as the more mature in building perfection will do well to accept patiently everything that self-love finds tantalizing and offensive. Steeling themselves to the quiet endurance of hardships, and getting the better of pain, they often experience marvellous graces and inner lights.

b) *Carrying our cross lovingly and willingly*

St. Bernard counsels us to embrace our cross willingly and gladly. A novice in the spiritual life may think that it suffices to take the cross as a matter of course, in the name of God. The mature person regards it as a blessing and will welcome it: *"Bonum mihi Domine, quia humiliasti me."* "It is good for me that Thou hast humbled me."[8] Humiliations, privations, fatigue, labor and pain—all are good, even excellent. Those striving to advance in perfection will not look upon hardships and reverses as unavoidable necessities to which they must bend themselves, but rather as benefits, gifts, graces, which we ought to cherish with spiritual complacency. United with Christ, we must offer ourselves completely in total dedication.

A twofold recognition transpires simultaneously in our interior in the spiritual life; the knowledge of God and knowledge of the cross. When in the light of God we behold the cross as an excellent gift from God Himself, He shows us simultaneously in the same light the wonderful value of sufferings and of the cheerful abandonment to

---

8 Ps. 118:71.

God's holy Will. They cannot be too highly evaluated. Father Alvarez, S.J., well versed in this unconditional surrender to the designs of Providence in whatever is imposed upon us, highly esteemed reverses and hardships of the most demanding; from them he extracted the precious gems that would shine in his eternal crown, he hoped, like pearls and precious stones, the more the better. If a veritable tempest of reverses broke in upon him, he would welcome the hoard of nuggets of the purest gold. No practical landlord would complain if such a storm laid waste his vast fields. Jubilantly would he gather the gold kernels. In the light of faith, ours is a similar case when crosses press heavily with unaccustomed severity. An act of resignation. "It is good for me, O God, that Thou hast humbled me."[9]

The Lord purifies us in the furnace of tribulations, "as silver is tried by fire, and gold in the furnace."[10] It is a mark of divine goodness to be asked to make this or that sacrifice for love of God, that we may be better able to realize fully the eternal value and merit of suffering and bearing the cross. The gain for our supernatural, eternal life is wholly inestimable. Our own experience bears us out. In a quiet moment of retrospect, do we not find that in times of special stress and trials we made the greatest progress in virtue, in a purifying process?

Sufferings are undeniably the furnace in which the heart is tried like gold. Disordered affections and attachments to creatures and to self are thrust aside like sediment and dross out of the furnace. Our apostolate of charity and

---

9 Ps. 118:71.
10 Prov. 17:3.

dedication will reach beyond our greatest expectations in personal sanctification and the spirit of sacrifice. Labors, fatigues, pains, and trials, are the plowshare by which the soil of our heart is loosened and made receptive for the implanting of God's best gifts. The light and warmth of Christ's love fructifies our planting and toiling for God and for souls.

Humiliations, misunderstandings, neglect, or things burdensome are in the mind of the great St. Augustine comparable to a winepress. Under tremendous pressure the grapes are crushed, but only to yield the precious wine. From the heart of the just, the zealous man, even if wholly crushed by sufferings, there stream forth all the more generously in rich abundance, the noblest virtues of humility, of the total renunciation of self, of total surrender and abandonment to God, who is infinite love.

In other words, sufferings rightly borne are the surest and the shortest way to perfection. They lend to us a divine beauty, investing our soul with incomparable dignity and splendor. The apostles and martyrs furnish splendid proof, as do the great saints, a St. Francis of Assisi, who in the midst of manifold reverses and dire rebuffs was a passionate lover of the cross; a St. Camillus, who regarded his greatest and most painful sufferings as a special proof of God's merciful love; of St. Teresa, who valued sufferings so much that she cried out, "To suffer or to die!" Such sentiments were conspicuous in the spirituality of St. Ignatius. Father Nadl, one of his own, asked him one day for the best way to achieve perfection most quickly. "This will happen when you have much to bear for Christ's sake," replied the Saint. "Beg God for this grace," he continued, "for to whom God grants this gift, He gives much indeed.

In this one gift, many others are included." The Saint spoke these words visibly moved amidst tears, perhaps of gratitude for the countless graces he himself had received along this same way.

They may also have been tears of sorrow and regret for the gross indifference toward such a vital truth. Why is it that high perfection and sanctity are rarely found? God Himself gave St. Catherine of Bologna the answer: The reason lies in the gross neglect of the necessary means, but more particularly in our unwillingness to meet trials and reverses valiantly with a will for the most perfect service. May this complaint from the lips of God Himself never apply to any of us. We are all called to genuine virtue, to holiness and complete surrender. Let us resolutely employ the means that will in the shortest space of time lead us to this desired holiness. Let us adhere to the second degree of the love of the cross, without yielding a foothold. It must be our earnest resolve, in spite of all the sighs and protests of self-love, freely and willingly to take from the hand of God what is painful to human nature.

What may be the most solid foundation of such noble sentiments and the assurance of our fidelity in persevering practice?

It is the sincere, earnest striving for perfection. Let us therefore be serious in the discharge of our vocational duties, for the endeavor to attain perfection is our foremost obligation. One who really wishes to be perfect desires nothing with greater avidity than the cross. He will also desire the means and occasions to lead to this end, to afford some satisfaction to the Divine Heart. Father Alvarez assures us that such occasions are counted by a blinded world as sufferings, painful visitations of the most diverse kinds, which only harass the soul. A zealous religious judges differently of such exquisite occasions for bearing some slight resemblance to Christ, Head of the Mystical Body, of which we are all members. He will regard them at their true worth as special favors and marks of divine affection, as privileges all the more precious the heavier the cross presses.

Let us not prove cowardly under the impact of these splendid examples on the part of our forebears. They often had roads to travel that called for heroism and fortitude of no mean calibre, though the world looked at it askance as all bitter loss. In such untoward happenings we must see the stuff of genuine virtue and holy living. The cross that I glimpse at the present moment, the contradiction, large or small, inseparable from my work, the office assigned to me now, the insipid details of my present undertaking, all these are splendid opportunities for me to manifest my love of the cross.

Without this deliberate attention to the demands of virtuous striving, my love of the cross is of little account; it is nothing more than an exteriorly attractive fruit, which is worm-eaten. Sad to say, like the fruits in the natural realm, so in the garden of the inner life, the virtues have their defects. And what are the shortcomings of our love of the cross? It is the lack of unconditional surrender. Indeed, we mean to work most diligently and shoulder heavy burdens, but to suffer *this inconvenience* and temporary disability seems beyond our strength. We are ready to bear privations, to be sure, but *this sudden curtailment* in my assigned work, we reason, seems most inopportune. To enlist our faculties in God's service and for the salvation of souls is fine and most fitting, and even at the cost of sacrifice and labor, we offer ourselves gladly. To do so *under the present circumstances,* however, in the present difficult situation, with the specific studies allotted to me seems almost unreasonable, wholly against the grain. It appears as so much wasted energy and lack of prudence. I am willing to accept everything—reproofs, neglect, lack of consideration, but *with certain restrictions and reservations.* What a host of "buts" and "buts" without end. What shortsightedness in one who professes to be cultivating the interior life, while completely ignoring the power, the superb excellence of the cross in its varied shapes and forms.

Nothing is fuller of dissonances than such specious objections, and therefore more displeasing to God. Inner harmony is here conspicuous by its total absence. God hears nothing with greater delight than the unconditional *"Ecce venio!"* "Here I am"; the wholehearted "Yes, Father!" Let us take the *"Ecce venio!"* of Jesus for our maxim and apply it on principle in all the circumstances that try our mettle, as the daily order precipitates it. With a determined resolve and surrender let us cultivate the inner spirit and ignore the designs of self-love with its insinuations and proposals.

This is truly a solid road to perfection and also the speediest. If saintly writers could speak to us from the beyond now, they would assure us that our progress in the inner life could be accomplished in the shortest space of time, by analogy, using the modern means of travel by flight or railway specials. It is ours to cooperate and to step in rapidly without counting the cost in sacrifice and self-effacement. Let us board the spiritual plane; the cost in self-denial never exceeds the divine help freely offered for every act of resolute determination to reach the purposed goal. Sanctity will never thrive except by suffering and denial, loving naught but the cross to afford some consolation to the Wounded Heart of Christ.

c) *Carrying our cross joyously*

The reward for this courageous, persevering self-denial is an unspeakably magnificent one. It can merely be indicated here. It is the most precious of all gifts of grace for which mortal man can hope on earth. I allude to the third degree of love of the cross. It is that enduring sentiment of heart in virtue of which we love suffering because of the resemblance to Christ it confers on us, with such vigor that it would be painful for us to be without the cross. Nothing more beautiful can be thought of.

St. John Chrysostom tells us that God's gift of joy in bearing the cross exceeds the power to raise the dead. The reward of persevering, faithful self-conquest in the daily frictions and occasions is often a very beneficial comfort even here below. Why do we so often lose the genuine, sweet, heavenly savor of Christ's comfort? Is it not because we lack the courage, figuratively speaking, to bite resolutely into the bitter rind of the cross? How often would we come upon a kernel which is nothing less than Jesus Himself, lifting the unaccustomed load to our shoulders, with His inexpressible meekness, satisfaction, and immolation.

"But above all things have charity, which is the bond of perfection."[11] Such an invaluable fruit is to be treasured. The work assigned us often has a rough, hard exterior, with

---

11 Col. 3:14.

much that runs counter to our tastes and desires. If with the grace of God we regard this as precious material for the practice of genuine virtue, and a source of blessing, a challenge to put on a resemblance to Christ Crucified, to protest to Him our love, little remains to deter us from an ardent love of our calling with the sacrifices it demands.

Finally will come the eternal recompense: *"Quod est momentaneum et leve tribulationis nostrae aeternum gloriae pondus operatur in nobis."* "For that which is at present momentary and light of our tribulations, worketh for us above measure exceedingly an eternal weight of glory."[12]

Christ Risen, the King of Glory, the King of Eternity, is here our Model, our Exemplar and Security.

---

12 2 Cor. 4:17.

CHAPTER XII

JOY IN THE SPIRITUAL LIFE

*"Serve the Lord with gladness,
come before Him with joyful
song."*[1]
"Take delight in the Lord."[2]

Joy is warmly recommended by St. Paul. It furthers our spiritual life in many respects.

"Gaudete in Domino semper, iterum dico: Gaudete!" "Rejoice in the Lord always; again, I say, rejoice."[3] He addresses the same admonition to the Thessalonians: *"Semper gaudete!"* "Rejoice always!" He admits that he himself is overwhelmed with joy in the midst of tribulation. "I exceedingly abound with joy in all our tribulation."[4] In his letter to the Romans he wishes them also the same grace of the Lord, a constant joy. *"Deus autem spei repleat vos omni gaudio et pace in credendo."*[5] "Now the God of hope fill you with all joy and peace in believing." The Apostle stresses the sentiment of joy emphatically, because of its tremendous value in the spiritual life.

---

1 Ps. 99:2.
2 Ps. 36:4.
3 Phil. 4:4.
4 2 Cor. 7:4.
5 Rom. 15:13.

1. THE EXCELLENCE OF JOY IN THE SPIRITUAL LIFE

Our own spiritual advancement demands joyfulness; we owe it to our fellow men. Our Heavenly Father by every right and justice expects it of us in His service. We shall briefly consider these three motives for joy. In truth, the service it renders us is not slight.

a) *First and foremost, joy eases and lightens our activity, our prayers and our work*

How different our actions in a time of joyful labor and good cheer from what they are when our mind is disturbed by clouds of sadness and ill humor! Cheerfulness perfects our actions; sadness mars them all too easily. The reason is very simple. The clearer our mind, the more unhampered our faculties, the more promptly and practically may they be employed.

It is impossible to do good work with rusty or defective tools. Sadness and moodiness are the rust that impairs our faculties in their daily toil. Cheerfulness—calm and equanimity—on the contrary, removes it, keeps them shining and fit for action. Under the foggy, dark northern skies vegetation scarcely thrives and yields sparingly. Under the clear, sunny heavens of the South, there is exuberant growth. If we wish our soul to resemble the sunny, fruitful atmosphere of southern climes, we must strive for cheerfulness and joy of spirit. Let it be the sunshine of joy, the supernatural joy of which the Apostle speaks: *"Gaudete in Domino!"* "Rejoice in the Lord!" The results of this joy are an inexhaustible source of fruitfulness and indefatigable energy.

b) *Joy is further an excellent means of defense against difficulties and temptations*

The archenemy knows this full well; therefore he makes every effort to disrupt the peace and composure that the presence of God imparts to the soul; he even tries to banish it entirely. At other times, under the aspect of good, he intervenes to foster discouragement, timidity, low spirits in every imaginable shape and form. Such states of soul prepare the way for his desperate attempt to disturb the mind and invest lower nature with a decided advantage. Here he is not so easily recognized, nor opposed so vigorously. The picture assumes a wholly different aspect when cheerfulness and genuine joy reign in the soul. This we have all experienced, beyond doubt.

Spiritual joy liberates the spirit, makes it strong to resist manfully, and reach out for the hand of God in hours of trial. In a cheerful frame of mind we are quick to wield the most effective weapons of defense with dexterity and determined resolve to frustrate his sinister attacks. It is clear that souls who work with positive joy in the Lord are less exposed to the tempter's wiles. He shuns the light, is repulsed by its glare, lest his snares and wicked designs be discovered, and shame and defeat be his just portion.

c) *A third advantage is still greater*

Cheerfulness in the Lord assures us of manifold graces and spiritual aids for greater alacrity and self-sacrifice in our vocational work. "*Delectare in Domino:*" says the Psalmist, "*et dabit tibi petitiones cordis tui.*"[6] Delight in

---

6 Ps. 36:4.

the Lord, and He will give thee the requests of thy heart."

Little wonder, for this sentiment holds one of the most essential requisites for being heard in prayer. By offering our sufferings and hardships, we can be true apostles for Christ and the immortal souls He died to save. for fruitful labor and sacrifice. "I will sing to the Lord, who giveth me good things:" the Psalmist declares, "and I will sing to the name of the Lord most High!"[7] Oh, the joy of this realization!

Childlike trust and unconditional surrender bears within itself the germ of deep, inner peace and joy in the Lord. The reverse obtains when the soul yields to ill-controlled sadness and dejection. Distrust and discouragement constrict the heart; if God chose to bestow His gifts, He would hardly find a willing heart to accept them. Let us rejoice in the Lord and set no limits to our confidence in His divine magnanimity.

"Blessed is he whom Thou hast chosen and taken to thee: he shall dwell in Thy courts." How fitting the words of the Psalmist, when we think of the divine enlightenment, of the stillness of prayerful moments and inner peace. And the consoling word continues: "We shall be filled with the good things of Thy house: ... Thou hast visited the earth, and hast plentifully watered it; Thou hast many ways enriched it ... Thou shalt bless the crown of the year of Thy goodness: and Thy fields shall be filled with plenty ... and the hills shall be girded about with joy; they shall shout, yea they shall sing a hymn."[8]

---

7 Ps. 12:6.
8 Ps. 64:5, 10, 12, 13, 14.

Our prayers will be answered, not in the time and manner of our own choosing, but in the moment eternally designed by a loving Providence. In very truth our "fields shall be filled with plenty . . . and the hills be girded about with joy." Our life of joyous sacrifice always begins at the foot of the altar, in the Sanctuary of the Most High. Religious life—the spiritual life in general—is one of combat and vigilance, which only the valiant souls achieve. The atmosphere of peace and trust is its life-source.

This attitude itself, though mute, is a constant and most effective prayer. If I could place words on its lips, figuratively, I would address the Father: "O my God and My All, my Father! In Thee I rest content. Do with me as Thou willest, what Thou wilt! Give what Thou wilt, I will devote it to Thy holy service cheerfully, to Thy greater honor and glory. I know but one care, namely, of pleasing Thee, devoted to Thee in all Thy divine dispensations."

A precious prayer! We may well apply the words of the *Canticle of Canticles*: *"Vulnerasti cor meum in uno oculorum tuorum."* "Thou hast wounded my heart with one of Thy eyes."[9] Oh, indeed, a single glance upward to God in such a state of soul touches the Divine Heart and opens His treasures. The sentiment itself, however, is a steady, even if unconscious, demand upon the munificence of Divine Providence. But the Lord cannot resist this plea, and graciously rewards such implicit trust with newer gifts of grace.

Souls that foster such a disposition of absolute trust, of supernatural cheerfulness, regardless of feeling or disgust, but with a resolute will, could many a time ask

9 Cant. 4:9.

whence that special uplifting help in daily work. They might wonder over the happy solution of difficulties in this or that emergency, or the ease experienced in the practice of virtue, no matter what the odds. Might they not wonder at the consoling victory in temptation, fortitude in meeting dangers and reverses, in bearing fatigues and labors with ease. Oh, the good God could respond by asking what joyfulness and contentment in His service might be other than an uninterrupted prayer in the apostolic spirit. "*Delectare in Domino!*" I said it through My prophet: "Delight in the Lord, and He will give thee the request of thy heart." Our own advantage, our own interest, calls for cheerfulness and joy in the simplicity of gracious giving in apostolic work. "And I have known that there was no better thing than to rejoice, and to do well in this life."[10]

2. JOY, A DEMAND OF FRATERNAL CHARITY

The first requisite of fraternal charity is not to be burdensome or annoying to others. The Sacred Word must be fulfilled: "*Quam bonum et quam jucundum habitare fratres in unum.*" "Behold how good and how pleasant it is for brethren to dwell together in unity."[11] Where selfishness yields to disordered sadness there can be no thought of such a pleasant dwelling together. There will be constant dissonance, the sky of friendliness will be overcast, and dark clouds dull or dim the eye; there is

---

10 Eccles. 3:12.
11 Ps. 132:1.

much coldness and frost to create the atmosphere of unpleasant things.

It is true, I may suppose my brethren to bear patiently with my foibles and defects, according to the exhortation of St. Paul: *"Alter alterius onera portate."* "Bear ye one another's burdens."[12] Still I have no right to impose upon them the burden of my unfriendliness and egoism, for their own cross is heavy enough. In the spirit of Christian charity, I am obliged to lighten their burden, to bring joy into their lives by charity and gentleness at every turn. By perfect love of my neighbor, forgetting self and being the servant of all, I can do much to strengthen fraternal charity.

a) *Fraternal charity calls for mutual edification*

In large measure it is the fruit of joyousness, not in the worldly spirit, but of joy and contentment in God. What a source of edification the life of a St. John Berchmans, a St. Francis of Assisi, a St. Teresa, to all about them! It was the beautiful flowering of their unselfish joyousness and good cheer in the love of God, forgetting self. It was the most natural thing, for is not joy a constant reminder of the eternal words: "My yoke is sweet and My burden light!"[13] It is nothing less than a tangible proof of the truth of the sacred words, encouraging us to bend willingly under the "sweet yoke," and to embrace the burden wholeheartedly.

---

12 Gal. 6:2.
13 Matt. 11:30.

b) *Among religious, joyousness of spirit is a forceful refutation of the prejudice of many worldlings*

They esteem solitude, retirement, and denial as hard and unendurable. Recollection and prayer, they insist, can have little that is agreeable, since it offers us a mere pittance of joy and delight. It is their benighted, blinded outlook upon spiritual values. The heart and countenance of a cheerful religious furnish proof abundant that to hold communion with God in a life of prayer is surely not tedious. *"Non habet amaritudinem conversatio illius."*[14] "Her conversation hath no bitterness." There is no bitterness in our communings with the Most High. To withdraw from everything, to immolate everything and rest satisfied with Him alone, to live alone with the Lord in the spirit of joy cannot engender anxiety or disgust... *"nec habet taedium convictus illius."* It generates only profound peace and joy of heart, *"sed habet laetitiam et gaudium."* Such an admission, however, you will agree, evokes joy and contentment and draws the soul to complete surrender to God, incites it to faithful imitation and, as fraternal charity demands, is a source of edification.

Daily association with our religious confreres, instead of being a hindrance, should, as St. Ignatius demands of his Sons, be a strong incentive to the praise of the Lord, whom each one strives to behold reverently in the other, as His Image. A religious who yields to selfish whims, to sadness and despondency, will not readily recall to his associates the mercy and love of God, nor the blessed

14 Wis. 8:16.

workings of His grace, or the riches of His treasures, lavished on the soul by the Holy Spirit.

These lovable traits will be conspicuous in a religious whose countenance and whole demeanor reflect the splendor of love that fills his heart as a reflex of the Divine Love burning in the Heart of Christ. It will manifest itself outwardly, elicit our admiration and incite us to ever greater generosity in fostering mutual charity in the apostolic spirit of our sublime vocation.

c) *One of the most beautiful aspects of fraternal charity is the desire to serve*

This, too, is strengthened through genuine joy in God. Charity is truly a heavenly growth, easily giving way in a joyous mood to others, reaching out a helping hand for body and soul, at a personal sacrifice. Disgruntled and morose characters have little leisure to forget their ego in order to confer a loving kindness on others. Absorbed in selfish designs, they miss the sweet savor of Christian charity. Joy in the Lord, on the contrary, is sunshine and light in which our field of vision is enlarged, enabling us to see and seize the occasions for serving in the ranks of Christ's closest followers.

With almost irresistible force, it induces us to seize the opportunity and utilize the occasions we have already glimpsed. Above all, it imparts something to our services to make them doubly valuable. Cheerfulness in rendering a service, the sweet forgetfulness of self that marks a kindly deed, is often more beautiful, comforting and beneficial than the act itself. A joyous disposition imparts an unusual fragrance to our least actions.

The Holy Spirit counsels us, therefore: *"In omni dato hilarem fac vultum tuum."* "In every gift show a cheerful countenance."[15] In a very special way this exhortation applies to the gifts we bring to the Lord, for the service of God. Joy and gladness we owe our brethren. In all things seek to "sanctify thy tithes with joy."[16]

3. JOY, A TREMENDOUS ASSET IN GOD'S SERVICE

We owe joy infinitely more to the Lord our God. He expects it of us and has countless claims to it; there is not a single reason that could justify and sanction sadness and dissatisfaction in His service. Neither the Lord, nor the work itself, nor the reward, offers the least incentive. A religious, St. Ignatius advises us, has no reason for yielding to undue sorrow or dejection, but many reasons for abiding joy in the Lord.

a) *The Lord whom we serve is the "King of Kings and Lord of Lords."*[17]

He is the Infinite Majesty, all-wise, powerful, great and exalted, so glorious that to serve Him is in truth reigning as being princes ourselves. *"Deo servire regnare est."* Indeed, to serve the Most High is to reign. Pondering the mercy and longanimity of Our Lord, His goodness and magnanimity, His ineffable loveliness, what could we find in the exquisite beauty of heaven and earth at all

---

15 Ecclus. 35:11.
16 Ibid.
17 Apoc. 19:16.

comparable? It surely deserves a cheerful surrender. It must be our joy and bliss to be dedicated to the incomparable Divine Majesty, to bask in the sunlight of His magnificence, even if a sacrifice be involved in this total surrender.

The service of God is neither hard nor oppressive. Worldlings who are still base slaves of materialistic motives may say what they will, corrupt nature may lift its head, the Evil One may seek to assail us with his sinister distorted pictures, yet the words of Eternal Wisdom ring undeniably true: "My yoke is sweet and My burden light." Most assuredly, the service of God remains a yoke and a burden, but Our Lord helps us bear it. He smooths away the rough edges and points to the light that radiates from a loyalty without compromise.

Oh, how beautiful and precious are the supernatural graces and consolations afforded us here below from divine munificence! All the dangers of sin cut off or minimized, the means of perfection bestowed upon us in lavish abundance, place us in a state of delightful security, provided we are alert for the momentary need. In the midst of enlightenments and consolations from above, which literally glorify the services we daily render, no child of the Heavenly Father could for even a moment yield to discouragement and anxious care.

b) *The manifold duties, the fatigue, and exhaustion that are an indispensable adjunct of our labors, often press heavily*

Privations and humiliations need be reckoned with, yet none of these will ever justify dissatisfaction or discontent. We shall feel the burden to the very last, to the last breath, but in this lies the glory of our inner spirit of total annihilation of all that savors of self and selfish endeavors. It would be unworthy of our sublime call to yield to base incentives in the face of such lofty associations in the Mystical Body.

Let us heed the advice of St. James: "My brethren, count it all joy when you shall fall into divers temptations."[18] But how can this be an occasion for joy? There is yet another side that still gives joy, despite the harshness that nature feels. Everything is in reality the stuff of virtuous living and the means to attain it and to amass copious merits. God in His merciful compassion grants us sufficient grace to achieve this goal. Provided we will it, we may belong to those of whom the Apostle declares: "Blessed is the man that endureth temptation; for when he hath been proved, he shall receive the crown of life, which God hath promised to those that love Him."[19]

c) *Oh, the reward! The glimpse of the recompense which Our Lord will bestow upon us!*

What joys He allows us to taste, not for thirty years, but for thousands and myriads of years, for eternity! It must make our joy wholly indestructible. "*Spe gaudentes,*" joyous in hope.

The Most Blessed Trinity in all majesty, splendor and power, the Infinite Beauty, amidst the blessed choirs of angels and saints in heaven, shall be for us joy and bliss

---

18 James 1:2-4.
19 James 1:12.

inexplicable, without end. Is there a sorrow on earth, sin excepted, capable of disrupting the peaceful hope of such a reward? Is there room for voluntary discontent and dejection or lassitude, when we can envision such future glory? They should serve the Lord, St. Paul writes to the Romans, full of joy in such hope. "*Spe gaudentes.*" "Rejoicing in hope."[20]

If amidst the trials, labors, and fatigues, which my God-given work imposes, I nourished sorrow and bitterness, while the Lord is fashioning a throne for me, weaving a celestial garment, and casting the most precious crown, I would be truly ungrateful. I owe my Lord the most disinterested and joyous self-sacrifice and service it is mine to give. His persuasive affability, His easy and gentle, sweet yoke, and His divine recompense deserve it. There is not a single reason to justify sadness and moodiness, but on the contrary there are many valid reasons for a joyous, loving service of the good Saviour. "*Nullam habet Religiosus moerendi causam, multas vero gaudendi.*" Let us admit that this constant joy in the Lord is not mere child's play. It comes not of itself; we must create it with the grace of God and persistent effort with renewed energy and zeal.

In this endeavor the first moment of the day is of the utmost importance. "*Venite adoremus Dominum!*" the Church accosts us each morning in the Hours. How is this invitation to be received? Assuredly in a joyful frame of mind, withholding nothing of our day's sacrifice and oblation in Adoration and Homage of the Most High. Whatever obedience enjoins for this day should redound to the

---

20 Rom. 12:12.

praise and glory of the Lord our God. Is there one who would not arise with fresh ardor and vigor at such a moment, no matter what nature feels momentarily at the beginning of a newborn day? We can do nothing better in looking at the hours ahead than envision our daily cross as our share in the Lord's own passion and death endured for love of us. Thus we literally pierce the sly machinations of the Evil One and laugh the enemy to scorn.

Similar acts must be renewed during the day, again and again encouraging ourselves. "Sursum corda!" Holy Church calls to us not in vain at Mass. "Lift up your hearts!" Here is indicated of what nature the affections should be. They must be supernaturalized. Were one to establish this joy in what is agreeable, what flatters nature, he would be building on sand, open to the least winds that blow across the lands. No lasting joy will there be found, and it will be lacking him at the very moment when God expects him to step out courageously as a true apostle of souls in the spiritual exercises.

The best means, finally, the inexhaustible fount of divine joyfulness can be merely suggested. "If you would be always cheerful and happy," says St. Ignatius, "be ever humble and submissive, and joy will infallibly grow in you, until it finally assumes the shape of that joy to which Jesus Himself invites us. 'Enter thou into the joy of thy Lord'," into the joys and delights that will flow to us eternally from God Himself, the Infinite Ocean of Divine Mercy and Bliss.

CHAPTER XIII

OF FAITHFULNESS IN LITTLE THINGS

"He who wastes the little he has will be stripped bare."[1]
"The teaching of the wise is a fountain of life. . .but the way of the faithless is their ruin."[2]

Fidelity in little things is enjoined upon us by Our Saviour Himself, when He says: "He who is faithful in a very little thing, is faithful also in much."[3] Faithfulness in smaller matters is highly recommended by spiritual masters. In the service of God the lowliest thing is important. It is one of the chief means of attaining perfection and walking steadfast in the Lord. It strengthens us to meet any graver trials more efficiently.

The Supreme Teacher, Eternal Wisdom, Our Saviour Jesus Christ, says: *"Qui fidelis est in minimo, et in majori fidelis est."* "He that is faithful in that which is least, is faithful also in that which is greater." This word from the lips of Eternal Truth should suffice for a rational human being to devote himself earnestly to fidelity in small matters to his last breath, with a sort of consecration.

---

1 Ecclus. 19:1.
2 Prov. 13:14, 15.
3 Luke 16:10.

1. "HE WHO IS UNJUST IN A VERY LITTLE THING, IS UNJUST
   ALSO IN MUCH"

In the spiritual life this is truly a terrific thing in its
consequences. Unfaithfulness in important duties is a
grievous matter, we realize, for it leads finally to a total
spiritual collapse. This does not come to pass after every
minor offense, but actually only in grave infidelities, thrusting conscience and its warning notes aside, for Scripture
tells us: ". . . He who wastes the little he has will be
stripped bare."

We naturally ask how negligence in small things can
conjure up such a misfortune. For all who have understanding of the inner life there is no riddle here. Such
negligence nourishes the passions. In certain grave matters,
we oppose them vigorously and practice self-control, fully
resolved to subdue them; gradually, however, we are weak
enough to yield again, two or three times or oftener. This
suffices to keep them fit for a strategic attack in a decisive
moment, to be victorious over grace. Only uninterrupted,
conscientious self-denial leads to dominance of the passions; once gained, it will be preserved only at the price
of eternal vigilance.

Constant alertness to the opportunities we daily meet
will help us in acquiring solid virtue. In the Heart of
Christ we will recognize clearly the way He has traced
for our sanctification. To render outstanding service to
God we need a substantial measure of humility, submission, purity of heart, and love of the cross. Youthful enthusiasm soon wears thin; the time when God treats us still
as beginners on the difficult road of holiness, and cares for
us tenderly, comes to an end; the yoke of Christ is more

pronounced and the burden weighs more heavily. Unless the soul is fortified by an abundance of inner strength and light from the Heart of God, it weakens and the yoke presses more insistently; finally we throw it off as unbearable. The words of St. Gregory the Great have often been verified: "When small matters are neglected, the soul gradually succumbs and commits graver offenses fearlessly."

How many acts of virtue to which God would attach copious graces are forfeited! How many graces in reward of our fidelity are never won, and what merits we could have amassed are forever lost! These are losses not in material things, but in heavenly, unchangeable, everlasting treasures of which the slightest measure far outweighs the whole world in worth. Let us always keep the eye of faith open and peer beneath the surface in matters we often regard as trivial. There we find a rich substratum of promise for a plentiful yield; we will more readily correspond to the Will of God in the least without anxiety. Supernatural gains will not be wanting.

2. THE BLESSINGS OF FIDELITY

It is a sense of security and guarantee for faithfulness in the greater. "*Qui fidelis est in minimo, et in majori fidelis est.*" ". . . faithful in that which is least . . . faithful also in that which is greater." Experience testifies to the truth of the Saviour's words. It is truly a surpassing reward. The pleasant assurance, the childlike confidence with which we can prevision fatigue, hardships, temptations and trials, and in all humility even expect them is heart-warming. We rest at peace in confidence at the thought of Jesus, whose Divine Heart is the safe refuge of faithful souls.

God Himself gives the soul this consoling trust, so that she may say with St. Paul: "I can do all things in Him who strengthens me." When the occasion arises to test our mettle in great things, the soul grown strong in the lesser observance will not prove weak and succumb. With docility to grace, she will approve herself in the finest sense of the term, acquit herself of all that God has imposed, and meet the challenge to her strength and best performances. What glorious fruits are these, plucked from the previous acts of fidelity in the discharge of every duty.

What brings this growth to such beautiful fruition? How is it that one who is faithful even in the lowliest actions, will be so in the greater and more considerable? The reason is simple, indeed. Every act of fidelity in our round of duties calls for greater effort in self-denial and complete fulfillment of God's Will. This is a never-failing source of strength and happiness in the practice of the different virtues. Stone is fitted to stone and gradually we have a powerful bulwark. The Evil One, observes St. Ignatius, who studies the soul in his attempt to ferret out a weak side, will finally be disillusioned. If he nevertheless plans an attack, he is bound to suffer defeat. His opponent is a servant of God, who not only harbors great strength within and is accoutered with the plenitude of divine power, but who also enjoys the special light and protection of God and is endowed with actual graces in overflowing measure. "*Veritas mea et misericordia mea cum ipso et in nomine meo exaltabitur cornu ejus.*" This finds fulfillment. God is at his side, not only with sufficient grace for him who cooperates with it, but He allows so much light to illumine his mind, so much courage to stir his heart, so much stimulation and energy to move his will, that cooperation is assured and the victory infallibly won.

This invaluable reinforcement of grace will be imparted particularly in matters of importance to those who manifest outstanding loyalty in little things. In such decisive matters, God delights to show His own fidelity towards them in the most tangible manner, to lead them in such wise that they may cry out jubilantly: *"Dextera Domini fecit virtutem, dextera Domini exaltavit me—fecit mihi magna, qui potens est!"* "The right hand of the Lord hath wrought great strength: the right hand of the Lord hath exalted me."[4] If they persevere in their fidelity, God will also continue the manifestations of His changeless love. He will then crown His loving dispensations and favors with the grace of final perseverance for all eternity. This is unquestionably true. If anyone may look with childlike trust to the gift of this most important of all graces, it is he who has always been solicitously faithful in the smallest things. Consider how great must be the wealth of merits such a soul may take with her into eternity.

There will not be many sins still to be cleansed in the purgative flames, for the soul was ever bent on avoiding even the smallest faults. The defects that still occurred through human weakness and instability, were regularly made good by increased fidelity and thus atoned for here below in great part. One who walks circumspectly gathers very little for the cleansing flames; in many instances, when the portals of eternity are flung wide, these minor matters will have long been atoned for. This is a great consolation, indeed. To have escaped purgatory with its

---

4 Ps. 117:16.

bitter sufferings and pains, entirely, or to be liberated in a brief space, soon to hear the consoling words: *"Euge serve bone et fidelis. . ."* "Well done, thou good and faithful servant, enter into the joys of thy Lord!" What a glorious gain!

In the hour of death, fidelity will be our supreme consolation if we assiduously cultivated it in life. Through fidelity in little things we are assured of valuable treasures for eternity. "Nothing," says St. Basil, "that conforms to the Will of God is to be regarded as slight. It is something sublime and of such a nature that it gains for us heavenly rewards." The acts in themselves may be small, but by repetition they mount up, and the merit that accrues to those who are conscientious will be considerable in the course of time. These facts are not to be ignored. In temporalities foresight and prudent solicitude are lauded as most reasonable. The future is worth being envisioned with a prescient mind and eye. Management plans are geared to the greatest efficiency for the sake of material gains in the business world. Should we not look well to our spiritual motivation where there is question of eternal profits?

Does not Jesus Himself say: *"Thesaurizate vobis thesauros in coelo."* "Gather treasures for heaven." One degree of heavenly glory more or less is neither indifferent nor is it a trivial thing. St. Teresa of Avila declared that in order to acquire the least degree of heavenly glory, she would be ready to submit to the greatest labors, fatigues, and hardships, as well as sufferings of this life to the end of time.

We must remember that we are not here for our own sanctification, but that there is question of the greater honor and glory of God. The more God is known and loved by His creatures, the more is He glorified. Therefore, every degree of the Beatific Vision, which is the most perfect knowledge and love of God, and lasts not only for several years, but forever, is of the utmost significance. All who love God truly and strive to promote His Honor are eager to amass merits here below, thus to prepare themselves for a more excellent praise of God in eternity. They use every opportunity faithfully, even the smallest, with a view to its inner worth. To do this for God's greater glory and renown must be our constant endeavor, in order to give joy to God and win His divine pleasure in a high degree. Oh, the inestimable happiness of serving God with loving abandon!

3. FIDELITY IN LITTLE THINGS DELIGHTS THE HEART OF GOD

"Qui fideliter agunt, placent ei." "Those who are truthful are His delight."[5] This is the third motive for faithfulness in little things. Naturally, this is true only of the genuine virtue, which is not reckless, nor assumes all sorts of petty annoyances beyond the measure of graces that God wills to impart and crushes them. It is not short-sighted and does not imprudently hold to a personal opinion where there is good reason for omitting some act or performing a better one.

Finally it is not motivated by fear bordering on scrupulosity, as if danger of sin lurked in every move, and as if on every occasion all imaginable losses and hazards threatened the soul. Genuine fidelity has nothing akin to these disorders. It is rather wise and prudently animated

---

5 Prov. 12:22.

by the spirit of childlike love. This is pleasing to God and gains sure access to His Sacred Heart. Fidelity is an approved means to perfection.

It is that, because in fidelity in small matters the desire for greater perfection is constantly and actually expressed. It affords God the greatest delight. He sees how we enter upon His favorite plan, for the realization of which He did not hesitate to offer what was dearest to Him and immolate His only begotten Son.

Through fidelity, the soul further expresses a magnanimous love of God, a love that finds the barriers of necessity, of stern obligation, much too narrow and constricting; a love that is determined without reserve to espouse what is pleasing to God; a love that really embraces and faithfully carries out what duty demands, whether it be something of note or insignificant. It suffices to know that it is most pleasing to God. *"Quae placita sunt ei, facio semper."* "I do always what is pleasing to Him."

Through such solicitude in fidelity, the soul proves her pure, disinterested love of God. How easily self-love intrudes everywhere, in things that seem noteworthy in the eyes of men; if it be something without external glamor, still in her own estimation it has importance and weight. In such situations nature is capable of great exertion and sacrifice. Nothing flatters man so much as the consciousness of having accomplished something of note. But the scope of fidelity in little things is almost entirely hidden from human eyes, and for the most part little may be found that is in accord with natural inclinations.

On the contrary, self-love finds there a bleak desert. Only a soul that is animated by the spirit of faith and moved by love of God will cheerfully persevere doing what duty prescribes, day by day, willingly and exactly, for weeks, months, and years. Only the pure love that seeks nothing outside the divine pleasure and complacence will persevere. But the eye of God dwells lovingly on such souls. "God looks," says a-Kempis, "more upon the desire and the love that prompts our actions than upon the magnitude of the work." Is not Our Lord Himself, supreme Exemplar and Model of fidelity, a splendid proof? Or was He less pleasing to the Father by His simple, apparently insignificant life in Nazareth than by His spectacular public appearance?

Let us follow Our Leader and King Jesus Christ! Let us be faithful to the daily routine, no matter how trivial it may be. We shall then more readily be steadfast in greater things, if God entrusts them to us. By our fidelity without stint, we will be most pleasing to God and finally deserve to hear the Blessed Word: "Well done, thou good and faithful servant! Because thou hast been faithful over little things, I will place thee over many. Enter thou into the joy of thy Lord!"

CHAPTER XIV

SPIRITUAL MOTIVATION
DIGNITY OF CONSCIENTIOUS OBSERVANCE

> *"Thou hast ordered all things in measure, in number, and weight."*[1]
> *"Divine Providence provides for all things according to their measure."*[2]

We link our momentary contemplation with the feast of the Purification of the Blessed Virgin Mary. A careful reading of the Gospel for Candlemas will impress us with the eagerness of St. Luke to depict the exactitude and fidelity of the Holy Family in complying with the Law of Purification. As soon as the time was accomplished, Mary and Joseph, without delay, prepared for the journey and set out for Jerusalem. In the Temple they observed most graciously all the regulations prescribed for the sacred rites of purification.

1. EXAMPLES OF FIDELITY IN SMALL THINGS

Yet there was much that we might choose to classify as trivial rubrics. No one had ever come to the Temple for whom the Law as such had so little significance as for the Holy Family. No one, finally, had so many apparently

---

1 Wis. 11:21.
2 St. Thomas Aquinas.

good reasons as Mary and Joseph for evading the Law, or at least some of its minor details. Still, they submit humbly and minutely; they observe every requirement as it is written in the Law of the Lord. Here we have a shining example of absolute fidelity and conformity in the smallest details, which invites our closest study and imitation.

a) *God Himself*

We have just pondered the beautiful example of the Holy Family. The highest and most sublime model, however, is God Himself. What exactitude and promptness in all His works! Full of admiration, the Wise Man cries out: *"Omnia in mensura et numero et pondere disposuisti."* "Thou hast ordered all things in measure, in number, and weight."[3] How minute His exactness in assigning to the stars their posts, and how promptly have they for centuries run their gigantic courses!

Everything is determined to the very second. How carefully is everything around us on earth in the plant world determined to the tiniest grain of pollen; in the animal creation we find even the single-celled organism possessed of all that is requisite and serviceable for its existence. For ourselves, for our body, everything is ordained to the utmost perfection and finesse, in accordance with our purpose in life.

Solicitous as God is in the act of creation, so is He in the conservation and government of the world; nothing, not the least, escapes His loving Providence. What is less than a flower of the field, than a sparrow on the roof, a

---

3 Wis. 11:21.

hair of our head? These are trivial things in this immeasurable universe. Yet Christ assures us that His Father cares for it, neglecting nothing. *"Videte!"* Augustine cries out, and see "How God does not despise the most insignificant part of His creation." The tremendous realization of the munificence of God our Father, shows us how close He is to us in the least we do. His generosity is limited by the barriers we ourselves interpose.

A glance at the supernatural order will show us that the Almighty Hand of God is active in the smallest details as well as in the greater. The divine finger never fails to support with His grace even the least we do for love of Him, the most insignificant good thought we entertain. Nor is a cup of cold water given in His name left unrewarded. The grace of God," says Pascal, "makes itself known in great souls in the little things."

"Fidelis Deus." God is faithful to the minutest detail. Though He is so great, infinite and superb a Spirit, He never rides roughshod over even the most trivial matters. Or should we say just because of His magnificent grandeur and perfection, He attends not only to outstanding conspicuous performances, but bestows the same solicitude and care upon the least. Faithfulness in small matters, with good intent for love of God, is the mark of a great mind. Our Divine Saviour exhorts us, when He says: "Be ye perfect as your Heavenly Father is perfect."

b) *Our Divine Saviour Himself set us the most beautiful example of this inestimable virtue*

How conscientiously the Lord adheres to the *Jewish Law!* Still there was no one who could more readily have disregarded it than Jesus. When John at the Jordan hesitated to baptize Him, it was a great moment. "Let me have my way for the present," Jesus remonstrated, "after all it is only so that we fulfill, as is proper for us, all justice demands."[4] Here we have the spirit of Our Saviour, one of His invincible principles. Nothing, not the least that pertains to the Father's Will shall remain unaccomplished. Even if it were not necessary, nor of great importance, just so it is pleasing to Him, that He expects it, takes delight in it. *"Quae placita sunt Ei, facio semper."* "What pleases Him, I always do."

We pass over many other instances cited by the Evangelists. One alone we will single out—the tiny word *"Sitio,"* spoken on the cross. What is more trivial in itself, what more insignificant than this word *"Sitio!"* But Jesus recalls that it was written, as it were, contained in Rules, and therefore He cries out: *"Ut consummaretur Scriptura dixit: sitio."* ". . . that the Scripture might be fulfilled, He said, I thirst."[5] "I have come to fulfill . . . all things."[6] What depths of love for His own is this cry from the Saviour's Heart!

How slightly would the Saviour's redemptive work have been impaired by this simple omission! It matters not, the Lord knows that it is agreeable to the Father, and He does not despise it. How easily would such forgetfulness have been exonerated! On the cross, in the throes of immense sufferings and dereliction, in moments of profound abasement, of what small import is such a trifle!

---

4 Matt. 3:15.
5 John 19:28.
6 Matt. 5:17.

None the less, Jesus does not disdain it. O faithful Heart, O Divine Model of Fidelity, of care for even the least! How must religious blush for shame, if they paid homage to the despicable principle: What does it matter, they are mere trifles? These would in very truth not be the sentiments of the Heart of Christ, therefore not those of His true disciples.

The solicitude for little points of observance rightly understood and carried out with wisdom in the spirit of love, must be the concern of a true disciple of Christ. Religious founders and spiritual directors never neglect to stress this point. Such fidelity, they hold, is a powerful means to perfection, and its neglect, no slight hindrance. Enlighten me, O Jesus, and strengthen me that by fidelity in little things as well as in greater, my life may be conformable to Thine.

2. THE COMBAT OF SATAN AGAINST EXACT OBSERVANCE

The Evil One is diabolically cunning and clever in his stubborn battle against conscientious observance in every shape and form. His chief concern is to undermine the conviction of its importance, so as gradually to weaken and destroy it altogether. He knows full well that if we underestimate the value of faithfulness and give ear to his insinuations, its practise will soon diminish and fall off. Having recourse to prayer and humbly manifesting our love of fidelity in the smallest precepts of the Rule, whether alone or in accord with others at work, we furnish eloquent proof of our willing surrender and love of God.

No matter how vague they may seem, we shall consider some of the enemy's stratagems, in order to arm ourselves against his despicable attempts to deter us from exercising absolute and prompt compliance with the least of our obligations.

a) Details are for beginners in the spiritual life, is Satan's first sinister advice

We should certainly be more mature in mastering our passions, avoiding imperfections, building upon the solid foundation of faith, he holds, than awkward, inexperienced and undisciplined workers. But his pretensions come to naught when the soul looks upon her sacred obligations, voluntarily assumed and loved for a lifetime of conscientious observance. Young and untutored souls will learn from the shining example of their elders, and one and all proclaim anew their loyalty to religious discipline in all its delicate, innate charm and beauty.

Divine Wisdom will enlighten our darkened minds if we persevere in patience and love of sacrifice. We may not delude ourselves, but joyfully reach out for the manifestations of the holy Will of God in the offices entrusted to us. Let us offer Jesus our heart as an oblation of fidelity, forgetting self in the spirit of loyalty and resolve in the strength of God. Such fidelity, St. Bonaventure assures us, is the most beautiful and the shortest way to holiness. The formative example of time-tried and mature religious will exert a powerful influence on those around them and be a source of edification to all.

It is true that at the outset in the spiritual life, great stress must be laid on the unimpaired discharge of their obligations to the minutest detail. These young aspirants to holiness must learn that Christian perfection consists in the disciplined life of acquiescence in God's holy Will. They must be grounded in the holy art of serving God wholeheartedly, no matter what the cost in sacrifice of self. It is something to be studiously acquired in Christ's school of perfection. These noble young souls, full of lofty ambitions, must be grounded in the holy art of personal surrender. This shining fidelity will shed its light over the latter years of difficult striving with spiritual gain; it will greatly aid in building the superstructure of their inner life, in making it a more beautiful thing and steadily adding to its growth and splendor. Disinterested zeal for souls will cheerfully make every sacrifice, not counting the cost of unreserved fidelity to every observance, no matter how tedious to nature. It is not a negligible thing in our spiritual life. "*Qui spernit modica, paulatim decidet*," cries the Holy Spirit in earnest admonition: "He that contemneth small things, shall fall by little and little."[7]

In the light of truth the holy endeavor to foster such devotedness and sacrifice rather increases through the years. It is of paramount importance. The grace of God will lighten the burden that seems tremendous to young shoulders. Beginners, we will admit, often work with a certain restlessness and anxiety at the start, but they grow accustomed to the formative influence of steady, thoughtful labor with purity of intention. Maturity and love, grown strong with the years, will help us bear the yoke of fidelity with delightful zest and elasticity. New under-

---

7 Ecclus. 19:1.

takings that appeal are easily discharged without difficulty, in perfect conformity to the holy Will of God.

b) *The wily tempter advances a second objection*

A certain freshness and elasticity of spirit, he maintains, are indispensable for religious observance. This is easily marred, he contends, through the care for small rules and prescriptions. A basic note in the enemy's second stage of strategy not to be overlooked! By his atrocious attacks upon religious living, he seeks to inject the spirit of liberalism and a flagrant love of freedom, in order to undermine and destroy our deepest convictions and loves. Humbly acknowledging our weakness and inefficiency, we will sanctify our labors by prompt obedience in complete surrender to the Will of God, lest we labor fruitlessly and in vain.

It is true that in the service of God joy must reign supreme. It is the deference we show the good God, whom our Superiors represent. "*Hilarem datorem diligit Deus!*" "God loves a cheerful giver." Well known and to the point are the words of St. Ignatius: "*Religiosus nullam causam habet moerendi.*" "A religious has no cause for yielding to sadness or being disheartened." Cheerful, even heroic acceptance of the smallest matters in the spirit of faith will rout the enemy and frustrate his subtle strategy and restore peace to the soul. There can be no monotony in the service of the Most High, who is pleased with our sacrifice of ease and comfort to embrace the cross gently laid on my shoulders and to radiate the love of the Crucified.

"Give me understanding and I will keep Thy law with my whole heart.... Give me understanding and I shall live."[8] It is basically false to say that the true *cura minimorum* injures and destroys the freedom and joyful liberty of the children of God. It rather enhances it, vivifies and ennobles it. Our shortcomings and defects alone might cause us momentary grief, but our trust and confidence are an inerrant source of deep soul-peace. There is beauty in the practice of unquestioned surrender; it is stimulating and fruitful. The Holy Spirit desires to enrich us with His grace, if we are but on the alert to note His gentle whisperings. Genuine faithfulness never conjures up unrest, discouragement, or disgust. It is something deep and holy, an oblation, a holocaust to the Most High.

The minute observance of the least injunctions of divine grace is an infallible mark of interior greatness and generosity in God's service. We recall St. John Berchmans of the Society of Jesus, perfect examplar of the *cura minimorum*, the most splendid exponent of the effects of this beautiful virtue. In this youthful religious, we see faithfulness personified, radiant in divine light. "Rather be torn to shreds," was his firm resolve, "than transgress even the smallest regulation." He lived it to the letter. Yet no religious among his associates was more congenial, more sought after and loved than this lovable son of Ignatius. His unrestrained hilarity and almost uninterrupted jollity was like a ray of sunshine in the midst of the busy life around him. It won him the admiration of time-tried religious of the Society.

8 Ps. 118:34, 144.

> c) *Again, we often hear the objection*
> *that these things are mere trifles,*
> *so what does it finally matter?*

We may, indeed, hold them to be infinitesimally small, yet they wield a power beyond words in the inner citadel of the religious who bows willingly to their demands. Silence, quiet and calm reserve, solicitude for the social amenities, short recollection before prayer, and other helps for our prayerlife, reserve in communicating with others— these are not obligatory under pain of sin. To call them mere trifles, of little import, is hardly just. They are a challenge to those who aim high, beyond what is of strictest necessity; perfection is their sole purpose and determined resolve.

Faults against these virtues and minor observances are ordinarily due to forgetfulness, to haste under pressure of work, and similar causes, and should not evoke undue alarm or regret. But, you say, they are trifles, why not disregard them outright? Here we have the *cauda serpentina*, the serpent's tail, slithering in at the oddest moments, the hallmark of the fiend of all virtues. Interior souls must guard against this pernicious snare. Is it not our earnest desire to achieve heights of zeal and loyalty far surpassing the mere *must* in this respect, beyond what is of obligation? Love and gratitude would seem to demand this of us.

All religious founders laid great stress on the faithful discharge of the little things that make up our daily routine. We give ourselves to God freely. Why hold back the least and minimize the grandeur of our oblation? How stimulating the examples drawn from the Rules and regulations of the Society! Clear and succinct, it reads: *"Omnes con-*

stanti animo incumbamus, ut nihil perfectionis, quod divina gratia consequi possimus, in absoluta omnium Constitutionem observatione ... praetermittamus." "We will perserveringly endeavor not in any point to remain behind the perfection that, with the grace of God, we can attain in the exact observance of our statutes." St. Ignatius could hardly have spoken with greater ardor of his profound esteem of those who excelled in the virtue of fidelity. A positive call to his Sons to recognize with joy the beauty and excellence of the Rule.

All his Sons, he insists, must be permeated with this spirit, "*Omnes!*" Not only temporarily, perhaps at the outset in the spiritual life, should they walk in its light, but they should persevere in it gloriously through the years: "*constanti animo incumbamus.*" This spirit should further prove so fortifying and all-embracing that nothing we can achieve with God's grace would ever be overlooked. Not mere regularity, but loving submission to the rules and customs must be our aim. The spirit of deep devotion to duty performed in the best possible manner, must increase and flourish through the years. Finally it must manifest itself outwardly, not only in the general observance of the important ones, but in the most perfect fulfilment of all without exception. "*. . .in absoluta omnium Constitutionem observatione.*"

The ardent Loyola will have nothing to do with a comfortable, laissez-faire attitude towards minor observances among his Sons. He was fully aware, however, that through weakness, frailty, forgetfulness, haste, and precipitancy we would miss out here and there and commit a fault, yet that matters little to him. But he insists irrevocably on the sincere, earnest endeavor to achieve fidelity in the minor points, with fresh energy in all the directions of our varied program under the holy sanction of Rule. Humility, charity, zeal for souls, self-denial will insure for you the friendship of Jesus Himself in your shining example of loyalty to the law.

In transgressing smaller rules, there is ordinarily greater danger than in more serious violations. In these latter, the danger at once becomes apparent, and we more readily guard against a second fall. In the former, we are hardly aware of the evil and realize it only when it is too late. Summing up, our greatest gain must be on the side of fidelity in small matters, persevering fidelity nourished by love. A religious character anchored in this spirit of self-immolation will wax strong in the great acts that lift souls Godward, out of the vitiated atmosphere of self-seeking and indifference.

We must constantly be on the alert for the opportunity to exercise ourselves in the least details of the Rule, with great loyalty and self-sacrifice. To wait for greater calls to practice mortification, patience and humility, genuine love of God and of neighbor, might prove disastrous. Unless steadily refurbished in these smaller observances, the inner spirit will lose its agility and collapse. Great, heroic, outstanding occasions are relatively rare, but there are many opportunities for conscientious regard for the Rule as the holy Will of God. Delicate concern for mutual love and charity in the daily experiences and routine observances will make life congenial, Christlike. It is the hallmark of a great soul tending toward perfection, supporting the fire of love in the hearts of our associates by mutual edification.

To speak of charity and mutual forbearance, we may ask what often disturbs the even tenor of life and casts a shadow? Countless opportunities are ours for selfless love and cordial esteem, as the Rules and the *Constitutions* require it. These deserve our utmost concern, solicitude, and love. How beautiful and delightfully agreeable would our religious families be if the least labor were perfomed with ardent Christlove and self-surrender, relying on His gracious goodness! Not for one moment would we be faithless to Him, who supports us so liberally by the outpourings of His grace. How lavishly we have been endowed with grace in the sanctuary of the religious life. It exacts perfect conformity. ". . . the Lord's generosity to you must be the model of yours."[9]

Love can never be achieved in its perfection, nor shed light across many beclouded pathways, unless we lend a docile ear to the faintest whisperings of grace. One who aims to excel in these smaller matters with lively faith and love, will have the divine grace to radiate the beauty of fidelity in greater moments. Trustful prayer is needed when severer trials confront us that we may cheerfully realize the charm of selfless surrender. With jubilant heart, it is saying with St. Ignatius, "take and receive all my liberty."

In a letter to the Scholastics of the Society, the heroic Xavier reverts to this point. Noting their intense zeal to exercise themselves on a grand scale for the glory of God, he cautioned them to guard against the delusion of overrating external splendor at the cost of deep inner values. No one will ever distinguish himself in great things, if he neglects the less conspicuous in the eyes of the world.

9 Col. 3:13.

This may be one of the hidden ways in which hyper-sensitiveness and self-esteem try to assert themselves. Fully conscious of our own insufficiency, we bow humbly before the Lord for stronger courage and high resolve. Only His divine pleasure is the concern of our souls—naught is done for mere human applause. "For better is one day in Thy courts, above thousands."[10]

Concluding with the admonition of Blessed Peter Faber of the Society, to his brethren, we resolve to make it our own: "Continue to exercise yourselves in the least that is enjoined, so that in all humility and trust you may merit the surpassing, immeasurable reward of eternal life." Then you will realize the truth of the beautiful word: "In that day the mountains shall drop down sweetness, and the hills shall flow with milk: and waters shall flow through all the rivers of Juda: and a fountain shall come forth of the house of the Lord, and shall water the torrent of thorns."[11]

10 Ps. 83:11.
11 Joel 3:18.

PART THREE

THE MOST EXCELLENT FRUIT OF
THE INTERIOR LIFE—ZEAL FOR SOULS

"You are built upon the foundation of the apostles and prophets with Christ Jesus Himself as the chief Corner Stone"

—*Eph.* 2:20, 21.

CHAPTER XV

THE SUBLIMITY OF ZEAL FOR SOULS

> *"That they all may be one, as Thou, Father, in Me, and I in Thee."*[1]
> *"You are citizens with the saints and members of God's household."*[2]

1. ZEAL FOR SOULS FRUIT OF THE LOVE OF GOD

This zeal originates in love, in the loftiest of all virtues. It demands a higher degree of this beautiful virtue. Not every love is able to generate it. Zeal is the fruit of an intense love, St. John Chrysostom assures us,[3] and St. Thomas Aquinas teaches us that it is an effect of love, which comes to light when it grows most ardent and intense.[4]

a) *Love of God*

It springs from the love of God. "There is no sacrifice more pleasing to God," St. Gregory observes, "than zeal for souls. In truth, if we are filled with love of God to such an extent that in total abandonment to God we know no other

1 John 17:21.
2 Eph. 2:19, 20.
3 Cf. Lanc. op. 13. 1. 3. c. 1.
4 I-2ae, q. 28. a. 4.

interests than those of His ineffable and infinitely loving Majesty, our heart expands. It bursts into flames of holy love; the rays of its participation and its activities penetrate to every place where the honor of God is concerned.

A heart so inflamed with love will not only grieve over personal sins, with deep compunction, but it will exercise the same potential fervor wherever sin is to be found. "I beheld the transgressors, and I pined away; because they kept not thy word."[5]

A heart aglow with love rejoices not only for itself in the knowledge and love of the Infinite Good. Not satisfied personally to fulfill the holy Will of God in all things, it longs incessantly to win many souls to participation in the knowledge that love imparts. It stimulates souls to the highest, the accomplishment of the Will of the Divine Majesty. Zeal for souls desires that God be known and loved by all men. The greater this love, the more effectively it ignites such a desire and the more selflessly it excels in genuine works of zeal.

b) *Love of Jesus Our Saviour*

If this love is so ardent that it unites us most intimately with our Saviour, our heart of necessity beats in union with His; it cherishes an irresistible desire to work for the salvation of souls. Love unites souls most closely, makes them one in mind and heart; naturally, they will admire and strive for the same things.

"Oh, My friends," Our Lord once said to St. Bridget. "Oh, you must know that I love these lambkins so dearly

---

5 Ps. 118:158.

and tenderly that if it were still possible for Me to die for them, I would gladly go into death for each individual soul, in order to save all from perdition." Again, "Even now I would willingly surrender My body with perfect love to all imaginable tortures and pains." Would it be possible for one united by the closest bonds of love with such a Heart not to be aflame with the holy fire that burns incessantly in His loving Heart? This union is so tender that the desire for the salvation of souls burns vehemently in a holy, passionate zeal for souls.

c) *Love of neighbor*

It is in fact nothing other than love of God, whom we find and love in our neighbor. In its marvellous light, there shines out the supreme value of every soul created by God and redeemed by the Son of God. It is impossible to recognize this interior worth in the light of grace and not to strive to promote the preservation of such a good.

Where true love of neighbor is fully at home in a heart, the eye will ever be open for dangers that circumvent the soul, for the misery and suffering that afflict countless souls, for the terrific assaults of the Evil One, and for the unspeakable anguish that threatens in the life beyond. But to be aware of this and to realize it as a personal danger, as a personal need, and not to look about for help and preservation is, again, unthinkable. "Citizens with the saints," we are and with the light infused into our soul by grace, we easily enter into the designs of God to do His holy Will.

Zeal for souls generates love of neighbor, provided it be genuine without selfish aspirations and interests. In the degree to which it spreads its charitable endeavors in search of the welfare and the happiness of the beloved, more than one's own, it is Christlike, giving "testimony of the Light."[6] Genuine fervor and zeal often ponders seriously the interior wealth of well-prepared souls, of good will and implicit trust. It longs to walk in the light of grace and rejoice with the riches supplied to souls through the Precious Blood of Christ. The soul thus endowed is skilled in depicting in the liveliest colors this intrinsic feeling of joy unutterable. To envision in such a light the beneficent peace that may be ours here below, the marvellous beauty and fullness of grace in which we may be clothed, the inexpressible glory and eternal heavenly delights awaiting souls, this is a privilege beyond compare. To realize all this and not endeavor to the utmost to make this wonderful happiness accessible to the souls we love in Christ, and not to bring all this spiritual wealth into their lives at the cost of sacrifice even, is wholly unthinkable.

2. THE EXCELLENCE OF ZEAL FOR SOULS

Zeal for souls, we repeat, is the fruit of love; it is the most precious and divine fruit of this supreme virtue. How valuable, how exalted in its origins, its endeavors! With restless, irrepressible ardor it tends toward the highest. It is the hidden principle of genuine love for souls, a love like that of Christ Himself in going about "making all things well." It is broad and all-embracing. In its innermost heart, the welfare of many is preferable to the welfare of only one. Tireless must be the roadmap of this divine

---

6 John 1:8.

virtue. Therefore, according to St. Thomas, a virtue is the more excellent the more it is directed to the welfare of many.[7]

a) *Zeal for souls is wide and all-embracing*

With its aspirations and endeavors, it reaches out beyond personal salvation and perfection. It embraces many, indeed, all men. Not as if it forgot its own sanctification and the constant interior effort it exacts. *"Miserere animae tuae placet Deo."* "Have pity on thy own soul, pleasing God."[8] Sterling fervor and zeal notes this well. It pursues holiness with all the greater tenacity, because of the opportunity offered of working efficiently for the salvation of countless other souls. Attention and solicitude for one's own perfection, far from cooling fervor and zeal, rather furnish new enrichment.

The increased knowledge and love that springs from the pursuit of our own advancement towards holiness, forcibly augments the wish that all without exception might know and esteem this ineffable Good, might love God, who created them, redeemed them, and wills to admit them to participation in His divine bliss. Thus zeal for souls, drawing new strength from one's energies to achieve perfection, extends over all souls. The clearer our concept from personal experience what purity and peace of heart signify, what fulness of grace and virtue, of union with God, and of heaven itself, of which a foretaste is often granted us, the more ardent will be our desire to share

---

7 I–2ae, q. 141, a. 8, n. 1.
8 Ecclus. 30:24.

these inestimable benefits with countless souls, who hunger and thirst for the truth. The more intense is our wish that all would enrich themselves and quench their thirst at this overflow from the House of God, which is so abundant that myriads of worlds would not be able to exhaust it.

Such was the zeal that glowed in the heart of St. Ignatius. Animated with this fire of love, he sends out his Sons with the challenge: *"Ite, filii mei, ite, incendite et inflammate omnia!"* "Go forth, my Sons, make haste, enkindle and inflame everything!" O sublime, divine virtue, all-embracing in its irrepressible love! It knows neither difference of persons, of age, nor of conditions of life or nationality.

b) *Wherever human beings are found, this virtue exerts itself for the loftiest aim imaginable, the salvation of immortal souls, in the strength of God*

Consonant with this zeal, we incline to the care of bodily welfare of men, and under certain conditions we endeavor to promote their scientific and cultural pursuits. This is done with the love and dedication of an apostle, but only in so far as it is conducive to the higher purposes of zeal, namely, the salvation of our neighbor. This must be our guiding star in all we undertake to spread the kingdom of God through selfless work for the souls within our reach. It is no hardship because it is a means of gaining strength in our own self-conquest. Fervent prayer will support our least efforts at disseminating the lovableness of generous concern in the spiritual life of another.

Should there be little or no satisfaction in our labors for the good of souls, neither honor nor recognition before men, this fact will certainly not impede our activity; it ought rather stimulate us to more intense fervor. How easily can we transform this privation, this sacrifice, into a fruitful source of grace and salvation for souls. "Should the Lord," cries St. Magdalen of Pazzi, whose heart was aflame with love of souls, "Should the Lord ask me what reward I desire for my labors, I would respond, 'I desire nothing, dearest Lord, save the salvation of immortal souls'!"

c) *Zeal for souls is finally tireless and persevering*

"*Ignis vero nunquam dicit sufficit.*" "The fire never says, 'Enough'!"[9] Genuine zeal is such a fire. Even if it lacked occasion for outward activity, it will nevertheless not grow cold, but remain alive and restless in acting for its lofty aim. Such work is inspired by love.

Could we ever find ourselves in a situation with no opportunities to exercise zeal for the salvation of souls? It is hardly possible. Prayer, we know, is most efficacious in advancing the kingdom of God and the world's salvation. "Pray for one another, that you may be saved. For the unceasing prayer of a just man is of great avail."[10] It is a turning towards the Infinite with unshaken confidence. "I desire, therefore, first of all, that supplications, prayers, intercessions, and thanksgivings be made for all men."[11] To St. Mechtild Our Lord said one day: "Pray for poor sinners, whom I have bought at such a dear price, and for

---

9 Prov. 30:16.
10 James 5:16.
11 1 Tim. 2:1-4.

whose conversion I long." He desired her prayers as an excellent means of imparting His plentiful graces to the souls of sinners.

Let us, therefore, pray much for the entire Church. Even if we ourselves are not directly engaged in apostolic work, we can certainly by our prayers entreat the Lord to send laborers into His vineyard; by prayer and sacrifice we ask Him to fortify, strengthen and encourage those He has sent, and bless their apostolic activity.

What should hinder us from devoting our activity, no matter of what nature it be, to this sublime purpose? If the desire to work for souls is strong within us and induces us to exercise the greatest care in the performance of our daily tasks, even the most distasteful assignment, we can offer it to the Lord with the stipulation that it may be acceptable in His sight as an apostolic deed worthy of His divine complacence. "You would do much," St. Ignatius counsels the Scholastics at Coimbra, "if in this spirit you dedicated your work to the apostolate of souls. Your labors assumed in this manner, offered to God and accepted by His paternal pleasure, would become a most efficacious instrument in the hands of God for the salvation of our neighbor."

The practice of virtue is yet another fruitful means of apostolic achievement in the immediate homeland or in the mission fields abroad. If the dear Lord sees how we strive to do good to our poor, benighted brethren by our loving docility to His every wish, He will in infinite mercy receive the erring and lost sons back into the Father's House. Genuine apostolic work thrives where souls are devoted to the unselfish and unremitting practice of virtue. It flourishes in the sunshine of divine pleasure. If in the same spirit we accept disagreeable happenings, sufferings, and reverses with the sentiments of St. Paul: *"omnia, sustineo propter electos, ut et ipsi salutem consequantur, quae est in Christo Jesu, cum gloria coelesti,"* how discerning we are. "Therefore," he says, "I endure all things for the sake of the elect, that they also may obtain the salvation which is in Christ Jesus, with heavenly glory."[12] To suffer thus in the apostolic spirit, will be most fruitful for countless souls. We may not forget that Christ redeemed the world primarily through His passion. Souls that cling to the cross when danger threatens, will reap richest fruits of the blessings of Our Lord's ineffable Sacrifice for all mankind. A thought to ponder on our knees.

How varied and excellent are the ways for implementing our apostolic fervor! Self-love may tempt us to desire work in accord with our personal choice, regarding the duties, the post assigned us in obedience. Let us not be caught unawares. All these things cannot quench zeal. They are a fabrication of the Evil Spirit, who aims at distracting souls and directing our interests surreptitiously toward externals. He thus seeks to hinder the spirit of sacrifice that lends dignity and transcendent worth to the least of our actions. Strong and noble souls are convinced that God is the Author of salvation, and that His grace and mercy alone endure majestically against the wiles of the Tempter.

The souls for whom we labor may be far removed from us, and we rarely come into communication with them; yet what does it matter? God in His paternal goodness is

---

12 2 Tim. 2:10.

close to them and everywhere He disposes events according to their best interests, in the light of faith. All who work for the welfare of immortal souls are the objects of His divine mercy; likewise, those for whom he exerts himself. In difficult hours in the apostolic field, there is need of lively faith, of a turning to Him who knows the hearts of all those whom we wish to serve. Strength from the Heart of God will refurbish the weapons of prayer and sacrifice in our hands unto deeds of saving grace for countless souls redeemed by the Blood of Christ.

Prayerful activity is always within our reach; it is of the utmost importance in the apostolic work entrusted to us. When the opportunity for direct service to souls has more or less ceased, the spirit of faith rooted deep in the heart that is consecrated to God's work, will perdure to the last in restless giving of self, to the last pulsation, which will still be for God and the immortal souls for whom Christ died on the cross. All this happens so unobtrusively as if Jesus Himself were still among us.

Little wonder that it is so inexpressibly dear to the Lord. "There is no sacrifice," observes St. Gregory, "that is so pleasing to God the Almighty, as zeal for souls." It must, therefore, be our earnest endeavor to acquire it more and more, even at the costly price of sustained effort and denial of various sorts, that may often hurt to the quick. It is for God alone. Through self-immolation and a close association with the Heart of Christ, let us try to increase our love for this tender, apostolic Heart. We do this in the spirit of silent thanksgiving for the overwhelming grace of our election.

We shall then be true apostles, cooperating every hour and at every step, in the most divine of all divine works. Full of confidence and trust, we may look forward humbly to the reward of zeal for souls, to shine as the stars in the heavens for all eternity.

CHAPTER XVI

ZEAL FOR SOULS

> *"Let this mind be in you which was also in Jesus Christ."*[1]
> *"Launch out into the deep, and let down your nets for a draught."*[2]
> *"For we are made partakers of Christ."*[3]

I. THE APOSTOLIC HEART

Zeal for souls is the noble sentiment that springs from love and is nurtured by it. It fills us with an intense desire for the salvation of immortal souls and incites us to do all in our power to promote it.

"*Vidi praevaricantes et tabescebam, quia eloquia tua non custodierunt.*" "I beheld the transgressors, and I pined away; because they kept not thy word."[4] All great and noble souls have felt the profound grief so forcibly enunciated by the Psalmist. They know of no greater sorrow than to see how the commandments of God and His divine injunctions are flagrantly ignored, how His service is neglected, how God, the Infinite Majesty all Goodness and Love, is so little known and loved.

---

1 Phil. 2:5.
2 Luke 5:4.
3 Heb. 3:14.
4 Ps. 118:158.

Today there are still countless souls who take well to heart the dire soul-need and the deep guilt of sinful man. The complaint of the Psalmist spontaneously rises to their lips: "I beheld the transgressors, and I pined away." This heartfelt sorrow calls forth the ardent longing that the insults may cease and the honor due the Divine Majesty be fully restored. Since this is possible only in so far as men know and love God, it is the glowing wish of these loyal hearts to diffuse the knowledge and love of God. Not for themselves alone would they envision it, but for all on earth, far and near. Thy kingdom come! The repeated cry of many hearts.

In these sentiments we see the genuine fount of zeal for souls. Through the instrumentality of our priests in their consecrated ministry, and of all those in direct care of souls, it is a shaping for Christlife. "O my God, be not Thou silent to me."[5] Consonant with the Holy Father's insistent recommendation, others cooperate with the Clergy in the vast and fruitful areas of Catholic Action, to bring Christ and His world-wide mission into the hearts of men; it is all God's work.

Only in hearts aflame with holy zeal, will it seek an outlet in deeds. Why is it so difficult to win faithful, loyal co-laborers for this apostolic work of Christian charity? It is nothing less than lack of zeal for souls and brotherly love, of self-dedication and denial that Christ in the Mystical Body may live. "Am I my brother's keeper?"[6] Our hearts

---

5 Ps. 27:1.
6 Gen. 4:9.

are narrow and constricted. So we think and care only for ourselves, unmindful of the dire needs, of the longing love of Christ for souls. That is no concern of mine, we say, as we pass by the poor who have been exploited and robbed of everthing by the archenemy, sin, and now lie prostrate in the dust unto spiritual death.

Let us briefly ponder some aspects of zeal for souls, that this fount of light may ever more copiously spring in our hearts. What is zeal for souls? we ask. It is growth in holiness, increase in perfection with the endeavor to help others attain it. Here we envision an ardent desire for salvation and the zealous effort to promote it, in other words both an apostolic heart and an apostolic activity.

1. THE APOSTOLIC HEART GLOWS WITH LOVE FOR CHRIST

An apostolic heart is the first distinctive mark of the lovable virtue of zeal for souls. It is a heart wholly absorbed in fraternal love, a heart that beats with burning desire for the salvation and happiness of all men. This longing must be a permanent, deep sentiment that reaches out to souls, not only under pressure of external circumstances, perhaps, but it must be constantly alive, a dominant inclination of the heart, glowing with love for Christ. "As the branch cannot bear fruit of itself, unless it abide in the vine, so neither can you, unless you abide in Me."[7] Three things are requisite for this desirable end, to be considered briefly.

---

7 John 14:4.

a) *To achieve the laudable end of implementing our zeal for souls, we must love and esteem immortal souls redeemed by Christ's Precious Blood*

We are solicitious about the welfare and happiness of others only in so far as we cherish and love them and their interests. Daily experience bears us out. The father of a family seeks the well-being and contentment of his dear ones because he loves them with fatherly affection. A friend wishes his friend all good things sincerely, because he loves him and thinks highly of him. The desire to save souls will live in us and grow strong in the strength of Him who promised His assistance, as we sacrifice ourselves for these souls, whom the Godman purchased with His Precious Blood. Let us learn from our Divine Saviour. In His breast there burns a truly apostolic Heart, for He beholds in each human being the image of God. A sublime thing, indeed! In every sentient human being the Saviour loves the marvellous work of the Creative Hand of His Heavenly Father. This thought of divine condescension fills His Heart with the unspeakable desire to restore this image, the wonderful handiwork of Divine Omnipotence, disfigured by sin, and to invest it with even greater lustre and divine splendor. To do the Will of the Father, to save souls is the food of Jesus, the first need of His Divine Heart.

A similar life animated the hearts of all true apostles. Paul, the ardent disciple, values souls as the object of the love and affection of the Heart of Christ. In the light of this love, he envisions each soul in wondrous beauty, and never can he forget the infinite redemptive price at which they were bought. He sacrificed Himself for us. This stupendous truth seizes hold of him anew at sight of his fellow men, whose souls are radiant in the crimson Blood of Christ. This spectacle presses him irresistibly to new efforts for their redemption, and fills his soul with the desire to be all to all.

The world-apostle, St. Francis Xavier, is another telling instance. What brings him to the outposts of India, China, and Japan? What enables him to shoulder the hardships of an unspeakably difficult life of sacrifice? Xavier comprehended the real value of one human soul; he recognized the startling truth that even a whole world is worthless in comparison with one soul. Here is the unfailing source of his insatiable thirst for its salvation. Hence his incessant prayer: "Give me souls! Take all, but give me souls!" And after he had received thousands upon thousands from God, his desire, instead of being stilled, burned with a brighter glow. Here we see clearly that love and high esteem of souls themselves is the basic condition for winning them to Christ.

Let me ask again: How do you regard human beings? With merely natural eyes? Do you take offense at mere externals, at defects, faults, and sins, which appear on the surface and often make men so unlovable? Are you, perhaps, given to unkind strictures and thoughtless disparagement of their good name? What bitterness, perhaps, may be in your heart.

How totally different does the entire world appear to a heart that loves souls. How lovingly a true apostle overlooks everything that might disturb, grieve, or embitter him. He looks deeper, views souls in the light of the divine sun of love, of the Heart of Christ breaking on Calvary. Would you like to share in the work of Catholic Action? Is there further need of a powerful incentive? This flows only from a profound concept of the value of souls in the light of faith.

b) *High esteem and love of the goods that constitute the salvation of souls*

If we value a thing—any good—but lightly, we will care little for it either for ourselves or for others. On the contrary, we desire a thing we much admire, not only for ourselves but for our loved ones, our friends, and for all for whom we cherish real affection. Obviously, then, we shall wish our neighbor grace, virtues, the pleasure of God, the bliss of heaven, all the more fervently the more we anticipate and love it even for ourselves.

Again we look into the Heart of Christ. How it burns with the desire to make all men children of His heavenly Father. No one knows better what the sonship of God implies than the only-begotten Son of the Father. No one values and loves the pleasure of the Father as much as He whose daily bread it was to do the Father's Will. "My meat is to do the Will of Him that sent Me."[8] No one can better appreciate the happiness of being beloved of the Father than He who in a solemn moment heard the words: "This is My beloved Son, in whom I am well pleased."[9]

All true apostles registered the same experiences in their search for souls. Why does St. Paul repeatedly feel himself pressed to preach the grace of Our Lord and Saviour Jesus Christ? Why is his heart filled with inexpres-

8 John 4:33.
9 Matt. 3:17.

sible desire and lips overflowing, that he never wearies of reiterating this wish again and again: "Grace to you, and peace from God our Father, and from the Lord Jesus Christ." *"Gratia vobis et pax a Deo Patre et Domino nostro Jesu Christo."*[10] He is, as it were, consumed with this desire, and we ask why. Because he himself values grace so highly above all else, the grace that was purchased at the dear price of the labors, hardships, fatigues, and the blood and sweat of the Godman. Because he knows no ideal more sublime than the restoration in the hearts of men of the kingdom that is justice, peace, and joy in the Holy Spirit. In his eyes these goods are of such tremendous worth that, when embraced wholeheartedly with ardent love, everything else the world may offer him in comparison, appears as dross and emptiness and vanity, as a hindrance. "I count everything loss because of the excelling knowledge of Jesus Christ, my Lord."[11]

Why is St. Ignatius wholly aglow with the desire to spread the fire of the love of God over the entire world? Why does he with a holy vehemence exhort his Sons to "Go forth and inflame all hearts!" Why does he shed copious tears at thought of the world's need of apostolic laborers? Why must he seek relief for the irrepressible flame that burns within his breast with the ardent ejaculation, "Oh, that all men would know and love Thee!" Is it not because Ignatius himself in his own person esteems the priceless goods of grace and love so highly that he neither wishes, loves, nor seeks any other good, save this one good:

---

10 Rom. 1:7.
11 Phil. 3:8.

"Give me only Thy love and Thy grace, with these I shall be rich enough and shall have no more to desire!"

And if Ignatius, permeated with zeal for souls, ardently desires that his Sons should not advance languidly like weary wanderers, but with giant strides hasten toward the heavenly Fatherland! If he burns with the desire that they come not alone, but with many others, whom by word and example and deed, they led along the same way, toward the last and blessed goal, the possession of eternal happiness, we ask, why all this? It is again a tribute to his own disdain of earthly things and his great esteem of the eternal goods, his longing for the heavenly Fatherland. He would see his Sons inflamed with genuine fervor, that with him they would cry out: "How despicable earth seems to me when I look up to heaven!" So will it be with us only on one condition. We must cultivate a profound esteem of grace and virtue, know and love it and utilize it to give pleasure to God, conforming our Will to the Father's holy Will. Provided our life is attuned to this beautiful ideal, we shall be able to make Jesus known and loved by all souls, since it is His Will that all be saved.

May the reign of Christ be established in every soul. May we love Thee, O Jesus, for those who love Thee not. How indispensable is the striving for perfection if we would win souls and diffuse the ardent charity of Christ in all hearts. We must confess that because of our sins we are not worthy of the grace to labor effectually and constantly for the eternal salvation of souls. O Jesus, cleanse our sinful souls, inflame our cold hearts and replenish them with Thy virtues that we may become worthy apostles of Thy love.

c) A *third source of zeal for souls springs in the heart of a true apostle and grows into a mighty stream of tireless labor for mankind*

It is the true recognition of the misery into which souls who lack the spiritual goods are thrust. Sin, offense against God, spiritual death, to be despised of God, cast away, lost forever as a victim of the tortures and eternal perdition! What a terrible reality!

Moses had understood this. He was, therefore, so intent upon the salvation of his people that he forgot himself entirely. Falling down before the Lord, he prayed: "This people hath sinned a heinous sin, and they have made unto themselves gods of gold; either forgive them this trespass, or if thou do not, strike me out of the book that thou hast written."[12] And what are the sentiments of the Psalmist at thought of sinners! He should like to die of grief: "I beheld the transgressors, and I pined away; because they kept not thy word."[13] And again: "My zeal hath made me pine away; because my enemies forgot thy words."[14] The Psalmist once more: "My eyes have sent forth springs of water; because they have not kept thy law."[15]

How is *Jeremias* immersed in grief, sitting on the ruins of Jerusalem! How he sighs and laments when he thinks of the sins of his people and of their dire consequences! "Jerusalem hath grievously sinned, therefore is she become

12 Ex. 32:31.
13 Ps. 118:158.
14 118:139.
15 118:136.

unstable: all that honored her have despised her, because they have seen her shame. Her filthiness is on her feet, and she hath not remembered her end: she is wonderfully cast down, not having a comforter."[16] So the Prophet continues his lamentations, and his tears are stilled; his grief is solaced only when the Lord vouchsafes him a glimpse of the future redemption.

What was the source of *Christ's restless zeal* when the fulness of time had come? What prompted Him to rend the heavens and to issue forth from the Father's bosom to come to earth? It was the *misery of sin in which mankind was enslaved,* in which Satan held them fast; this so touched His Heart that He could no longer brook the hideous sight. For our sakes and for our salvation He came to earth. What was the *sorrow* that from the first moments of His earthly life to the last breath never left Him, which the Prophet had long since envisioned in his heart and caught up in the words: "My sorrow is continually before me."[17] Our sins, our misdeeds are ever present to Jesus, as an infinite offense against the Father, implied in them, the crushing guilt they load upon us, the eternal flames of hell which they invoke upon us. These are the things that the all-holy gaze of Christ's Divine Heart cannot endure. Jesus lives for love of souls alone, and the more He realizes how men themselves are so cold and indifferent, the more eager He is to be baptized with the baptism of blood for the world's redemption. "*Baptismo autem habeo baptizari, et quomodo coarctor, usque dum perficiatur.*" "I have a baptism

---

16 Lam. 1:8 f.
17 Ps. 37:18.

wherewith I am to be baptized: and how am I straitened until it be accomplished."[18]

In overwhelming measure the earth is covered with sin, but still more intense is the desire that burns in the Heart of Jesus, through His passion, to release an overflow of graces. Endless is the irrepressible desire kindled in the Heart of Jesus to wipe out the guilt of sin with His own Blood by His death on the cross. The cold death which sin has brought into the world is terrifying. Its power is irresistible; no man can wrest its victim from his grasp. But the love of Christ is strong as death and stronger still the flames that burst from His loving Heart, charging it with an inexpressible desire to destroy the sting of Satan by His death on the cross.

The *flames of hell* are terrible, an ocean of fire that will never die; more unquenchable, still, is the fire that burns in the Heart of Christ. In that Heart is enkindled the fire of which we sing in the Canticle: *"Lampades eius lampades ignis atque flammarum."*[19] "The lamps thereof are fire and flame." And again: "Many waters cannot quench charity, neither can the flood drown it."[20]

A boundless ocean of sorrow has broken loose upon Jesus, but it was powerless to quench the fire of His love. He was eager to suffer still more, His Blood had flowed in streams, the purchase price was offered a hundredfold and more, overwhelming redemption was made: "With Him there is plentiful redemption," the prophet observes, "and yet He thirsts." *"Sitio!"* I thirst for sufferings, for souls. To

---

18 Luke 12:50.
19 Cant. 8:6.
20 8:7.

St. Bridget Our Lord said: "I created you, and did not spare a single member of My body; I offered them to be tortured for you; in spite of it all, I would even now, if it were possible, offer Myself to be crucified again rather than lose one immortal soul. So intense is My love for souls."

2. THE HEART OF JESUS, THE IDEAL OF A HEART CONSUMED WITH ZEAL FOR SOULS

The Heart of Jesus glowing with love is, indeed, the ideal of an apostolic heart, with an insatiable longing to save immortal souls.

a) *He loves souls as images of the Father,* as temples destined for the indwelling of the Holy Spirit, and this consuming fire of love knows no measure.

b) *Jesus loves virtue and holiness, as the true ornament of the house of God; therefore His desire to see it radiate its beauty.*

The Father's delight and the eternal bliss of union with Him is joy supreme; therefore He cries out with longing trust: "Father, I will that those whom Thou hast given Me, may be where I am." Ponder briefly the delicate beauty of Our Lord's sentiments.

c) *He knows no greater distress than to be forsaken of the Father.* "What does it profit a man to gain the whole world and to suffer the loss of his soul?" Here is the secret of Christ's irrepressible longing to wipe out sin, to ward off from souls the misfortune of eternal perdition, and even the slightest damage of sin. Sin is abhorrent in the sight of the gentle, self-immolating Christ. His Heart is charged with boundless zeal for souls; it is a deeply-bedded, irresistible passion.

Our zeal for souls must be similarly constituted. It may not lag, nor depend upon outward conditions and contingencies, being agile and alert only for exterior purposes. It must be rooted deep in the soul's inner depths. It must function as a main artery and incentive for our soul-life which is interior, and is, therefore, active every hour and every day in a truly apostolic life. An apostolic heart beats in unison with Christ for souls. Of ourselves we cannot possess such a heart; no one claims it by nature. On the contrary, being sensually minded, we love earthly goods and lavish on them greater care than upon immortal souls. Then, too, we have little understanding for genuine virtue and holiness; being blind and thoughtless, we are only lightly touched by what may bring ruin to souls. In this regard our heart is indifferent, cold, and hard as stone. *"Cor lapideum,"* says the Holy Spirit, "a stony heart."[21]

There is some one who has promised to take the stony heart out of our breast and replace it with a new one: *"Auferam cor lapideum de carne vestra."* "I will take the stony heart out of their flesh."[22] He has deigned to work this marvel of grace in us. He has chosen us out of the world, or at least allowed us to see its vanity. He has drawn us to Himself in tender mercy, in closest intimacy through the grace of sonship and of Confirmation; through the steadily increasing love, which He pours into our hearts in Holy Communion.

---

21 Ezech. 11:19.
22 Ezech. 11:19.

In the marvellous light by which we walk: ". . . You are a chosen generation, that you may declare His virtues, who hath called you out of darkness into His marvellous light,"[23] we see more clearly the terrible darkness in which countless souls lie buried. In view of the beauty, the delights, and the riches that we behold in the Divine Heart and already enjoy, we realize the absolute wretchedness of blinded and hardened sinners. What an abominable sight! Finally, in the union with this Heart, our heart takes fire, with deepest longing that all may partake of the light, the joys, and the wealth of our Lord and God.

Let us therefore keep close to Him who is not only our Ideal, but also the Creator of an apostolic heart. Let us endeavor to foster ever closer harmony in perfect union with Him. Since this is possible only in a pure and humble heart, we must endeavor with restless fervor to acquire this lovable virtue. Inflamed with true zeal, we will with cheerful ease perform the beautiful works of our vocation and so garner rich fruits from our labors in the Lord's vineyard. It is our consoling privilege to look forward to a crown resplendent in twofold celestial glory.

II. Apostolic Activity

1. PRAYER—WORK—SACRIFICE—OBLATION

Three times a day we are invited by Mother Church to recall in fervent prayer the sublime mystery of the Incarnation of Our Lord and Saviour. "The angel of the Lord declared unto Mary, Behold the handmaid of the

---

23 1 Peter 2:9.

Lord, And the Word was made flesh!" In the course of the Ecclesiastical Year, especially in the holy Adventide, our thoughts dwell reverently on this miracle of the love of God. We then recall vividly the merciful compassion of the Heavenly Father, as told by St. John: "For God so loved the world, as to give His only-begotten Son; that whosoever believeth in Him, may not perish, but have life everlasting."[24]

Let us momentarily contemplate this mystery of love, which incites us to similar love of our neighbor. The love we here admire is above all zeal for souls. Love is powerful in winning souls.

Let us enter the holy House of Nazareth, and hear the Archangel Gabriel saluting the Blessed Virgin: "Hail, full of grace, the Lord is with thee!" Our spiritual eye discerns much more; it beholds the Heavenly Father, as He executes the decree of the *Redemption, the divine thought of peace and reconciliation,* as Isaias styles it. The fullness of time has now come. What will the Father do? Heaven and earth stand in utter amazement as they see the Father's glance looking for a means of redemption, as it rests on His Son. It is in truth His only-begotten Son, whom He is about to immolate for love of us, by eternal decree. What inexpressible love for our souls.

The Eternal Son of the Most High, the Splendor of the Father, by whom all things were made! Oh, see with what readiness He wills to be the Victim for us, with what love He is determined to clothe Himself in our human nature to suffer and die for us that we may have life everlasting. *"Ecce venio!"* "Behold, I come!" He says, here I am, Father.

---

24 John 3:16.

"In the head of the book it is written of Me that I should do Thy Will. I have desired it."[25]

Presently the heavenly messenger speeds toward Nazareth to announce the happy tidings to the Virgin, that she is chosen to be the Mother of the Redeemer, and to await her consent. Contemplate this holy messenger. It seems as if the love for us that he beheld in humble adoration in the Father and the Son in heaven is resplendent in his whole being and sets his spirit aglow. Note with what zeal for souls he discharges his sublime office of a divine messenger. Look into his heart. Admire the love for us poor mortals his presence radiates. What joy is his that the hour of redemption is at hand, and that he is the chosen one to transmit the heavenly word.

We hear the salutation, the message, and then the great Word for which the millenniums have waited, for which, says St. Bernard, heaven and earth, and the nether world, breathless in anxious expectancy, waited and longed. *"Ecce ancilla Domini, fiat mihi secundum verbum tuum!"* "Behold the handmaid of the Lord, be it done unto me according to thy word!" Mary pronounces it sweetly with ringing accents of love. Love for the children of men prompted her joyous assent. What a model again of zeal for souls!

Hardly has he spoken the word, when the heavens open and drop down dew . . . and the clouds rain the Just. *The Holy Spirit*, the personal love of the Most Blessed Trinity, hovers over Mary, overshadows her with His creative power. In her virginal womb sprouts the celestial Flower, the Saviour of the world. The Heart of Jesus beats close to the heart of His Mother. The Eternal Word was made

25 Ps. 39:8.

Man. The only-begotten Son of God is ours, offered by the Father, that all who believe in Him, all who wish to love Him, may not be lost, but have everlasting life.

Oh, how love radiates from this marvellous mystery! Love for our souls! All the persons in the sacred scene are animated with zeal for souls in thought, word, and action. Who could ponder this mystery attentively without being himself inflamed with the divine fire that envelops him here? At thought of the great heroic things done here for the salvation of souls, for the redemption of mankind, must we not be strongly impelled to imitate as best we can such examples, and offer ourselves to take part, as far as possible, in this most divine work?

2. THE APOSTOLATE OF PRAYER

For a proper understanding of the apostolate of prayer we need but call to mind who is the proper and last author of the salvation of souls.

a) *Intrinsic excellence*

It is God the Lord. Only with His grace can we be cleansed of sin, made capable of performing good works, merit rewards, live in a manner pleasing to Him, and finally die happily and enter eternal bliss. What is the logical result? Obviously this: everyone who entreats God to impart this grace and opens His hand, as it were, that He may fill all living things with blessings, is a genuine co-worker for the salvation of souls. He is in a unique manner active for immortal souls and is a genuine apostle.

Prayer is the powerful means at our disposal for moving

the Heart of God, for disposing the Father of Lights, the Giver of every good gift, to grant us His grace. If we prostrate ourselves in reverent adoration before the Lord and Creator of mankind, whom to know is eternal life; if with contrite hearts we approach the Infinite Holy and Just One, Him who is all-merciful, who does not will the death of the sinner, but that he be converted and live; if we cry incessantly to Him, the Almighty Helper in every need, whose ear is open for the least cry of distress; if, finally, we immolate our most ardent desires and longings to the infinitely perfect Highest Good who is ever ready to impart of His perfections to all men, to sanctify all, we shall surely move the Heavenly Father to open the treasures which His beloved Son Jesus Christ earned for humankind with His Heart's Blood.

He will allow the light of faith to shine for those who are still in darkness and in the shadow of death; again, He will receive lost sons in grace, press them to his paternal Heart, imprint upon their foreheads the kiss of peace, and restore them to the full rights of sonship. Lovingly He will raise up and protect a desperate soul, free one sorely tempted and tried, fortify the dying, or set free souls from the cleansing flames of purgatory, and lead them home to the heavenly Fatherland.

Oh, that we could see with our own eyes the powerful effect of truly apostolic prayer, and the marvels it has achieved in the Lord's vineyard. Our attitude toward this kind of apostolic activity would change considerably. We would embrace it with greater fervor, with even greater confidence than heretofore. We would gladly surrender our selfish designs and preconceived cogitations. But time and means are still at our disposal for remedying this untoward situation; there is ample opportunity for devoting ourselves with zeal and sympathetic understanding of the need of souls we are able to relieve in this fruitful apostolate of prayer. We cite a few examples of this apostolate.

b) *Examples of this Apostolate*

From time immemorial the Holy Spirit has mightily incited the faithful servants of God for this apostolate of prayer.

We recall how *Moses* prayed for his people, incessantly entreating mercy and pardon for them. It is well known how imploringly he raised his arms in suppliant prayer when his people faced the enemy in battle, who were also God's enemies. God's warriors in the New Testament should certainly not be denied similar help, least of all from those whom the Holy Spirit so eminently deigns to instruct in the art of prayer.

The Prophet Daniel is in captivity, banished from Jerusalem, far from the Holy of Holies, but he does not forget to pray. Thrice daily he falls on his knees in his solitary cell and turning towards Jerusalem, he importunes God in fervent prayer. Even after his enemies had wrested from the king the mandate that anyone who asked in prayer from any God other than their king, would be cast a victim to the lions, even then the holy man continued to pray as often as before with the utmost trust.

His love is stronger than death. Nothing is able to stem his intense longing for reconciliation, for salvation, and the sanctification of his people. *"Peccavimus!"* "We have sinned; we have committed iniquity, we have done wickedly, and have revolted: and we have gone aside from thy commandments, and thy judgments. But to Thee, the Lord our God, mercy and forgiveness. O Lord, hear: O Lord, be appeased, hearken and do: delay not for thy own sake, O my God: because thy name is invocated upon thy city and upon thy people."[26]

Behold how a loving heart, full of compassion for the salvation of his neighbor can pray! But what a marvellous answer it receives! We see it in Daniel. While he was still speaking and praying, behold, the Angel Gabriel "swiftly touched me at the time of the evening sacrifice. And he instructed me, and spoke to me, and said: O Daniel, I am now come forth to teach thee; . . . to show it to thee, because thou art a man of desires; therefore do thou mark the word and understand the vision. Seventy weeks are shortened upon thy people, and upon thy holy city, that transgression may be finished, and sin may have an end, and iniquity may be abolished; and everlasting justice may be brought."[27]

The application is left to the individual soul in this awful realization. There is no need of further exposition of our duty, as exiles of these newer times, when we see how the true Jerusalem, the holy Catholic Church, the people of God, is made an object of scorn and contempt, how it is assailed and persecuted.

When we reflect that every soul is a sanctuary of God, and in how many the "abomination of desolation," mortal sin, reigns, must not our zeal burst forth in ardent flames? Must we not more and more, like Daniel, become men of

---

26 Dan. 9:5, 9, 19.
27 Dan. 9:21-24.

desires, of longing for the conversion and salvation of poor sinners?

Such were, like *Daniel*, an *Isaias*,[28] and all the just of the Old Dispensation, who never wearied of crying out with intense fervor: "Drop down dew, ye heavens, from above, and let the clouds rain the just. Let the earth be opened and bud forth a Saviour."[29] This was their heart's desire, and for that they incessantly cried to heaven, not for themselves alone, but for their people, for the whole world. *"Emitte agnum, Domine, dominatorem terrae."* "Send forth, O Lord, the lamb, the ruler of the earth."[30] "And all the kings of the earth shall adore Him: all nations shall serve Him . . . and in Him shall all the tribes of the earth be blessed."[31]

c) *What admirable examples of the efficacy of prayer for souls!*

By word and deed these men were zealators for souls, but far more efficacious was their activity through prayer. The Holy Spirit Himself, the author of salvation, was their inspiration. What shall we find in the *New Testament?* It is self-evident that there this manner of the apostolate is developed in a far higher degree.

We catch a glimpse of *the Queen of the Apostles,* the Blessed Virgin Mary. What transpires in her heart? What desires and wishes sway her mind from the first dawning of reason? "The most abundant," observes Bernardine of

28 45:8.
29 Isa. 45:8.
30 Isa. 16:1.
31 Ps. 71:11, 17.

Siena, "were those with which she prayed for the salvation and redemption of mankind." "We are hardly able," the Saint continues, "to represent to ourselves the heavenly ardor with which she longed for the redemption of mankind." When the Word took flesh in her virginal womb, these holy desires were augmented, for she prayed that the hidden God and Redeemer might become incarnate, to be known and loved by all men. How diligently she must have prepared the way for her Son by her prayers! How she pleaded with the Lord lest the labors and fatigue, and finally the passion and death of Jesus might be lost in a single soul! And with what assiduity must she later have followed the Apostles in spirit on their apostolic journeys. What blessings may her incessant prayer have called down upon their labors and their missionary activity! What is Mary doing still today? The very thing that has absorbed her maternal pity for these 1900 years. Mary is active. She works for the salvation of souls through prayer. She stands at the throne of her Divine Son as Mediatrix and intercessor for the whole human race.

Are we in need of more examples to show how irresistibly the Spirit of God incites us to exercise zeal for souls through prayer? May it suffice to cite *St. Paul,* who calls God to witness that he incessantly is mindful of all in prayer. "For God is my witness, whom I serve in my spirit in the gospel of His Son, that without ceasing I make a commemoration of you."[32] *St. Ignatius, Francis Xavier, St. Peter Canisius* and *Brother Alphons,* with fiery ardor and intensest longing sought to set a world afire. Think of a *St. Teresa of Avila,* who amidst tears and sighs, often

---

32 Rom. 1:9.

spent the night in prayer for the conversion of heretics. A *St. Magdalen of Pazzi* in spite of prolonged dryness and aridity in prayer cherished a glowing desire for the salvation of souls. She incited her religious with the same fervor in pleading especially for the conversion of sinners. These examples are among the most encouraging and convincing in hagiography, yet their number could be indefinitely multiplied.

What must be our concern in this efficacious apostolate? The more restricted our field of labor exteriorly, and remote, the more eagerly must we devote our best efforts by prayer and sacrifice to help the world still caught in the meshes of misery and sin. There will be a moment, sooner or later, when many a soul whom we never recall having met on earth, will salute us as her saviour and be grateful to us for all eternity in heavenly bliss.

III. THE APOSTOLATE OF SACRIFICE AND OBLATION

"I sat down under his shadow, whom I desired: and his fruit was sweet to my palate."[33]

The mysteries of the life of Jesus may be compared to a shady tree richly laden with ripe fruit. It is prohibited to none to seek refreshment under the shadow of this mystic tree. All are invited to come and taste of its fruits. There is a simple requisite—that we desire them, pluck them in fervent meditation, and sitting beneath the tree, that is, remaining in silent contemplation close to Jesus, enjoy the delicious fruits. They will be sweet to the soul, will mellow the bitterness of earthly sorrows, fill us with

---

33 Cant. 2:3.

love of our dear Lord, and give us strength to bring forth genuine fruits of patience and of salvation.

Beyond doubt, we have all, at one time or another, in patient perseverance, cherished such sentiments, as we tried to lift the Saviour's cross. Oh, how numerous and precious are the *fruits* that invite us by their sparkling lustre from the *mysteries of the Sacred Passion!* And how marvellous are the *effects* of their delightful taste in the soul!

Devout meditation on the passion opens our eyes to the stark reality of *sin*, since to atone for it a Godman suffers the most excruciating pain. As we ponder this mystery, we adore profoundly the *immeasurable mercy and love of God,* who withholds from us, the guilty ones, the full measure of justice and punishment, but inflicts it upon His own well-beloved Son, the Holiest and Innocent Lamb of God.

Our hearts expand in limitless *confidence and trust.* What could God still deny or refuse us after having immolated the highest and dearest that is His, His well-beloved Son? After giving us in His Precious Blood the pledge of every grace and everlasting bliss to be with us to the last? *Love of God* burns more brightly in the soul, and fastens us indissolubly to Him who has first loved us and delivered Himself for us.

Love of our neighbor is likewise increased and fanned into flaming *zeal*, not only ready to suffer everything for the neighbor's spiritual good but actually attempting the utmost. Pondering these truths, we will be stirred anew to a deeper appreciation of this holy mystery, and of our obligation to sacrifice ourselves as a propitiatory victim. Meditation on the passion of Christ generates solidity and unreserved surrender for the welfare of souls. No more powerful motives for nourishing our zeal could be offered us than the profound and prayerful study of the Passion, with its almost irresistible impulse for exercising zeal.

1. SURPASSING WORTH OF AN IMMORTAL SOUL

Zeal for souls is nourished by the thought of the *value of an immortal soul*. Now, let me ask, where could we find a more conclusive and convincing answer than in the contemplation of the passion and death of Our Lord? Could the Heavenly Father, Infinite Wisdom and Omnipotence, give us a more obvious proof of the value of a soul in His eyes than He did when He offered His well-beloved Son to suffer the most ignominious death for its ransom?

Zeal for souls is heightened, secondly, by the thought of the *terrific disaster that awaits the reprobate forever*. Could Jesus, with His divine eloquence, depict for us the direst misery of sin more effectively than He did through the inexpressible pain and anguish He suffered in the Garden, sorrowful unto death? Or at the pillar of the scourging, where His Sacred Body was mercilessly reduced to but one wound—a "Worm and no man." On the cross, finally, where on His bed of martyrdom, distended between two thieves, maligned and mocked by the rabble, abandoned by heaven, He voiced His final lament: "My God, My God, why hast Thou forsaken Me?" If this is done on the green wood, what will happen to the dry?

A third motive for working toward the perfection of our neighbor resides in the *precious goods* that are destined for him: *grace and virtue*, heaven and everlasting bliss. Even if one had the gift of tongues, of angels and of men, he could not find words to extol adequately the grandeur of these goods so vividly as Christ's passion and death presents them to us. If we contemplate the Blood of Christ as it trickles from every pore of His Body in Gethsemane, or streams from His Sacred Body at the pillar of the scourging and in the crowning with thorns, we are moved to compassion and adoration of this inestimable Gift. Ponder silently the Sacred Countenance bedewed with blood, the shoulders lacerated, the cruel nailing of hands and feet on Calvary, the issuing of the last drop from the thrust of the lance, from His most Sacred Heart. What a deep mystery this, in which we are privileged to participate, by offering the merits and graces that spring from this everlasting Flood for the salvation of many whom Christ died to save.

The fruit of our contemplation of the sublimity of this divine work is a final, powerful incentive to let nothing undone to help in Christ's redemptive work. Christ was not satisfied to divest Himself of heavenly glory, to become Man, and to toil for years in the sweat of His brow. For this stupendous undertaking everything of which love made Him capable had to be pressed into service; every member of His innocent Body, every movement and surrender of His Sacred Heart, every faculty of His Divine Soul, even His own precious life had to be immolated.

What must be the divine import of the salvation of souls, for which a Godman makes such tremendous sacrifices? Truly, it is the most divine of all divine works to contribute to so noble an end. For us it is a pleasant opportunity of doing our utmost to excel in this apostolic work. Since this is our God-given privilege, we must labor incessantly to cultivate the spirit of absolute surrender in the quest of souls for the love of God.

2. SACRIFICE AND IMMOLATION FOR SOULS

This is nothing less than to suffer for the salvation of souls, and where it is expedient even to die and immolate life itself. This is the *apostolate of sacrifice and oblation.* Jesus Himself designates it as the most sublime manifestation of true love of our neighbor and of the desire for his salvation. *"Majorem hac dilectionem nemo habet, ut animam suam ponat quis pro amicis suis."* "Greater love than this, no man hath, that a man lay down his life for his friends."[34] St. Paul depicting for us the zeal of Our Saviour for souls, exclaims: "He loved me, and delivered Himself for me."[35] *"Dilexit me et tradidit semetipsum pro me."*

To immolate Himself for us, to suffer all imaginable pains, to die a Victim for our salvation—this it was upon which Jesus fixed His gaze and toward which His most ardent desires were directed. At His entrance into the world, St. Paul testifies, Jesus offered Himself to the Heavenly Father for this kind of activity. "Sacrifice and oblation thou wouldst not: holocausts for sin did not please Thee . . . Then said I: Behold, I come to do Thy Will, O God: *'Ecce venio'!"* Here I am to fulfill Thy Will. But how? "A body thou hast fitted to me."[36] I am ready to suffer and finally die, a Victim for My brethren.

Well we know how the *thirst for suffering* accompanied Jesus *all the days of His earthly life.* Not the total renunciation and profound humiliation in His Mother's womb, nor

---

34 John 15:13.
35 Gal. 2:20.
36 Heb. 10:5, 9.

the utter poverty in Bethlehem, nor the privations and fatigues of the flight and exile in Egypt; nor yet the hidden life and hard labors of Nazareth, not the inconvenience, the weariness, and the persecutions during His public life— none of these were able to quench His thirst.

Even after having suffered all this, the desire of His Heart for further suffering and pain for the redemption of mankind is not yet allayed. He is unable to stay it, He breaks forth into the cry: *"Baptismo habeo baptizari, et quomodo coarctor, usque dum perficiatur!"* "And I have a baptism wherewith I am to be baptized: and how am I straitened until it be accomplished."[37] Indeed, He felt an irrepressible impulse to implement His zeal for souls. No one is able to hinder or restrain Him. Peter attempts it one day and begs Him not to go to Jerusalem, and so evade the passion. What was His response? "Go behind me, Satan, because thou savorest not the things that are of God, but that are of men."[38]

Oh, of what significance must sufferings be to which we submit for the love of immortal souls, which we bear patiently and gladly for their salvation! Borne in this spirit as a whole burnt offering to God, how efficacious they must be for the good of souls. What fruits will they garner in the Father's vineyard! No one knows this better than Jesus, consequently He chooses for Himself this sort of apostolic labor, with all its hardships and trials. He retrenches His immediate work for the salvation of mankind; for suffering He recognizes no limits. He teaches in public for three years only, but suffers for a lifetime. From the first breath

37 Luke 12:50.
38 Mark 8:33.

in His Mother's womb to His last sigh on the cross, He is a Victim of immolation. Many have spent a longer time in apostolic preaching, but no one has ever suffered like unto Him for souls, and no one will ever be able to do so.

What a lesson for us! Oh, that we rightly understood it! May the example of Our Lord give us a better perspective of the manifestations of zeal for souls in bearing pain; may it show us what a distinctive place the apostolate of sacrifice must hold in our activity for the good of souls. Let us often and earnestly pray for this understanding of so profound a mystery in the service of God.

Though we may be in the most diverse ways employed in working directly for souls, this manner of activity remains somewhat limited. We must study how to equalize desire and performance. Unless we would allow days to slip by without accomplishing anything worth while in the apostolate, we must remember that prayer and suffering are unexcelled means of bringing home to souls the merits of the passion of Christ. In a special way, we wish to be fervent disciples of Christ in His insatiable hunger and thirst for the salvation of souls. Let the apostolate of sacrifice and suffering, therefore, be our cherished portion.

There is never a dearth of opportunity for stilling our desire for apostolic work. The distasteful and disagreeable things and reverses, troublesome vexations, the fatigues of daily duty, pains of body and soul, taking all as it comes and bearing it gladly, heroically, without alleviation, this and much more are precious nuggets in the chalice of our dedicated service to share in Christ's redemption and take an active part in aiding others to love suffering and the cross.

Our Lord appeared to St. Bridget one day. To give her

an idea of the magnitude of His love for all men, He said; "If it were possible for me to die as often as there is a soul in hell, and I could suffer death for each soul, I would even now most cheerfully, with perfect love surrender my body to the greatest tortures for all mankind." These are the sentiments of Our Saviour. Pondering these sublime sentiments, we must be forcibly impressed and moved to embrace the apostolate of suffering. But we must be ready to exercise it at the place assigned and for the specific work with all the opportunities it offers for self-denial and cheerful surrender.

Such opportunities give a clear indication of the genuineness of our love for souls and for the ways and means designed in holy obedience, with attendant humiliations and trials. We believe ourselves misjudged, neglected, or otherwise unduly tried. In such moments we may easily succumb to the wiles of the tempter. A feeling of disconsolateness, discouragement and a weariness inexplicable assails us, within and without. We are aware of our insufficiency. Let us not forget that these moments are precious for testing our virtue and our willingness to be a victim with Our Lord for the salvation of men. The cheerful offering of our hardships and sufferings will bring light into many hearts that still sit in darkness. It will engender compunction of heart for sinners hardened and bitter. We may in this spirit, alleviate the suffering souls in purgatory, afford relief to the sorely tempted, and help restore peace and joyous resignation to those who are laden with trouble and distress.

If the Heavenly Father beholds our willingness to sacrifice all in order to join the ranks of apostolic workers, He will afford us countless opportunities to work for souls, whether we are actually engaged in personal service in Christ's ranks or not. He will look upon us as good and useful instruments in His hands, and regard us as His victims, like unto Our Lord. He will confer on us the most precious of all graces, untold sufferings, together with much love to bear them resignedly. We may never know which souls profited of our sacrifice and oblation, but the Master of the Vineyard knows it. In the great Beyond, in the Land of the Blessed, we shall one day enjoy forever the gratitude of those we have helped to save, members of the Mystical Body of Christ.

PART FOUR

MEANS FOR CULTIVATING
THE INTERIOR LIFE

"Now we have received the Spirit that is of God; that we may know the things that are given us from God."

—1 Cor. 2:12.

CHAPTER XVII

MEANS FOR THE PURIFICATION OF THE HEART

> *"It is I who wipe out for My own sake your offenses. Your sins I remember no more."*[1]
> *"He who created thee without thee, does not will to save thee without thee."*[2]

I. The Sacrament of Penance Viewed in the Light of Faith

"My little children . . . if any man sin, we have an advocate with the Father, Jesus Christ the just; and He is the propitiation for our sins."[3]

1. THE DIGNITY OF THE SACRAMENT OF PENANCE

What happens when the Sacrament of Penance is administered, viewed by human eyes, is slight and very simple. In the light of faith, however, showing forth the reality, we behold a sublime action, a divine work, God Himself bending over us in merciful compassion and forgiveness.

---

1 Isa. 43:25.
2 St. Augustine.
3 1 John 2:1, 2.

We do, indeed, approach a human being in confession, but he does not act in his own name. The Godman, our Lord and Redeemer, acts through Him, hears and absolves us: *"Dominus noster Jesus Christus te absolvat,"* says the priest, and does so only at His command, in virtue of the power conferred on him. *"Ego auctoritate ipsius."* "In virtue of His power." The priest pronounces the absolution, but the power that operates in these words is not his. Who can forgive sin save God alone? *"Ego te absolvo."* "I absolve thee." True, but *"in nomine Patris et Filii et Spiritus sancti,"* "in the name of the Father and of the Son and of the Holy Spirit."

Christ Himself absolves us. The same moment when the priest pronounces these words, the Three Divine Persons, the Most Holy Trinity, are truly and really active in the soul. It is not only a natural cooperation—concursus—which is operative in all creatures. Nor does it grant only the support of grace, which enables us to perform supernatural works, but here it is active in a loftier degree. By the word of the Confessor, it effects the marvellous remission of sins and the infusion of grace. Christ is present in the grace of sacramental Absolution, imparting peace to the soul and strength to be more conscientious in the love of God, who suffered untold pain for our redemption.

Holy Mass and Communion excluded, nothing in this life could even remotely be comparable to this Divine Action. It is stupendous in the sight of God and works wonders of grace and mercy in contrite souls. Our labors and studies, our prayers and meditations are and always remain human actions. Christ offered Himself in expiation for the sins of humanity.

Here in this august Sacrament, the Infinite Being acts in our behalf. Here is a wholly divine activity. The mercy of God pardons without considering our inability of ourselves alone to do the least to merit such love. Oh, how generous is the Saviour in pardoning! Our Redeemer is a fount of mercy. He cleanses in His own Most Precious Blood every contrite soul.

Infinite Justice provides for a satisfaction worthy and condign by reaching into the treasury of the merits of Jesus Christ. Infinite Holiness restores or perfects Its Supernatural Image in our hearts, by infusing sanctifying grace, or if still present, increasing it. All this happens at the moment when the priest absolves us. The Blood of Christ has been shed for all. It is a medicine for everyone. The action of this Blood is intensive. It cleanses the soul of human guilt.

O truly sublime action, most holy ceremony, divine work! We see only a simple Sign of the Cross, hear a few words, perceive in our interior hardly more than ordinary devotion. But this makes no difference in the reality and efficacy of the Divine Act, before which our Guardian Angel falls prostrate in adoration of the marvellous condescension of an incomprehensible divine mercy and love. With what reverence must we be filled, since our heart is the scene of the divine transformation!

No matter how often we receive this holy Sacrament, this frequency may not in the least diminish our sentiments of reverence and holy awe. In despite of the simple exterior, despite the frequency, it is and remains a sublime, most holy, a divine action. We need only the spirit of faith, which reveals to us in some measure the sublime reality. Let us cherish this spirit and remind ourselves every time of what happens in reality, though invisibly. This Sacrament of the purifying Blood was instituted by Jesus in an outburst of great love for men.

St. Ignatius advises us, when going to meditation, to ask ourselves whither we are going and to what purpose. *"Quo vado et ad quid?"* Is this suggestion not more applicable whenever we approach the Sacrament of Penance? I am going to the Eternal Father, whom I have again offended, but who awaits me with open arms and after a few moments will impress upon my forehead the kiss of peace. I am going to Jesus Christ, who stands as Mediator with the Father and now impetrates for me with the Father through His Infinite merits. *"Filioli, . . . si quis peccaverit Advocatum habemus apud Patrem, Jesum Christum justum et ipse est propitiatio pro peccatis nostris."* "My little children, if any man sin, we have an advocate with the Father, Jesus Christ the just. He is the propitiation for our sins."[4]

I am going to the Holy Spirit, who is essential, infinite Holiness, but who is at the same time the immeasurable, boundless love of the Divinity. To the Holy Spirit, whom I have often offended, but who, none the less, in infinite goodness, longs to cleanse my heart and to embellish it as His Temple more richly.

I am about to approach the Most Blessed Trinity to experience in a few minutes that in the eyes of this Infinite Majesty I am not an object of disdain, to call God's holy anger and justice upon myself; in those sublime moments I realize that I am rather a vessel of mercy into which the Three Divine Persons pour new graces for Their glorifica-

---

4 1 John 2:1, 2.

tion. "That He might show the riches of His glory, on the vessels of mercy, which He hath prepared unto glory;"[5] "*ut ostenderet divitias gloriae suae in vasa misericordiae, quae preparavit in gloriam.*" O action truly divine, soon to rejuvenate my soul! Sublime work, which I will endeavor to perform with reverence and devotion. The richer will be the fruits to be garnered for my spiritual life, in renewed consecration and loving service in a sinless soul. "The justification of a sinner is surely one of the most beautiful works of God, and deserves our most loving contemplation."

2. HOW THE SACRAMENT OF PENANCE OPERATES IN THE SOUL

The Blood of Christ produces the most precious and richest fruits to be gathered by the devout penitent. In the Sacrament of Penance it is the Precious Blood that works primarily with the greatest spiritual efficacy.

a) *The Precious Blood purifies*

When the priest in the tribunal of penance raises his hand and makes the Sign of the Cross over me, then is fulfilled what we so often entreat by the lips of the Psalmist: "*Asperges me, Domine, hyssopo et mundabor: lavabis me, et super nivem dealbabor.*" "Sprinkle me with hyssop, O Lord, and I shall be cleansed. Wash me, and I shall be made whiter than snow."[6] "For if the blood of goats," says St. Paul, "and of oxen sanctify such as are defiled, to the

---

5 Rom. 9:23.
6 Ps. 50:9.

cleansing of the flesh: how much more shall the Blood of Christ, who by the Holy Ghost offered Himself unspotted unto God, cleanse our conscience from dead works, to serve the living God."[7] "The Blood of Jesus Christ," writes St. John, "the Blood of the Son of God cleanses us from all sin. If we confess our sins, He is faithful and just to forgive our sins and to cleanse us from all iniquity."[8]

What a grace in such a cleansing! With the grace of God it is relatively easy for us to live in the religious state without committing a mortal sin. A sinless life is the ideal of religious living under holy Vows. The Sacrament of Penance, therefore, should never need to cleanse us of them. Yet the Blood of Christ is a medicine for all, wiping out our guilt and giving strength for the leading of a sinless, holy life. Even if a religious had sinned grievously, the cleansing power of the tribunal of penance restores to the soul the grace offered us in the bountiful mercy of God.

Confession is for all sinners the plank of salvation in shipwreck. What a grace and what a blessing! But the cleansing of venial sins is, likewise, an inestimable grace, and it is ours in every confession. It is a spiritual bath for the soul, rejuvenating our whole interior. It does still more. The semi-voluntary faults and imperfections that cling to us in spite of our best efforts, are brought under the powerful focus of the Sacramental blessing, when we receive it with glowing love.

The more fervent our preparation, the more efficaci-

---

7 Heb. 9:13, 14.
8 1 John 1:7, 9.

ously will the Blood of Christ bedew and cleanse our soul more and more of all inordinate inclinations and destroy the poisonous roots of sins and faults. Oh, to what a degree of purity and beauty of soul can we attain, since we have such easy and frequent access to the wonderful means generously offered us: *"Lavabis me et super nivem dealbabor."* "Wash me and I shall be made whiter than snow."

b) *The Precious Blood enriches us spiritually*

"Apud Dominum misericordia et copiosa apud eum redemptio." "With the Lord there is mercy: and with Him plentiful redemption."[9] Whence this wonderful spiritual privilege? It is possible because the price of this redemption is infinitely great. Christ's Blood is so precious and of such worth that it suffices not only to forgive sin, but beyond this to purchase countless treasures for our spiritual enrichment. This we experience preeminently in the Sacrament of Penance. The absolution I receive is God's act. In the name of Christ, the priest pardons my sins and remits the eternal punishment due to sin. The better my preparation, the more efficaciously will the temporal punishment due to sin be removed through the merits of Jesus Christ.

At the same time, it infuses sanctifying grace, or, if not lost, increases it. The powerful, divine gift thus conferred on souls need hardly be stressed. If we always viewed these marvellous spiritual advantages in the light of faith, and pondered the many other treasures that ac-

---

9 Ps. 129:7.

company this Divine Act, our inner life would be materially fortified and strengthened. In addition to sanctifying grace we receive numerous other graces and gifts, that tend to subdue and quiet the passions. Graces that liberate us from sundry temptations and occasions for sin; graces that enlighten and strengthen us in order to help us walk unscathed through the maze confronting us; graces that incite us to a more fervent and more perfect use of the opportunities for a sinless and holy life in the spirit of atonement.

How unspeakable the mercy, the love, the goodness and magnanimity of our God! May our eyes always be open to behold God's paternal hand depositing these graces in the soul as often as the words of the priest imparting absolution fall upon the ear in the stillness of the confessional. "May the passion of Our Lord Jesus Christ, the merits of the Blessed Virgin Mary and all the saints (and) whatever good you have done and evil endured, be unto you for the remission of sins, an increase of grace, and life everlasting." Oh, how the Blood of Christ enriches us! In a far higher degree and more frequently we shall experience in ourselves the third effect of this fruitful Sacrament.

c) *The Precious Blood infuses joy and consolation*

Is there one who would not be consoled on hearing the words of Christ's representative in the sacramental absolution: *"Ego te absolvo a peccatis tuis"*—"I absolve thee"? He who pronounces these words speaks in the name of God, for God alone has power to forgive sin. These are the words for which we long as often as we pray with the

Psalmist: "To my hearing thou shalt give joy and gladness: and the bones that have been humbled shall rejoice." *"Redde mihi laetitiam, et salutare tuum da nobis."*[10] Who should not rejoice on seeing himself enriched with so many graces and precious gifts! Purity, beauty, riches console, and of necessity give joy. All this spiritual wealth is ours in virtue of sacramental absolution. We are lifted out from dangers of sinful excesses. The Precious Blood flows from an inexhaustible fountain, purifying our conscience and imparting strength for uprooting perverse habits and tendencies.

A clean heart is created within me, Holy Scripture tells us, and a right spirit is renewed within me. I am newly accoutred with the princely spirit. Joy of itself floods the soul. *"Redde mihi laetitiam salutaris tui."* "Restore unto me the joy of thy salvation, and strengthen me with a perfect spirit."[11] Here it is taking place. Not only because purity and plenitude of grace automatically arouse these sentiments in the soul, but because God calls them forth through special lights and inspirations, inundating the soul with peace and joy in the Lord.

"Beati, qui lugent, quoniam consolabuntur." "Blessed are the sorrowful, for they shall be comforted." We come with contrite, sorrowful hearts, and the Heavenly Father, seeing it, fulfills His Son's promise. He turns a compassionate and merciful eye upon us, and the sweetest heavenly feeling flows into our veins. His divine glance dispenses

---

10 Ps. 50:10.
11 Ps. 50:14.

light and joy greater than the sun's brightest rays; *"adim-plebis me laetitia cum vultu tuo."*[12]

But the Holy Spirit, comforter and consoler, in renewing the face of the earth, adds to justice, "Peace and joy." Thus He builds up the kingdom of God within us. *"Regnum Dei justitia, pax et gaudium in Spiritu sancto."* "The kingdom of God is justice and peace, and joy in the Holy Spirit." In the depths of our heart, we hear the testimony that we are children of God. Nothing on earth, however, can give us joy and delights even remotely comparable to this testimony. The Holy Spirit encourages and moves weary souls, offers them healing ointment to strengthen their souls. The Good Shepherd stands at the gate of which Our Lord said: "I am the gate," to watch the returning flock to see if any of the lambkins need healing and loving care.

3. THOUGHTS FOR THE FRUITFUL RECEPTION OF THE SACRAMENT OF PENANCE

Tremendous realities are being enacted whenever the Sacrament is received with the solicitude and zeal that corresponds to God's most holy and merciful designs. The Blood of Christ, the Blood of the Son of God, purifies, enriches, gives joy, and strength, and new life. If we fail to experience these marvellous effects in so high a degree as we would wish and could easily do so, it must be ascribed to our lack of earnest endeavor. There is question here of a Sacrament, a superb and holy Act, a Divine Work.

---

12 Ps. 15:11.

a) *One who considers this truth will not delay his preparation to the last moment before entering the confessional*

He will strive earlier in silent prayer and earnest searching into his soul, to arouse sentiments of compunction, of humility and longing for the healing touch of God's merciful pardon. What might hinder us from this wholesome procedure? No special time is required. Ejaculatory prayers are so lavishly furnished us in the Penitential Psalms, in the offering of the Precious Blood, and in various indulgenced prayers tending toward mercy and pardon. We can easily create a humble and contrite heart in ourselves, which the Lord will not despise. Why should we neglect such a wholesome privilege of cleansing and purifying our soul, of strengthening it for the valiant encounters with the soul's enemy? If we have endeavored to draw healing from this wonderful divine institution, with the use of grace, our next confession will be more deeply imbued with the holy fire of love that burns away our sinfulness and spiritual torpor.

b) *A second hindrance why so many draw sparingly and less generously from this fountain source of God's mercy is the lack of confidence and childlike trust*

The tender mercies of the Heavenly Father are open to all. In the Sacrament of Penance God is the mild and benign Father, full of mercy and compassion. Mercy and boundless love radiate towards us in everything that happens. It is hardly worth mentioning what justice asks of us.

All that is due to justice has been lovingly assumed by Jesus Himself. May this the only true aspect of the Sacrament of Penance ever burn brightly in our mind. Then the Evil One will in vain endeavor to conquer our hearts, to disturb our peace. We shall make our preparation quietly, and at the moment of confession itself our attention will turn with childlike love to the Triune God, who deigns to work such wonders in the soul. We shall oftener and with deeper joy ponder the treasures we receive and be more grateful for these divine manifestations of generosity and pardon.

c) A deficient or hurried thanksgiving after confession is not seldom a positive hindrance for reaping the salutary fruits of the Sacrament

Since we hardly take time to become vividly aware of the wealth of spiritual gifts and benefits we have received in this Sacrament, we forfeit to some extent the treasures of grace infused into our soul. Their full unfolding is hindered. Let us, therefore, dwell more fully on these marvellous effects of interior transformation and renew ourselves thoroughly in the use we make of the holy Sacrament. We should always approach it with reverence and devotion, for it is a sublime, divine work.

Childlike confidence and the spirit of love should be our guides in the careful examination of conscience, in arousing contrition, and in the accusation itself. Mercy and boundless love give light to the soul. A devout thanksgiving is of prime importance. Adequate time should always be allotted to this worthy act; the special graces and precious treasures given us in the holy Sacrament should be cherished as exceptional gifts. May the love of Christ motivate us to such zeal. May His Sacred Heart find genuine delight in the loving atonement we offer Him for the abuse of so many with regard to this holy Sacrament, for the indifference with which they offend His merciful Heart.

It will give joy to the loving Heart of Jesus to see in our hearts, at least, the fruits that spring from His Most Precious Blood yield a bountiful harvest. Divine longing, thirst for Christ, for the healing waters that flow incessantly from the Sacred Wounds He suffered for us in His bitter passion and death will refresh our soul.

"Nothing shall separate us from the love of God, which is in Christ Jesus our Lord."[13]

---

13 Rom. 8:35.

CHAPTER XVIII

INTERIOR ENLIGHTENMENT

"O House of Jacob, come, let us walk in the light of the Lord."[1]
"You were once darkness, but now you are light in the Lord. Walk then as children of light."[2]

I. THE SPIRIT OF FAITH IS THE FOUNDATION OF THE INTERIOR LIFE.

Faith is compared to light in many instances in Holy Scripture. It will not suffice for us to possess this light, we must also walk in it. We should be children of light. Our whole life should be spent in the radiance of this inner light, making bright the drab stretches along the way. May the stars of our faith, the light of God, illumine our life.

The feast of Epiphany again reminds us of the inexpressible happiness that is ours in the call to the true faith. We rejoice in the splendor of the light that has come to us; we are filled with joy in the rays of the glory of the Lord that has risen over us. We treasure this divine gift all the more as we realize how dense the darkness that often reigns elsewhere. The world is verily caught up in an almost impenetrable darkness.

---

1 Isa. 2:5.
2 Eph. 5:8.

How readily we Christians can apply to ourselves the words of the Prophet: "Behold darkness shall cover the earth and a mist the people: but the Lord shall arise upon thee, and His glory shall be seen upon thee."[3] "God has delivered us from the power of darkness," St. Paul declares, "and has translated us into the kingdom of the Son of His love."[4] He has called us "into His marvellous light," St. Peter assures us.[5]

Well may we rejoice and tender profoundest thanks to God the Father, who according to St. Paul "made us worthy to be partakers of the lot of the saints in light."[6] This is not yet enough. Our joy because of the star that has arisen for us, is well in place, and we owe thanks to God the Father of light, from whom comes "Every best gift and every perfect gift."[7] There is still more. "O House of Jacob, come, let us walk in the light of the Lord." *"Ambulemus in lumine Domini."*

The truths which are the deposit of faith in us, should gradually guide all our steps, the spirit of faith, rule over all our thoughts, sentiments, and endeavors, all our actions and omissions. In short, our whole life should be spent in the realm of this supernatural light. We must be children of light. "You were heretofore darkness, but now light in the Lord. Walk then as children of the Light."[8]

What are the requisites? What must we do that we may walk in the light of the Lord? that we may live by

3 Isa. 60:2.
4 Col. 1:13.
5 1 Peter 2:9.
6 Col. 1:12.
7 James 1:17.
8 Eph. 5:8.

faith as we read: "The just man liveth by faith"?[9] The response is simple. This light must illumine all our ways, penetrate into all our circumstances, and there enjoy the full freedom of shining. "The more the saints enjoy the light of God, the more conscious they are of their nothingness."[10] "Be ye holy, because I, the Lord your God, am holy."[11] We must surrender our free will in an act of noble homage to the Most High, in complete abandon.

As every age in history, so the present time is beset with divers ills, with many errors, which release untold misery that engulf a large part of the world. What shall we designate as the chief error?

What this may be we gather from the words of the great Pontiff, Leo XIII, when in his *Allocution* to the College of Cardinals, on December 8, 1879, he stated: "The chief error of our time, the error including all others, is this cold naturalism which has interpenetrated every phase of public life and has forced its entrance into the sanctuaries of private living. It is the naturalism that puts human reason in the place of divine authority; nature in the stead of grace, in order to banish Jesus Christ everywhere, in order to make null and void the fruits of His Redemption." This is the true situation.

Public as well as private life would have to be thoroughly reconstituted if the higher light, which has arisen for us in Christ Jesus, should again permeate and vivify all the circumstances and conditions of Christian living. This goes against the grain with the modern man. He

---

9 Heb. 10:38.
10 St. Gregory.
11 Lev. 19:2.

prefers to be guided solely by the views and prejudices of blinded and perverted reason and the efforts of corrupt nature. Therefore, with impunity, he shuts out the higher light, the beneficent rays of the Sun of Justice.

And though this Sun stands high in the heavens and has arisen, as St. John says, to enlighten every man that comes into the world, and to illumine the paths we must tread from the first moment of the dawn of reason to our last breath, we open wide only, at best, the realm of human life which concerns the immediate service of God. And, oh, how sparingly its rays may enter even here! How narrowly we draw the limits of the supernatural! How quickly the supernatural point of view in all endeavors pales and vanishes! *"Diminutae sunt veritates a filiis hominum."* "Truths are decayed from among the children of men."[12] It is truly the basic evil of our day. Like a vitiated atmosphere it broods over the whole present generation. How many have completely succumbed to its sinister fumes! How many have been victimized, infected, and contaminated!

There are Catholics who otherwise lead good and wholesome lives, for the greater part without much sin, it is true, yet they seem to lack the spirit of living faith; they are listless in their response to grace and careless of acquiring merit for eternity. How many, too, who have begun well on the path of perfection and kept to it for long years, deserve the reproach of Jesus: *"Adhuc et vos sine intellectu estis?"* "Are you also yet without understand-

---

12 Ps. 11:2.

ing?"[13] Are you still the base slave of natural impulse, without the understanding that faith imparts?

In fact, much of the misery, the hardships that religious often suffer, without the supernatural spirit, stems from the basic ill of our day, of which they are victims, the lack of the spirit of faith. If many fail to achieve the heights of virtue, which is relatively easy in view of the generous means at our disposal, it is to be ascribed to the same cause, the collapse of faith. Their supernatural vision is blurred; it hardly extends beyond the area of spiritual exercises and prayers. Strong and living faith scarcely permeates even the surface of their activities; its absence leaves them cold and insensible to loftier motives. This higher light is but a faint glimmer across their path. Numerous opportunities for the practice of virtue are consequently not even noticed, let alone utilized. "There is now no saint: truths are decayed from among the children of men."[14]

For our time and for all who live in it, the exhortation of the Prophet has a special appeal: *"Surge illuminare Jerusalem!"* Arise, be enlightened, O Jerusalem!"[15] The light has come, "the glory of the Lord is risen upon thee." The supernatural order of things is reality, more than all we behold with bodily eyes, or touch with our hands, all around us.

The Sun of Justice, Jesus Christ, stands high on the heavenly ramparts. Nothing should ever evade its beneficent, scintillating light, its vivifying warmth. And the Saviour Himself invites us with a summons of special

---

13 Matt. 15:16.
14 Ps. 11:2.
15 Isa. 60:1.

import: "I am come a light into the world: that whosoever believeth in Me may not remain in darkness."[16] "Believe in the light, walk in the light that you may be the children of light," "*ut filii lucis sitis.*"[17]

We are to be children of the light, living wholly in and through its beneficent radiance. All our thoughts, our wishes, our actions and omissions, must be brought under its gentle influence. Eternal thanks be to God for the blessing of our vocation, with its marvellous organization in accord with this higher light. The training and education as well as guidance offered in religious Congregations and Societies are all geared along the principles of faith.

With the basic principle St. Ignatius enunciates in the "*Foundation of the Exercises,*" everything without exception is drawn within the supernatural order. "Everything else on earth," he says, "is created for the sake of man, to serve him in the attainment of his aim, that is, to glorify God, to offer Him due praise and reverence, and thus save his own soul." In stressing the aim of the Society, Ignatius makes it clear that our own perfection is of prime importance, with the grace of God. But with the utmost zeal, however, we must be concerned in the salvation and perfection of the neighbor, for which grace will be allotted abundantly by Divine Dispensation. Is there still room for a purely natural, materialistic point of view?

The beautiful *Seventeenth Rule* of the Society states this still more concisely and clearly: "All should zealously endeavor to have an upright intention, not merely in their state of life, but even in all its details. In these they should

16 John 12:46.
17 John 12:36.

always honestly aim at serving and pleasing God for His goodness and for the love and very special blessings which He first bestowed upon us, rather than for fear of punishment, or hope of reward, though they should also find help in these motives. They should seek God in all things, stripping themselves as far as they can of all love of creatures, so that they may give their heart entirely to their Creator, loving Him and all creatures in Him, in accordance with His most holy and divine will."[18]

So completely does this Rule circumscribe the situations of our whole life with the spirit of faith that there remains not a step, not a breath, nor pulsation, as it were, outside the sphere of faith. "All should zealously endeavor," we read, "to have an upright intention." How far must this intention reach? What is its goal? We should strive for it not only concerning our state of life in general, but also in the minutest details.

St. Ignatius desires still more. He is not satisfied to lead us into the higher light of faith in all we do. He would have us approach so near to the Sun of Justice and dispose ourselves so favorably to its fullest splendor that all its rays fall directly across our pathway. "We should seek God in all things, stripping ourselves of all attachment to creatures and giving our heart entirely to Him, the Creator, loving Him in all creatures and all creatures only in Him." Even if we need not exclude the less perfect motives of faith, the fear of punishment, or hope of reward, we should try in all our actions to serve and please Divine Goodness much more for the sake of His love and generosity, with an upright heart.

---

18 P. III, c. 1, n. 20.

What luminous paths Ignatius marks out for us! or rather, God Himself through the Saint. Little wonder that Pope Paul III, after having approved and examined the *Constitutions* of the Society, exclaimed: *"Spiritus Dei hic est!"* "The Spirit of God is here!" Indeed, the Spirit of God, who is Himself Light inaccessible, has led us along these ways. All the more imperative is the duty of walking in this way with eager delight. "O House of Jacob, come ye, and let us walk in the light of the Lord!"

We want it, and the more our present generation despises the light, the more we will love it and seek its shining. And the less the children of the world live in accord with the truths of faith, the more we will make them our safe guide in all we do. *"Lucerna pedibus meis verbum tuum et lumen semitis meis."* "Thy word is a lamp to my feet and a light to my paths."[19] *"Thy mercy is better than lives: thee my lips shall praise."*[20]

Thus shall it be. Not only that we may find protection and security against the chief evil of our time, but also in the spirit of atonement to the Most High for the infidelity of the masses, and the lack of the spirit of ardent faith among so many of the good. "In this has the love of God been shown in our case, that God has sent His only-begotten Son into the world that we may live through Him."[21] But the world rejects the precious treasure offered. Through His Incarnation, the Eternal Word desired to bring the

19　Ps. 118:105.
20　Ps. 62:4.
21　1 John 4:9.

Divinity with its infinite wealth close to us, as it were, visible to the eye, to captivate our hearts with irresistible love; yet we close our eyes and remain cold and aloof towards the Infinite Good. We foolishly try to find our happiness in earthly things and to rest in the pitiful, trivial goods of this mundane natural life.

What an insult to the Divine Majesty! What a contemptible detestation of His Infinite Goodness and Love! What a shameful gesture of dishonor of His Majesty on the part of creatures, whom He has created for the sole purpose of their praising, loving, and serving Him. Through the Redemption He willed to lift them out of the misery of their fall and to reinstate them in a new life, in a life that is infinitely exalted over the purely natural, and which leads to nothing less than to a participation in His own divine, unchangeable, eternal Beatitude.

Oh, how Love is despised! Who will and ought to make amends? Surely, we above all must have a vital part in it, we who by his grace walk in the Light and become intimately conscious of its vivifying brilliance. How shall this be done? By our personal efforts to make satisfaction of honor to the Most High where His reverence is most grievously assailed. If our time more and more tends toward the total loss of faith, we will bend our best and strongest endeavors toward holding high the immutable standards of living faith.

If the world seeks drastically to shut out the light of faith, as far as possible, from all human considerations, from the total area of public and private living, it is our privilege and a sacred duty all the more solicitously to look to the light and to walk with a steady tread in its undimmed rays. "O House of Jacob, come ye, and let us walk in the light of the Lord."[22]

The children of the world, in the glare of their false, deceptive lights, move farther away from the truth; they drift blindly into a darkness so terrifying and dense as the darkness that enveloped Egypt, and so impenetrable that it might be felt with the hand. "Stretch out thy hand towards heaven: and may there be darkness upon the land of Egypt, so thick that it may be felt."[23] We will abide near the unquenchable fount of truth, and more and more endeavor to live and move in the splendor of this light. In the spiritual sense the marvel of Egypt should be renewed in our midst. "Wherever the children of Israel dwelt," we read in the Sacred Scriptures, "there was light," or as Wisdom has it, "over them (the Egyptians) has spread a heavy night ... But Thy saints had a very great light." *"Maxima erat lux."*[24]

With Thy saints! We are such if we are true Christians, for does not St. Peter speak of us as a "chosen generation, a kingly priesthood,"[25] and St. Paul, "The elect of God, holy, and beloved"?[26] With the saints, remember, there must be not only light, but a very great light, *"sanctis autem tuis maxima erat lux."* Are we not called to ever greater holiness? Light must remain with the saints, with us, and like a burning pillar of fire guide us through all devious ways. "The fire on the altar shall always burn."[27]

---

22 Isa. 2:5.
23 Ex. 10:21-23.
24 Wis. 17:20; 18:1.
25 1 Peter 2:9.
26 Col. 3:12.
27 Lev. 6:12.

Thanks be to God, it is relatively easy for us. Our good God, the Father of Light, "by whom you are called unto the fellowship of His Son Jesus Christ,"[28] has placed at our disposal a means of inestimable worth and efficacy. In the first place we have contemplative prayer, to which an hour is daily allotted. Upon awaking we are summoned into the Divine Presence to ponder the truths of faith. *"Venite Adoremus Dominum!"* We have ample time to let heart and soul taste the delights of supernatural faith and love; to regulate our thoughts and aspirations, our judgments, wishes and endeavors for the day, and to predispose ourselves for assigned work in this admirable light. Our prayer will be all the more effective if in our meditations we behold Him vividly before our eyes, the very heart and centre of our spiritual life, Jesus Christ, the Light of the world. Seculars, too, more and more reach out to the quieting moments of prayerful repose and thought of God in the midst of the stress of active duty, willingly shouldered for love of God.

The daily examen finds us again viewing our thoughts, words, and works in the light of the same truth. Whatever is not irradiated by the gentle light of truth, and has been done in a purely natural way we reject as loss and harm, deeply contrite. What corresponds with faith, we alone cherish as gain, thank God and seek to fortify and perfect ourselves with unalterable love in the pursuit of holiness. Our life will thus be more and more supernaturalized as we endeavor to put on the new Adam, created in justice and holiness. This will necessarily come to pass if we

---

28 1 Cor. 2:9.

nourish the spirit of faith in all we do, invoke it on the various decisive occasions and let its light shine.

In this spirit our attitude toward *Superiors* will take on a beautiful meaning. Seeing in them Christ's representatives, we will gladly render them reverence, love, and implicit obedience. No matter how contrary or uncongenial an order may seem, we simply acquiesce in the challenge because God has spoken. God has designed it in the minutest details, and the mists of human cogitations, or criticisms and conjectures will vanish before the bright light of the holy Will of God. Charity among our associates —and with all men—furnishes us with frequent opportunities to act in the spirit of faith. Seeing in a *brother* an image of God, a member of the Mystical Body, another Christ, we will tender him esteem, kindness and humble deference, in the manner of a great soul.

Our *daily labor, enjoined by obedience,* is the work of God. In the light of faith it will be performed in a manner worthy of God, with inner strength and confidence. Difficulties, temptations, fatigues, sufferings of soul and body will take their toll. But hear St. Paul: "For that which is at present momentary and light of our tribulation worketh for us above measure exceedingly an eternal weight of glory, while we look not at the things which are seen, but at the things which are not seen. The things which are seen are temporal: but the things which are not seen are eternal."[29]

What glorious truths of the faith are ours! God has placed at our disposal a whole heaven of stars. It is ours to summon at will these wonderful bodies, that they may

---

29 2 Cor. 4:17, 18.

appear on our life's horizon and, as the Prophet puts it, "give light at their posts,"[30] namely, on the respective occasions when most needed, in God's design. And if we desire to enjoy their full splendor, the full strength of their shining, let us be solicitous for purity of heart. The fruitfulness of their light will then be, in the words of St. Paul: "every good, justice, and truth." We shall belong to those of whom it is written: *"Justorum autem semita, quasi lux splendens, procedit et crescit."*[31] "The path of the just, as a shining light, goeth forwards and increaseth even to perfect day."

II. PRAYER THE SOURCE OF SUPERNATURAL LIGHT AND DIVINE STRENGTH

St. Paul writing to the Thessalonians, bids them, "Always rejoice. Pray without ceasing."[32] Is this not a peculiar counsel and admonition? The worldly-minded and natural man will find it strange, indeed. In his eyes prayer denotes solitude, a desert; spiritual exercises are for him a tedious, fatiguing pastime. In such an atmosphere, how could constant joy in the Lord be at home with much prayer? For him there is no thought of it. He finds it a startling contradiction. A truly interior man, however, thinks altogether differently. He has only too often experienced the fruitfulness of prayer in giving light and strength, and by that token holy joy. Therefore he values leisure for recollection and the time of prayer highly. We

---

30 Bar. 3:33.
31 Prov. 4:18.
32 1 Thess. 5:17.

must surely have experienced this ourselves personally. To fortify ourselves in this practice, we will ponder the fruits of prayer more closely. It sheds *light* over our path in life and *vitality* and *well-being* for our resolute advances along this way. Interior joy is the inevitable fruit.

1. PRAYER A SOURCE OF LIGHT

Light gives joy. In its splendor we can walk securely, beneath its holy shining, work and be active; under its beneficent rays life in its fullest aspects grows and flourishes. Every new day furnishes positive proof in the rising sun. This is all the more true in the supernatural world. The light that shines confers a delightful feeling of security, of activity, and fulness of life. Therefore the Prophet invites us to come and walk in this light. "Come ye, and let us walk in the light of the Lord."[33] And the Psalmist often entreats the Lord with intensest longing, from the depths of his heart, to be enlightened by this light. "Send forth Thy light and Thy truth," he entreats the Lord. And why? "They have conducted me, and brought me unto Thy holy hill, and into Thy tabernacles."[34] In other words, beneath the splendor of Thy light and Thy truth, I shall scale the pinnacle of perfection and rejoice in the peace and wealth of Thy house.

At thought of the darkness that broods over the earth without the shining of this light, he prays at another time, as the Priests of God do daily in the Breviary: "Have mercy on us, O Lord, and bless us, and let the light of Thy

---

33 Isa. 2:5.
34 Ps. 42:3.

countenance shine upon us that we may know Thy ways."
"Illuminet vultum suum super nos." This is a clear, beneficent, vivifying light, in a word, "a marvellous light,"
"admirabile lumen," St. Peter calls it.[35]

a) *The Source of this supernatural light*

Where does this light shine upon us? Where do we
feel its clarity and power? Above all in the hours of
prayer, of converse with God, in contemplative pondering
of eternal truth. There is the spring whence flows this
mighty fountain of light. Therefore the Psalmist exhorts
us: "Come ye to Him and be enlightened."[36] Why do
many of the heavenly bodies always dispense so bright
and clear a light, though they have no light of their own,
being dim, and dark? For the simple reason that they are in
the sun's radiance, remain there, and regularly run their
course around the fount of the light whereby they shine.

We, likewise, who of ourselves are darkness walking in
the shadow of death, shall be enlightened in the degree
of our nearness to our Sun, to the Most High, in prayer
and meditation, as we closely follow in the course marked
out for us day by day in our religious life.

b) *Fruits of this light*

The more faithfully we persevere in this course, the
more we love to commune with God, the richer and more
generous will be the rays we receive from the Divine Sun,

---

35 1 Peter 2:9.
36 Ps. 33:6.

God Himself. Gradually, so much light will be dispensed for us that it will not only suffice for our personal needs, but will enable us freely to impart of this heavenly largesse to others. "You were heretofore darkness, but now light in the Lord," St. Paul cries out to the Ephesians.[37] How does this apply to us? Perhaps at one time we walked as children of darkness and participated in the unfruitful works of darkness, but now we are able to walk as children of the light, manifesting more and more the fruits of which the Apostle again speaks: "the fruit of the light is in all goodness, and justice, and truth."[38]

At one time, perhaps, we were of the number of those who shun the light, because their works are evil, and because they are reluctant to relinquish even these works. Now, however, with a joyous heart we approach the light. It has so transformed us that the Heavenly Father, who has kindled the light in us, can set us up as light-givers to others. It may come to pass that the exhortation Christ addressed to His Apostles and also to us be fulfilled: "So let your shine before men, that they may see your good works and glorify your Father who is in heaven."[39]

How we must love prayer because of such beautiful results, and how zealously devote ourselves to it! With what love and fidelity must we discharge our spiritual exercises, for we are friends of the light, children of the light, praying *with* Jesus, and *through* Him and *in* Him. We long for heavenly wisdom and for the precious fruits it brings to maturity in the soul.

---

37 5:8.
38 Eph. 5:9.
39 Matt. 5:16.

c) *We ordinarily have greater reserves of light than we think*

We do not always esteem the light sufficiently. It would come home to us with greater impact, if we realized how slight our grasp of the supernatural has always been. A brief elevation in prayerful thought would be more highly cherished, if we considered the utter unawareness of spiritual goods and their utter disregard by the masses, even among the cultured.

In the humble realization of God's merciful goodness in leading us out of a similar darkness, we shall more readily enjoy the simplest rays of supernatural light afforded us so generously. These are the real, even if less brilliant, rays of the marvellous light which the merciful Lord grants us, in spite of our total unworthiness: *"de tenebris vos vocavit in admirabile lumen suum."* "Who hath called you out of darkness into His marvellous light."[40] In our prayerlife we can easily find peace of soul and serenity in renunciation of self.

d) *The lights must be guarded solicitously*

If we received them with greater reverence, they would be dispensed to us more generously. They belong to the "good gifts, the perfect gifts, that come from the Father of Lights."[41] It is important, therefore, to desire them sincerely and perseveringly. St. Ignatius would have us be imbued with these sentiments at our meditation, after a

40 1 Peter 2:9.
41 James 1:17.

fervent preparatory prayer and vivid preludes have given life and light to the momentary exercise.

In the second prelude we entreat the fruit sought in our prayer. The Lord hears the man of desires. "I am come to show it to thee," said the Angel to Daniel, "because thou art a man of desires."[42] "He hath filled the hungry with good things,"[43] must be a source of vitality and strength.

Perfect prayerlife, union of the soul with God, must characterize every religious. All who would lead a sinless life, enkindled with divine fire, must dwell much alone with God in prayer. Sanctity is intimate communion with God, who rules our thoughts, words, and all our works. Christ is with us radiating light to support us in our endeavors in silent converse with Him. Of the inward nobility of the apostolic life, of union with God in prayer, Holy Scripture again assures us: "Daniel went into his house, and opening the windows toward Jerusalem, he knelt down three times a day, and adored, and gave thanks before his God."[44] Let us often in spirit kneel to adore the God of our heart and offer Him the momentary task in humble thanksgiving.

The hour of meditation, of interior prayer, is of unquestioned worth. It is impossible for a religious to live by faith unless he meditates well, unless Christ be the centre of his affections. "Sing to the Lord a new song of praise in the assembly of the faithful . . . For the Lord loves His people and adorns the lowly with victory."[45] Interior souls,

---

42 Dan. 9:23.
43 Luke 1:53.
44 Dan. 6:18.
45 Ps. 149:14.

in general, who would lead a Christlike life must cultivate silent prayer and contemplation to refresh and invigorate the spirit.

The celebrated Francis Suarez, S.J., declared himself ready to forfeit all the knowledge accessible to mortals, rather than a single hour set aside by the *Constitutions* of the Society for prayer. St. Peter Canisius reminded his religious very earnestly of the account we must one day render to God of the use we made of the time allotted to prayer and the spiritual life. St. Ephrem gave beautiful expression to God's infinite mercy and His readiness to hear our prayers. Full of joy and thanksgiving, he cries out: "Before the petitioner puts his foot on the threshold, Thou openest to him. Before he falls on his knees before Thee, Thou reachest out Thy Hand, O Lord! Before he sheds tears, Thou dost overwhelm him with Thy mercies."

"Prayer," says St. Laurence Justinian, "transforms men; out of the blind it makes enlightened souls; the weak become strong, the sinners, saints." Pray with the spirit and the mind of Christ, live and work for God. Recall the beautiful Pontifical Prayer:[46] "Keep in Thy Name, those whom thou hast given Me ... Sanctify them in truth."[47] "Come ye to Him and be enlightened, and your face shall not be confounded."[48]

2. PRAYER A SOURCE OF STRENGTH

Health is beneficial, strong resources inspire courage and trust and enlarge the heart. Where, we ask, is the

---

46 John 17:11.
47 John 17:17.
48 Ps. 33:6.

wonderful fount of health in which the soul finds rejuvenation and well-being? Where is the source of the noblest
and the most vital powers of soul, namely, genuine, solid
virtues and the fullest cooperation with divine grace? After
the reception of the Sacraments, which themselves form
so intimate a part of our spiritual program, our prayerlife
itself is the most efficacious and prolific means of finding
God, dispensing in merciful love abundant graces for a
deepening of our inner life.

a) *Prayer preserves us from spiritual lassitude*

Our interior prayerlife, our Eucharistic devotions and
aspirations help us subdue our disordered passions, which
affect the soul much as unwholesome humors act on the
body. Contemplative prayer and the daily examen call our
attention to these tendencies and make us aware of their
presence more readily. In this light we see clearly that
they have been the final and actual cause of sin, and are
still the poisonous roots of our dominant passions. Recog-
nizing their sinister effects, we detest them; eagerly and
humbly we implore God's grace and light in throwing
them off. In all confidence and trust, we bow profoundly
before the Lord, resolved to fight the battle against the
evil powers waiting to attack us at the most unexpected
moments. Mortification and self-denial are indispensable
weapons in this soul-cleansing and healing process.

b) *Prayer imparts new strength and energy*

Mere health will not suffice. Virility and necessary
skills are required if we would discharge with relative ease
and efficiency the duties incumbent upon us in our onerous

vocation. Even the difficult and cumbersome details inseparable from this obligation demand our utmost dedication.

How can these interior forces and assets be acquired? There is no better means than fervent prayer, the devout reception of the Sacraments, and the holy Sacrifice of the Mass, with its unquenchable flow of divine grace. There Christ is the Victim, immolating Himself to the Father for us. Inner strength and energy will be generated as we press close to His merciful and compassionate Heart and unite ourselves intimately with His Ineffable Sacrifice. Our spiritual life gains solidity and depth, strikes deeper roots, under the influence of grace, enabling us manfully to meet temptations and trials.

Though sanctifying grace is immeasurably increased in our souls and countless actual graces are conferred upon us through the reception of the Sacraments, *ex opere operato,* as well as by prayer and virtuous acts, *ex opere operantis,* yet the faithful discharge of our prayerlife enkindles in the soul a holy fire aflame with living intensity to grow in Christ Jesus.

Christ Himself reaches out to each of us individually to draw us closer to His Heart, the abode of consummate virtue and holiness. His virtues reflect so beautiful a light that we can but love them and ardently strive to make them our own. What is the result of our intense longing to put on Christ, our supreme Ideal of every virtue? The spirit of sacrifice is a grace beyond comprehension. It is the rich fruit of a life of prayer and childlike surrender to the infinitely loving Father in heaven. Since prayer wins for us an abundance of actual graces, we are bound to make steady progress and to strike out resolutely for a life of absolute detachment and interior consecration to our assigned apostolic work.

"The path of the just as a shining light, goeth forwards and increaseth even to perfect day."[49] Glorious heavenly goal! And it is within our power, within easy reach. Prayer is essential for spiritual growth, and it is so plentifully put at our disposal. From the first summons into the divine presence at dawn, until the last moments when with thoughts of the morning's meditation we seek repose, our day is an uninterrupted communing with the God of our heart. How often, how easily can we draw near to the Eucharistic Christ in loving self-oblation! He is our light, our strength, our joy, inviting us to share the immense riches of His Holiness.

Eternal thanks to Thee, O Lord, for such an inestimable grace, a gift surpassing all other gifts! Our gratitude and esteem must find expression in virtuous deeds and in the giving of self in the charity of Christ, more than in words and sentiments.

Our profound recognition of heaven's gifts draws us irresistibly to the perpetual fount of these living waters. Not the smallest fraction of the time allotted to prayer may be culpably neglected. "Deprive not yourself of present good things, let no choice portion escape you."[50]

Nature may grow weary, distractions, dryness, aridity, and petty annoyances may set in to rob us of the delights of prayerful intimacy with God. Courageously we resist the tempter's insinuations. In prayer the supreme ideal of all virtues is again and again envisioned. His meekness

---

49 Prov. 4:18.
50 Ecclus. 14:14.

and humility, His divine patience and obedience, His love of God and of neighbor incite us to acts of implicit trust and confidence, and the victory will be ours. The example of His Blessed Mother and of the Saints inspires us with confidence and filial surrender to His Love. This loving abandon to His holy Will is more precious in the sight of God than scientific knowledge and skills and consolations. The Lord will soon return with His comforting assurance. Provided we have been faithful, He will give us to taste the delights promised by the Holy Spirit: "Her conversation has no bitterness, nor her company any tediousness, but joy and gladness." [51]

III. Obedience in the Spirit of Faith—Its Splendor and Strength

"The mind of the just studieth obedience" [52]

Faith invests it with its supreme consecration. In these words the Holy Spirit points to a significant mark of a truly virtuous love. "The mind of the just studieth obedience." Ponder the beauty of this word. Not only his mind, but also his heart values obedience highly; charged with love, all his actions and omissions are keyed to the practice of perfect obedience. For the truth of this word Jesus Christ Himself, the Sun of Justice, has vouched. His first thoughts in His Mother's womb were fixed upon this virtue. "It is written of Me that I should do Thy Will, O Father. Behold, here I am!"

During life, as He Himself avers, His meat, His daily

---

51 Wis. 8:16.
52 Prov. 15:28.

bread was to do the Will of Him who sent Him. Thus He was obedient to His death on the Cross. The Most Sacred Heart of Jesus constantly dwelt on obedience. We, too, wish to be just and excel in fear of the Lord. St. Ignatius wished his Sons to distinguish themselves by obedience, because it is a virtue "which of its own accord generates the other virtues in the soul," as St. Gregory observes, "and keeps them there." Therefore all our thoughts and desires must be directed to the virtue that implants all the rest, namely, holy obedience. This consciousness should reanimate our faith, strengthen our hope, and inflame our love anew. Thus will our obedience be a service of God truly worthy of the Divine Majesty. St. Ignatius desired that obedience should be the characteristic virtue of the Society.

1. "I WILL HEAR WHAT THE LORD GOD WILL SPEAK IN ME"[53]

The spirit of faith imparts to obedience its greatest dignity and consecration. It must be a service of God, but a service worthy of the Divine Majesty. What could obedience otherwise be?

a) *Mere human service, prompted by the ignoble motive of human respect for the person of the Superior, vitiates the act in God's sight*

If his experience, his competence, and understanding are to be won, or his gentle, cheerful ways admired, or his displeasure to be studiously avoided, I am rendering a lowly, undignified service in the sight of the Most High.

---

53 Ps. 84:9.

How apropos is the word of St. Paul in this regard: "Am I now seeking the favor of men, or of God? Or am I seeking to please men? If I were still trying to please men, I should not be a servant of Christ."[54] The spirit of faith lifts us above the inordinate desire to please men, court their favor, or cherish similar imperfect sentiments. It points to the Superior as the representative of the Most High, the mediator of God's holy Will. In this supernatural light we submit, indeed, to man, but we do it for the sake of God, do it, as St. Paul exhorts us, "in the Lord," or "like Christ." We are thus not mere slaves of human expedience, or like those who "seek to please men," but true servants of Christ the Lord. In this manner we are joined to the ranks of the heavenly princes, who find their greatest honor and renown in fulfilling the holy Will of God.

These angelic spirits, indeed, behold God face to face and bend low in adoration of the Infinite Majesty, yet it is one and the same Lord before whom we bow profoundly in the person of His representative. Our obedience is truly a distinct service of the Most High, a hymn of praise, as it were, glorifying the Triune God.

b) *Service of self*

Only too often, sad to say, our obedience stoops so low. Self-love prompts the unwary soul. We submit and perform the task because it is agreeable, congenial, and flatters self-love; we find the charge to be honorable, nourishing pride and sensual delights in the performance. This

---

54 Gal. 1:10.

is hardly genuine obedience. Oh, no; these are unworthy, lowly motives, short-sighted views. They enervate the act of surrender and make of it a wretched exaltation of self, with hardly a shred of genuine virtue left to merit the glorious name of obedience. Obedience that bears even a trace of self in its make-up, St. Gregory maintains, is either no obedience at all, or at best only an inferior, diluted sort.[55]

c) *The Spirit of Faith banishes the lowly spirit of selfishness*

It lifts obedience beyond the narrow confines of self-love. It shows us in the command of the Superior the Will of the Most High, which every creature must fulfill entirely, for the Father's Will must be done in heaven and on earth. Faith teaches us not to place too much stock in the natural pleasure we find in obeying, but rather rule it out energetically. Obedience opens the fount of an infinitely noble and dignified enjoyment in the conscious knowledge that we are corresponding with the designs of the Heavenly Father and accordingly with His divine complacence. It is the spirit of faith that transmutes our obedience into genuine service of God, in loyalty and oblation.

2. "I SET GOD ALWAYS IN MY SIGHT"[56]

What may be the requisites? The Apostle tells us: "Be servants of Christ doing the Will of God from the heart. With a good will, serving as to the Lord, and not to men."[57]

---

55 cf. S. Thom. 2. 2ae q. 104 a. 2 ad 3.

56 Ps. 15.

57 Eph. 6:6, 7.

Here we have enunciated the unassailable foundation of religious obedience.

a) Joy—The spirit of faith imparts this interior readiness and joy

A purely natural external observance is wholly unworthy of God. Religious who, indeed, do what is enjoined, but do it grudgingly are, St. Ignatius observes, to be counted as pitiful slaves. If we are animated by the spirit of faith, we will not tarry on this lowly step of subservience. With a readiness and a quick resolve to obey, we will carry out an order of the Superior as the order of Christ Himself.

We then no longer regard only the human eye of authority in our striving, but fix our gaze upon God, who discerns our inmost sentiments. "For man seeth those things that appear," as the prophet says, "but the Lord beholdeth the heart."[58] He not only sees it, but desires it: "My Son, give Me thy heart!"

b) Holocaust—The Spirit of faith makes of the obedient man a living holocaust before his God

Where this spirit reigns, will and understanding are docile in executing what is enjoined; the sacrifice of obedience will be perfect, a true holocaust, worthy and dignified in the presence of the Divine Majesty. To carry out an order only half-heartedly is to offer the Most High, instead of a holocaust aflame with love, merely the empty chalice.

---

58 1 King 16:7.

c) *Love of God—The spirit of faith finally transforms obedience into purest love*

The holocaust kindled with the fire of love will ascend in fragrant odor to the throne of God. This is the last and the highest degree of the consecration that obedience can have. It is the spirit of faith, again, that imparts it as the final touch, the crowning act of so noble a work. "One does not serve with forced servitude," says St. Leo, "when one loves and esteems what is ordered."

The truly obedient man beholds God, his loving Father, in all things, whom he wills to please in all he does, and for whose sake he performs with alacrity what his Superior enjoins as the Will of God. And God in return looks lovingly upon him. This paternal glance is love itself, and it evokes love. "I will give you a new heart, and put a new spirit within you: and I will cause you to walk in My commandments and do them."[59]

Childlike love and submission will more and more be the mainspring of our whole life. A new heart, according to the Heart of Jeus, will beat in our breast. As good children of the Heavenly Father, we behold only His Will in everything we do. We do not act by force or coercion and fear, nor do we carry our yoke reluctantly. We embrace it lovingly, willingly, as the sweet yoke and the light burden, and we walk trustfully and joyously along the paths that not a mere man, but our Heavenly Father Himself through him points out to us. "I have run the way of Thy commandments when Thou didst enlarge my heart."[60] Through the love that lightens every burden Thou

---

59 Ezech. 36:26.
60 Ps. 118:32.

"didst enlarge" it. Obedience thus becomes the obedience of love, love interwoven with gold. This is truly worthy of God; such service motivated by love and rendered with loving surrender is worthy of His Infinite Majesty, Goodness, and Love.

d) *The life of St. Peter Canisius furnishes a beautiful example*

He was essentially an apostle, born for his day. In his very active life he distinguished himself by rendering obedience in the spirit of a tremendous faith and love. It was the spirit of St. Ignatius. The thought of the divine mandate given him by his Superiors filled him in the midst of arduous, distracting labors with inner peace and contentment. He had to travel far and wide through Europe, from Poland to Sicily, through Bavaria and Austria, in the countryside washed by the waters of the Rhine and the Danube. His tireless foot stood firm, for he was solely guided by obedience.

It is partly due to his heroic exertions that the Rhineland and Austria remained loyal to the Holy See. The greatest spiritual energies are heroically brought under control through holy obedience. Keep straight on the lines marked out, even if through a tunnel. Such was the obedience of Canisius. He was naturally of an impulsive temper, but his pious tutor in Cologne, Nicholas Esch, knew how to bring this tempestuous character into subjection by training him to true obedience and submission. His heart was wounded with arrows, as it were, when from the lips of his tutor he heard words of truth: "To serve

God is to reign. One thing alone insures salvation: the service of God; all else is empty show and deceit."

Later St. Ignatius himself in Rome deepened this sentiment of loyal and loving service and submission in his conscientious subject. As from all his sons, he demanded of Canisius complete readiness to everything and, therefore, total detachment as prerequisites of true obedience. When during Canisius' stay in Rome, there was question of selecting several Fathers for a new collegiate foundation in Messina, Ignatius asked the members of his household to signify in writing their sincere sentiments concerning a possible transfer to Sicily, and of the nature of the obedience that might be assigned. St. Peter Canisius possessed the Ignatian characteristic of allowing nothing to stand in the way of the driving power of his love. After three days of prayerful thought specified by Ignatius, among the responses came that of Canisius in his own handwriting, still preserved in the archives in Rome. Canisius declares himself ready to remain in Rome or go to Sicily, to India or to any other part of the globe. If he is sent to Messina he will gladly fulfill there every charge entrusted to him, teach every subject assigned to him; he is also willing to serve as cook, or porter, or whatever it be.

This is true humility, a perfect readiness for obedience in its fullest significance. St. Ignatius sent him to Messina, where the learned theologian, who had recently shone at the Council of Trent and had published several scientific works of great worth, might in Messina teach Latin to little Italian boys. For his whole life, Canisius never swerved an inch from his ideal of perfect obedience. In obedience he later crossed the Alps headed for Germany, Vienna, Prague, Augsburg, and Innsbruck. In holy obedience he participated a second time in the Council of Trent. He traversed the Germanic countries as emissary to the Pope in order to announce and proclaim everywhere the decisions of the Council. In the midst of unremitting labors, he took up his pen and wrote his *Catechism*; later he compiled the gigantic work to combat the Protestant revilings of the faith, not without marked success in disconcerting these hostile groups.

"Holy obedience," he once wrote, "makes every place for me a paradise." Let us not imagine, however, that his heroic obedience demanded no sacrifice. When compiling his *Catechism*, he once admitted that the work cost him endless labor and fatigue. He would much rather have discharged other pastoral duties than write for hours at his desk. He often told his Superiors that he would gladly hear Confessions, distribute Holy Communion, visit the convents, prisons, hospitals, there to work directly for souls, yet the *Catechism* detained him. It was entrusted to him by obedience and was for him the voice of God; he rested not until he had accomplished it with the thoroughness of profound scholarship.

Of the first recruits of the Order, Canisius was probably the one who showed forth in the most wonderful harmony the ideal of perfection, learning, and initiative, which dominated the mind of Ignatius as the ideal of the true companion of Jesus. When there was word of sending him to the religious conferences at Worms, he wrote to the Vicar General in Rome: "I would rather go a-begging in India, but God will speak to me through my Superiors. In obedience I find all my hope and my strength." Then he added a psalm: "I desire to be naught but a beast of burden in the house of God all the days of my life." A front line fighter, Canisius knew nothing of hesitancy or relaxation when obedience spoke. It was the voice of God and triumphantly in the strength of his humility he took up the psalm.

Canisius was delegated to Worms, where he utilized his powers to the full. Afterwards he himself wondered that he did not succumb to the exceptional burden. God blessed his fatiguing labors and his surrender. "From that moment," comments a Protestant historian, "dates the beginning of the decline of the stream of Protestantism in Germany." His missions on behalf of four Popes to German Bishops and princes stemmed the Protestant advance and brought about a revival of Catholic life.

3. "I HAVE ACCOMPLISHED THE WORK THAT THOU HAST GIVEN ME TO DO"[61]

Let us give Him all in holy obedience. *Service of God is always sublime. Its strength derives from faith.* A too natural view of its essence interferes with joyful obedience. The spirit of faith, on the contrary, invests it with invincible strength and vitality. St. Ignatius desired of his sons the "purity and perfection of obedience, with true renouncement of their own wills and denial of their own judgments."

4. "IF GOD IS FOR US, WHO IS AGAINST US?"[62]

The spirit of faith shows us God's representative in every Superior. No matter of what rank he be, the subject

---

61 John 17:4.
62 Rom. 8:31.

looks not to externals, is not captivated or influenced by them, but lifts his eye of faith above the natural vantage point and views with complacence the Most High, God our Lord. In all I do, the man of faith muses, I bend humbly before the same Infinite Majesty of God, for whose sake I obey His subjects.

Faith likewise helps us discountenance any purely *human qualities of the Superior.* The human eye loves to investigate whether the one who directs is of an agreeable disposition or personality, experienced and well read in the vicissitudes of the heart; he should like to know whether he is loving and kind, in general, well versed in the good things that attract hearts. The obedience thus conditioned surely rests on a very unstable foundation. Such a one will vacillate in his allegiance when the qualities he seeks are not in evidence, and not seldom he will suffer shipwreck, clinging merely to a semblance of the beautiful virtue.

How different is the situation where obedience is charged with living faith. It enlarges our horizon, lets us glimpse God's glory and power, His Wisdom and Providence, His Goodness and Love, far outstripping any excellences our Superiors may have. Merely using the Superiors as instruments, He will in all instances incline lovingly to me when I fail to find in my Superiors the splendor and the qualifications I seek. Oh, what confidence, readiness, cheerfulness and superb energy such a point of view generates! It will be clearer, brighter, and unchangeable in its steadiness, tending toward the ultimate goal of faith.

"Nolite dubitare," St. Ignatius counsels us. "Do not doubt, but be assured that the Lord, so affable and faithful,

will guide you on safe and secure paths by your Superiors."
Of this we may rest assured. It is not so much the different
Superiors, holders of office, whom we see with the bodily
eye, as prefects and rectors, not these are our guides, but
rather our Heavenly Father, our Lord and God. *"Dominus
regit me, et nihil mihi deerit."* "The Lord ruleth me, and
I shall want nothing. He hath led me on the paths of
justice. For though I should walk in the midst of the
shadow of death, I will fear no evils, for Thou art
with me."[63]

God, indeed, is with us when we render perfect obedience. The spirit of faith allows us to glimpse His Divine
Providence and His consoling powerful nearness in every
individual case, no matter what our limitations or the
final outcome. Keeping close to God by purity of conscience and prayer, communing with the Divine Presence
in the depths of our soul, makes our obedience a more
dignified service of the Most High.

5. "THAT MY FOOTSTEPS BE NOT MOVED"[64]

The spirit of faith shows us in the most difficult and
disagreeable happenings the Will of God, which is more
precious than gold and costly jewels, and sweeter than
honey. Even what is humiliating, the spirit of faith allows
us to accept as a loving service of God, always glorious and
honorable. In the most insignificant and trifling things, it
reveals to us God's interests and wins us over to admiration and loving acceptance. In every successful under-

63 Ps. 22:1, 3, 4.
64 Ps. 16:5.

taking, finally, even in apparent lack of success, this spirit calls attention to God's infinite designs, lets us recognize His dispositions in the fulfilment of His fatherly plan.

This is always wise and to the point; it challenges consent and invites imitation of those who shone as models of this virtue of complete renunciation of self in the execution of the special tasks assigned them. It is fraught with blessings. Even if nothing be achieved save the simple perfect performance of our obedience, it would still be wholly satisfying, as we ponder the words of the Prophet: "In peace in the selfsame I will sleep, and I will rest, for Thou, O Lord, singularly hast settled me in hope."[65] The obedient man is at home in the realm of divine dispensations, for he has taken up his abode in the Heart of God.

According to the testimony of the Founder of our Society—and this holds of all religious Congregations—no one is a more useful member than the obedient man. He need never fear to be doing nothing for souls. One who loves to do what God the Lord of the vineyard disposes as best for His divine purpose, and does it to the best of his ability, accomplishes much for the salvation of souls. Ignatius would have his Sons sanctify themselves through their work for the sanctification of others. No one contributes more for the greater honor and glory of God than he who walks conscientiously and fearlessly along the way by which Jesus achieved the supreme honor of His Heavenly Father. This is inerrantly the way of obedience, heeding the slightest whisper, shaping our souls in spiritual harmony with Thy holy Will, O God.

---

65 Ps. 4:9, 10.

Let us also walk this royal road with renewed zeal in the exercise of the sublime virtue of obedience. *"Mens justi meditatur obedientiam."* Guided and penetrated by the spirit of faith, may our submission realize in each of us its greatest consecration. May it receive and preserve its invincible strength and vigor, until it shall be crowned with the blessed Vision of Him whom the obedient man ever keeps in view.

Sharing spiritually in the glory of our Leader and King Jesus Christ, who was obedient to the death on the cross, but on that account infinitely exalted, who received a Name above all names, and enthroned at the right of the Father, will reign through all Eternity—a grace which enhances the growth and stability of our inner life.

IV. "LEARN OF ME ... MEEK AND HUMBLE OF HEART"[66]

Humility is the favorite virtue of the Divine Heart. It should be our adornment when we appear before Him. One who wishes to be a disciple of the Sacred Heart must esteem humility, the best loved virtue of this Heart, must love and practice it. Let us ponder how Jesus Himself sets us a marvellous example through His earthly life and in the Most Blessed Sacrament of the Altar, as well as by His teaching.

Daily we appear before Jesus in the tabernacle, we converse with Him familiarly as a friend with his friend, we approach His throne to testify to Him our love, our homage and adoration. On approaching Him, must we not

66 Matt. 11:29.

be clothed in the garb that pleases Him above all others, namely, humility?

1. THE HUMILITY OF JESUS IN HIS LIFE ON EARTH

No one has ever descended from such heights as Jesus, the humblest of all men. From all eternity He was in the Father's Bosom; from all eternity, Light of Light, true God of true God, from all eternity exalted with the Father above the heavens and all creation, which ever shall be.

He assumed the guise of a servant. He laid aside all His glory for love of us. In the direst poverty He saw the light of day as a helpless Infant in the manger among His beasts. For thirty years Jesus led a hidden life in Nazareth. Though the plenitude of the Godhead dwelt in Him who possessed more wisdom, whose Heart harbored more virtues than all angels and men could ever attain, yet we know little more of Him than that He is the Son of a poor artisan. "Is not this the Son of Joseph, the carpenter?"

What ingratitude for benefactions did He experience! What slanders were heaped upon Him in the course of the holiest, purest life! Did anyone ever end a life of inexpressibly loving service, so overwhelmed with shame and sorrow as was Jesus, who breathed His last on the wood of the cross between two thieves? For all this He longed, sighed for it, as for His chosen portion here on earth, embraced it with inexhaustible patience and resignation to the end.

Jesus, the humblest of men, humility personified. *"O humilitas virtus Christi!"* "O humility, the virtue of Christ," St. Bernard exclaims. Must we who call ourselves disciples and venerators of His Heart not excel in humility? May we appear before Him devoid of similar sentiments of profound abasement? "Let this mind be in you, which was also in Christ Jesus."[67] "Who being in the form of God, thought it not robbery to be equal with God, but emptied Himself, taking the form of a servant, being made in the likeness of men, and in habit found as a man. He humbled Himself, becoming obedient unto death, even to the death of the cross."[68]

Oh, never may we approach such a Saviour without sincere compunction and humility of heart. The more profound our sentiments of abasement, the more beautiful the simple garb of humility, the greater delights the Saviour takes in our manifestations of affection. He "Who dwelleth on high and looketh down on the low things in heaven and in earth."[69]

2. THE HUMILITY OF JESUS IN THE HOLY EUCHARIST

Jesus who dwells in the highest heavens wills to dwell among us in the profoundest abasement, under the Sacramental Species, in our Tabernacles. "*Qui in altis habitat!*" "He who dwells on high!" High above the heavens, Jesus is enthroned. Since for the course of His whole life on earth, He abased Himself so infinitely beyond comprehension, the Father has elevated Him to His right, clothed Him with surpassing glory as King over His holy Mount Sion and over the whole heavenly Jerusalem; He has given

---

67 Phil. 2:5.
68 Phil. 2:6, 8.
69 Ps. 112:5.

Him a Name before which all should bend their knees in
heaven, on earth, and under the earth. This glorified Jesus
is present on our altars. Oh, the marvel, but in what
vesture! Again the deepest lowliness comparable to that
of His earthly life, in a certain sense surpassing it! Who can
compass the profundity of such humility? On bended
knee we ponder this immortal, unfading beauty of the
humility of our Beloved Christ in the Sacrament of the
Altar, of our ineffable Redeemer in this Mystery of Love.

He dwells among us in *our chapels, in the House of God.*
No matter how beautifully adorned this place for Him
whose glorified Humanity fills heaven and earth, for the
Lord of the universe it is but little. Even the costliest
marble, exquisite silver or gold would still be nothing to
tender fitting honor and glory to the King of Kings, the
Lord of Lords, the Lord of heaven and earth.

What is the *Monstrance* for Jesus? Even were it of the
purest gold, glittering with precious stones, what is this
receptacle for Him in whose glory heaven and earth are
clothed, in whose splendor myriads of glorified spirits
radiate unspeakable beauty. Oh, the humility of Jesus in
the Monstrance! With a holy trepidation we look upon
the little white Host. It compasses the Godman Jesus
Christ, who reigns in heaven and of whose kingdom there
will be no end. How much of all His grandeur and glory do
we perceive? A few paces removed from us, He is before
us in reality who as Man is the Eternal King, the Father's
well-beloved Son. Does the eye perceive the least sign of
the Infinite Grandeur and majestic Power which that very
moment bears up heaven and earth? *"Omnia portans verbo
virtutis suae,"* "upholding all things by the word of His

power,"[70] by the merest act of His Will. But here, we must consider in adoration, He is present in the form of a tiny piece of bread, which is incapable of movement unless the priest holds and elevates the Sacred Host. *Oh, how profoundly does Jesus renounce all His majesty and power!*

We hear nothing of Divine Wisdom, of whom not a ray gleams forth, before whom all hearts are laid open, and who probes even into the depths of the Godhead. He is present in the fulness of His Sacred Humanity. Have we heard even the slightest sound from this Host to speak of such ineffable Wisdom? *Oh, the perfect silence Jesus maintains concerning Himself and His Infinite Wisdom!*

What does He reveal of His scintillating *beauty and magnificence?* Can we marvel in amazement at even a single ray of His charming fulness of grace and virtue? Our human eye may look upon Him, day in, day out, never will it detect even the faintest glimmer of the Infinite Perfection and Holiness of the Divine Heart. At the same time this Heart radiates such splendor in the heavenly Jerusalem that it no longer needs sun nor moon. *"Claritas Dei illuminavit eam et lucerna ejus est Agnus."* "The glory of God enlightened it, and the Lamb is the lamp thereof."[71]

Oh, the hidden life of Jesus in this Mystery! To this Jesus we wish to have access, to give joy anew to His Sacred Heart. In how far shall we achieve this goal? Obviously only in so far as we cherish similar sentiments in

---

70 Heb. 1:3.
71 Apoc. 21:23.

our heart. *"Hoc enim sentite in vobis, quod et in Christo Jesu."* "Let this be in your mind as it was in Christ Jesus."

The more we try like Jesus to disappear before God and to submit ourselves wholly to Him in view of our sinfulness and incompetence; the more we love to be unknown and counted as naught; the more we divest ourselves of disordered desires of self-complacency; the more we strive to serve all in humble submission and simple fidelity to duty; in short, the more we strive to establish in our hearts the spirit of the Divine Heart; all the more shall we be fit to be in the vicinity of our wholly hidden God; with all the more confidence may we prostrate ourselves before His Veiled Majesty. We may, then, rejoice in the knowledge that we are pleasing to His Heart, which beats in such infinite condescension, in our closest nearness, in His quiet and unpretentious repose on our Altar.

On the contrary, whatever offends against humility and modest reserve is in crassest contradiction to the Heart of the humble Christ and His divine mission. This obtains particularly in the presence of the Blessed Sacrament, where He remains among us in uninterrupted manisfestations of His profound humility and His love of modesty and reserve. For the sake of the humble Heart of Jesus who during His earthly life and in the Blessed Sacrament sets the example of humility personified, we will take to heart the admonition of St. Peter: "Do you all insinuate humility one to another; for God resisteth the proud, but to the humble He giveth grace."[72] Uniting ourselves with the

---

72 1 Peter 5:5.

priest at the Altar of the Clean Oblation, we should be flaming lights for the rest of the day, radiating love of the humble Christ.

Our Lord has clearly expressed His Heart's one desire: *"Learn of Me, because I am meek and humble of Heart."*[73] A good child gladly fulfills the father's will, and a friend, his friend's. But Jesus is to us more than father or friend. What does He ask of us? He does not say: "Be humble of heart, as I am," but rather, "Learn of Me!" We can all without exception learn this holy art and prove true disciples of such a Master. In the school of Jesus, humility is a prerequisite, as it is the principal science pursued there. "If you ask," says Augustine, "what is the first requirement in the school of Christ, I will answer, humility, and you ask for the second time, I answer again, humility, and for the third, humility." Humility is the heart and center in the school of Christ.

Here we clearly see to whom Jesus addressed the word: "Learn of Me . . . humility of heart." To all those who in a special manner are docile pupils of the Sacred Heart and desire to excel in this school of humble learning, this challenge applies. Among them we may count all who by their state of life, whether as priests or religious, or by special vocation, are obliged to strive for perfection of love. To all these Jesus confides a beautiful message: "I have called you out of the world and drawn you near Me. That before all others and more than they, you may learn of Me to be meek and humble of heart." What a wondrous thing—to be called! By the Divine Saviour! Indeed, this

---

73 Matt. 11:29.

is the first episode, the chief task of the true disciples of Christ. The more enthusiastically we discharge it, the more will we be granted the joy of realizing the last and the highest intentions of the Sacred Heart, in a moment of ecstatic joy.

3. "IT IS WITH CHRIST THAT WE JOURNEY, AND WE WALK WITH OUR STEPS IN HIS FOOTPRINTS"[74]

Only when built on the solid foundation of humility will poverty never waver, this rampart and indispensable bulwark of the Society and of religious organizations in general. *Oh, how necessary is humility for genuine holiness!*

Only if grounded firmly in humility can obedience take root, the strength of the religious state.

Only in the soil of humility will spring the fresh blossoms of the lily of chastity and remain uncontaminated, as the ornament of the religious state.

Only from humility arise richest blessings of zeal for souls, which germinates in the love of God and unreserved surrender.

Only in humility, in self-effacement, is there room for the love of God, the heart and center of religious life.

Only where true humility reigns, will flourish unity and brotherly love, the consummate happiness of religious life.

We now understand why the founders of religious orders, when formulating their Rules for the Congregation, stress humility so insistently and ask their sons and disciples to excel in its practical observance. Among others, we think of St. Benedict, of St. Francis of Assisi, and of

---

74 St. Cyprian: *De idolorum vanitate,* C. 15.

11

St. Ignatius of Loyola. They sought to instil into their sons the greatest regard for the superb excellence of true humility. They desired them to overcome resolutely all attachment to personal honor and recognition and their own individual interests; they should not be guided nor dominated by undue concern for their own gains in worldly honor and renown. They should generously look to God and His divine complacence and try to promote His honor and glory, no matter if their insignificant self remain wholly disregarded or contemned.

Sons they would rear who for love of the humble Son of God espouse valiantly all that makes them resemble the Saviour in His unspeakable abasement, poor, despised, and derided. St. Ignatius asks of the members of his Society a genuine discipline in this indispensable virtue. They should resolutely despise what the world loves and craves, avidly seize hold of and willingly accept whatever Christ Our Lord loved and embraced for love of us. We, too, must stand high above petty worldly aims in the business of honors and distinctions, all for Christ's sake. His admirable example will be our light in a life divinely ordered and centered in God.

We pause to see how our love of humility is constituted. Are we really clothed with the humble robe of Christ? Do we wear His uniform, His livery with predilection? And do we wear it gladly? Are we intent upon embellishing it daily with new precious gems? Do we love the lowly, insignificant, unseemly labors that necessarily fall to our lot, yet are so often listlessly pushed aside? In the little hardships and crosses that hem in our way, and in the casual humiliations, in lack of success, in neglect and censure, which despite all efforts on our part take their toll, in casual slights and disregard of all that hurts self-love, do we behold them as most precious nuggets, costly stones and jewels to be fitted in a sparkling crown of love to rejoice the Heart of God?

O happy Christian soul, who ardently desires to resemble his Creator and Lord in this manner, to imitate Him perfectly in wearing His garb and His distinctions! (cf. 11th Rule of the Society of Jesus). O happy the Christian whose expectations, hopes, and prayers culminate in the sincere longing to bear such humiliations with the humble Saviour. Happy he who, in using the daily opportunities, proves the sincerity of his intense desire for the abandonment, the repudiation, and the Cross of Christ.

Imitating the saints we, too, will love this vesture of humility and appear before our beloved Saviour clothed in this garb. In these ornaments of lowliness, we will prostrate ourselves before Him to offer reparation and atonement to His Sacred Heart. The saints ardently loved this vesture of humility. They always appeared in the presence of their Eucharistic Saviour clothed in this garment. Let us not prove untrue to the sublime thought of the children of God. Strength and immolation are paramount in this holy striving for the lovable virtue of humility.

How the memory of our secret acts consoles Him! Is not pride the final cause of the base injuries and offenses which the Heart of Jesus must endure in the Mystery of His Love? Refusing to submit their understanding, some reject all belief in the Infinite Condescension of Jesus, "meek and humble of Heart." Others, again, are apprehensive of the revilings of worldly judgments and opinions; hence, they fail in the fitting reverence they owe the Sublime Mystery of the Altar and frigidly absent themselves from the Table of the Lord.

How can we account for the coldness and tepidity of so many religious, which as Jesus Himself declared is especially painful to His loving Heart? Is it not because they are reluctant to break with the spirit of the world, to take the final step toward perfect love of the "meek and humble Heart" of Jesus? They shun humiliations and lowliness, forgetting that the saints rejoiced to suffer difficulties and hardships, with loving abandon to the Will of God. Our Saviour, therefore, dwelling close to them in the Blessed Sacrament remains estranged from them. Manifestations of His Goodness and Divine Compassion leave them cold and indifferent. When they draw near, their converse with the Source of Light and Strength leaves them arid and lifeless.

Pride is ever the chief source of countless insults and indignities offered the Divine Heart. Humility, therefore, remains the rich fount of ardent love and veneration, of self-dedication each morning anew, as we kneel in adoration of the Eucharistic God enthroned on our Altar. In union with Our Saviour, let us emulate His lowliness in the daily discharge of our duties in the Mystical Body. The ascent of the mount of holiness is often steep and trying, yet it is fraught with intense joy and hopes of an eternal reward.

For love of the Heart of Christ, we will make a thorough study of His humility and meekness in the school of this Divine Teacher, that we may enter fully into the hidden life of Christ Himself. Jesus will then verify His everlasting, glorious promise: "And you shall find rest to your souls."[75] A final note from the Prince of the Apostles: "All of you practice humility towards one another . . . Humble yourselves, therefore, under the mighty hand of God, that He may exalt you in the time of visitation."[76]

---

75 Matt. 11:29.
76 1 Peter 5:5, 6.

CHAPTER XIX

UNION OF THE SOUL WITH GOD

*"I am with you all days, even unto
the consummation of the world."*[1]
*"My soul yearns and pines for the
courts of the Lord."*[2]

I. "Sacred With the Sanctity of Christ"

The Most Blessed Sacrament of the Altar is Jesus Himself among us, the Eternal Word of the Father. It is Jesus, our Saviour, our Redeemer, our Teacher and Comforter, our Leader and King, our God. All this is veiled under the form of bread, but therefore not less truly and substantially present, with Godhead, and Divinity, and Humanity. If ruled by love, our heart will tend to the Most Blessed Sacrament, the "symbol of that one Body of His, of which He is the Head," according to the Council of Trent.

If we are in earnest in maintaining our union with Jesus, we will be eager to strengthen our devotion to the Mystery of Love. Fired with the sentiments of Christ, we will above all seek and surely find therein light, consolation, courage, and strength, contentment and peace. At

---

1 Matt. 28:20.
2 Ps. 83:3.

the Sacred Banquet we are fortified for our daily toils and encounters. In this sublime Mystery there dwells none other than He Himself, who invites us lovingly: "Come to Me, all you who labor and are burdened, and I will refresh you."[3] Here our wounds are healed, light is given us, and our supernatural life is reinvigorated.

What are my sentiments, what our relations towards this Mystery of Love? Do we nourish and cherish them as they justly deserve, with due reverence and esteem? Is our high regard for the Sacrament of the Eucharist profoundly fitting, worthy, dignified, and do we manifest these sentiments in the manner in which Jesus expects it of us, by way of a slight recompense for His self-elected loneliness and abasement in our Tabernacles?

1. OUR ESTEEM OF THE HOLY EUCHARIST

It is unnecessary to prove to the truly beloved of Jesus that we owe His Eucharistic Presence the highest reverence and esteem; that we must treasure It as a good that wins our heart's whole love and constitutes our supreme happiness on earth. We silently ponder realities that we have innumerable times pondered, and whose overwhelming grandeur and blessedness we know far better than words can express. Love is our watchword in this Adorable Sacrament. It strengthens and fortifies our faith. Let us make atonement and reparation to our Sacramental God for the insults heaped upon Him by the infidelity, the utter neglect and indifference of countless souls.

---

3 Matt. 11:28.

We know the Eternal Word of the Father, the Second Person of the Divinity, the only-begotten Son of God, the most perfect Image of the Father, who constitutes the unending blessedness of the Father, who full of joy announced it: "This is My beloved Son, in whom I am well pleased."[4] And the Blessed Eucharist is a gift, this only-begotten Son of God Himself, whom the Father bestows on us incessantly.

We know Jesus, *the Incarnate God,* who assumed our nature in the Virginal Womb of Mary, through the Holy Spirit. But it was our human nature adorned with such a plenitude of privileges, advantages, gifts, and graces, that it is the crown and fulfilment of the whole Creation. It hardly needs a word of elucidation what the Blessed Sacrament is, unless we belong to those who deserve the just rebuke: *"Medius autem vestrum stetit, quem vos nescitis."* "In the midst of you there has stood one whom you do not know."[5]

We know Jesus who traversed the whole of Palestine, dispensing benefits, making all things well, relieving misery and suffering wherever He was met with implicit trust and living faith. His Heart beat only of love, goodness, mercy and compassion. His frequent tears testified to the depths of His infinite love for us. In our Tabernacle dwells the same Jesus, and we can say: *"Ecce Deus Salvator meus!"* "Behold, here is my God and Saviour," not merely in sign and symbol, but Himself personally, really present in the same place with us, as close as the one kneeling beside

---

4 Matt. 3:17.
5 John 1:26.

me in the chapel. His Flesh and Blood—the purchase price of our soul.

We know *the Redeemer of the world,* who magnanimously offered Himself to the Father as Victim for us, in the first moment of His life; who devoted years of poverty, of humiliations, and fatiguing labors to the same purpose of love, until on Calvary, with the immolation of His own life on the cross, He consummated the work of the Redemption. He willingly shed His Blood for us and continually bestows upon us proofs of His infinite mercy.

The Blessed Sacrament is the selfsame Redeemer of the world. It is Jesus, who was not satisfied with having accomplished everything that the Infinite Holiness and Justice of the Heavenly Father demanded in expiation and atonement for sin; not satisfied to have earned with His own hands in the sweat of His brow, at the price of His Precious Blood and Life, the immeasurable wealth of graces, sufficient to enrich myriads of souls and ensure their eternal happiness; not satisfied to have left us in the other Sacraments equally fruitful sources of grace flowing to us in richest abundance—He desires still more.

To still His thirst for souls, His supreme love instituted the Most Blessed Sacrament, in which He continues to offer Himself to the Heavenly Father, a Sacrament of blessings, in which Jesus applies to us personally all the graces He Himself has earned for us, a Sacrifice in which He gives Himself as Gift! O inexpressible Mystery of Love! Jesus, my Redeemer, my Mediator, my Sacrificial Gift Himself! O endless Love! *"Ecce Deus, Salvator meus!"*

We know *the King of Glory,* enthroned at the Father's right. His beauty and glory captivates myriads of heavenly spirits, and rewards with divine munificence the ever growing number of saints, His faithful servants. He possesses all power in heaven and on earth, and He will come again to judge the living and the dead, and of His kingdom there will be no end.

The same King is enthroned on our altars. Him we justly salute with the jubilant: *"Tu Rex gloriae Christe, tu Patris sempiternus es Filius!"* What a blessed reality! What a blessing for us Catholics! How happy religious are in these marvellous privileges and heavenly benedictions! In our religious homes or in the nearness of the church, we can kneel in adoration before the Most Blessed Sacrament. Is there anything on earth comparable to the perpetual presence of Jesus, Our God, close to us under the Eucharistic Veils? Jesus, through whom all things were made, *"per quem omnia facta sunt,"* Jesus, who preserves everything in virtue of His power, *"omnia portans verbo virtutis suae,"* Jesus, the Godman whose holy Humanity is the crowning achievement of Creation!

Jesus is my Saviour and Redeemer, to whom I can say: *"Quid mihi est in coelo et a te, quid volui super terram?"* "What have I in heaven and what will I on earth?" He Himself dwells among us under the same roof, just a few steps away from the place of our activity, our prayers and our entire day's observance. His Heart beats incessantly for us. My God, what return shall I make? How shall I requite Thy love, O Jesus! "Heart of Jesus, Victim of love, make me a living holocaust, pleasing to Thee!" O Jesus, help me understand ever more clearly this glorious, incomprehensible Mystery, Thy love and condescension to us in our state of exile. "For we are made partakers of Christ," St. Paul assures us in Heb. 3:14.

2. OUR PERSONAL LOVE AND ESTEEM OF THE MOST BLESSED SACRAMENT

a) *Frequent Eucharistic Visits*

In these we manifest our personal love of the Sacramental Presence of Jesus. We hardly need an exterior incentive to draw us close to the Mystic Christ in the Adorable Sacrament of the Altar. Is it not the most natural thing for love to seek out the Beloved in the Tabernacle frequently, with eager longing and to bide with Him in loving contemplation, heart to heart? Jesus, Joy of Angels, Rapture of the Saints, Treasure of the Church, King of hearts, Glory of Heaven, Source of all grace, is present on our altars and is our Food in Holy Communion. The privilege that is ours in this wonderful intimacy of surpassing bliss is beyond compare with anything the world might offer. To become one with Christ, in the words of St. Paul: "It is now no longer I that live, but Christ lives in me."[6]

It is easy for Religious in virtue of their horarium, frequently to visit the Living God in the Tabernacle, but theirs is the sacred obligation to reproduce the holiness of Christ in their lives and in the apostolate of their vocation. In the early morning hours we make haste to answer the call, *"Venite Adoremus Dominum!"* We thank Him for His watchful care through the night, offer Him our heart anew, in union with His own immolation to the Father, and we dedicate to Him our day's work with fresh vigor, that we may grow in the likeness of Christ. As we gather about the Altar for the Holy Sacrifice of the Mass our love

---

6 Gal. 3:20.

kindles anew as the Sacred Mysteries are reenacted and we become one with our Eucharistic Christ in the Breaking of Bread. In the flaming Heart of Jesus we kindle the fire of our love with redoubled fervor and zeal. It is spiritual calisthenics, making us fit to cope with the unforeseen happenings of the day that are sure to try our mettle.

We are so intimately united with Jesus in the Most Holy Mystery that no greater happiness could be even imagined. There is no need of words in His Living Presence; He alone is to the soul complete satisfaction, the summit of love. Churches in larger cities speak eloquently of the power, the mercy, and love that draws hearts irresistibly to the surpassing Mystery of the Altar in odd moments at every hour in the course of the busy day. Young and old feel the impact of the power of the Christ in the Eucharist. Religious may not be outdone in generosity; by their living example of faith and ardent devotion, they will give themselves more perfectly through Christ to the works of the Christian apostolate of charity.

It is the hour of grace in the present critical world situation. *"Custos, quid de nocte?"* we may well query with Isaias. "Watchman, how much longer the night?"[7] What amazing examples many Sons of St. Ignatius, no longer at the front in the firing line, have given to posterity in their dedicated lives. From the Blessed Sacrament they drew the strength and the energy that marked them as true followers of Christ and of the holy Founder of the Society. Their memory still lives, calling down blessings upon the Church and upon the whole world. Renunciation of selfish plans and a reaching out for the hand of God in apostolic

---

7 Isa. 21:11.

dedication must be our aim. Not in vain do we rise joyously at the early morning summons: *"Deus meus, ad te de luce vigilo, sitivit in te anima mea."* Perhaps the seven or eight hours since the last Visit at night were much too long for the loving soul, which brooks no delay.

Personal visits in the course of the day are dear to His Sacred Heart and beneficial to us. Prompted by His overwhelming love and mercy, we thank our Sacramental God for His gracious presence, transforming our very environment into a paradise of inexpressible delights. As we listen to the silent whispering of His understanding Heart, we imbibe lessons of holy living and total submission, finding no sacrifice too great in the spirit of thanksgiving. Contempt of the world, charity and zeal for souls will enrich our lives in a generous response to Christ's infinite goodness.

b) *A spirit of intimacy with Christ, love for love*

"I am with you all days, even to the consummation of the world."[8] The religious house belongs to Him. He dwells there not as a guest or casual visitor, but as the Head of the House. The Superiors are but His representatives, charged with the guidance of the community in His Name. Everything in the day's round of duties comes under His provident disposition; all the work, all undertakings, even the most trifling matters fall under His omniscient eye; they share His paternal sympathy and understanding. The overwhelming goodness and compassion of Jesus, concerned in everything in the House of God, flows from His

---

8 Matt. 28:20.

Sacred Heart and is the amazing reality of the Mystery of the Tabernacle. Though we taste the joy of Christ's nearness to us in the Blessed Eucharist, we bow profoundly before this Miracle of Love unutterable. It exacts our utmost fidelity. Christ Himself said: *"Vos amici mei eritis, si feceritis, quae praecipio vobis."* "You shall be My friends, if you do what I tell you." And again, "This is My commandment, that you love one another," and finally, "Work while it is day."

These are the ardent wishes and desires of His Sacred Heart. He Himself abides with us to give us grace to correspond to His desires. To the young recruit and to the mature religious, He proffers abundant grace and strength. "All My things are thine," He says, "and all thine are Mine."[9] He watches closely to see how we acquit ourselves of this holy endeavor; He rejoices in the fruits of virtuous living that we strive to yield, in a more prayerful, Christ-like life, glorifying the Father. By our fidelity and self-sacrifice we can draw down blessings on countless souls and help them "Put on the Lord Jesus Christ."[10] Sacrificing ourselves in the service of souls in the effort to win them for the love of the Eucharistic Christ, we afford ineffable delight to the patient, humble Heart of Christ.

Oh, how these thoughts charge the soul with intense desire and firm resolve to return love for love! Jesus loves our desires and our good will of abandon to the more perfect following of Christ in His Eucharistic Presence, full of life and light. The Christian family, the Church, the members of a religious family, share in the rich fruits

---

9 John 17:10.
10 Rom. 13:14.

of this Holy Banquet. *"O Sacrum Convivium!"* "O Sacred Banquet in which Christ is received; the memory of His passion is renewed; the mind is filled with grace; and a pledge of future glory is given us!"

c) *Unchanging happiness and contentment*

A child is the happiest in the parental home. A friend counts the days he was permitted to spend in the home of his friend among his finest and best. Mutual interests of bride and bridegroom in the fulness of marriage blessing make it easy for them to forget home and earlier associations in the family circle.

What will be our sentiments, I ask, privileged as we are, in living close to the Most Blessed Sacrament in our cloistered homes or religious institutes? What are the sentiments of a companion of Christ, who finds in his Saviour father and mother, brother and sister, friend? Dissatisfaction, sadness, and timidity have no place in a family circle whose Head is Jesus in the Tabernacle. Jesus is present there really and truly in His own person, to be with us all days. This tremendous gift of God we do not sufficiently ponder. O Heart of Love! O Jesus Bridegroom! Love unutterable, comforting and invigorating consciousness of the Divine Presence! It is a wonderful incentive for us to put forth our best efforts. How much more courageously would we shoulder the hardest tasks in the apostolic outlines of our intense dedication.

The happiness of the continued abiding of Jesus with us in the Tabernacle is one of the greatest blessings of our religious life. More especially in the formative years of noviceship, the wealth of the Eucharistic Presence is to the young recruit an invaluable source of light and fresh resolves. The injunctions of religious authority for the laborers advanced in the apostolate, who have borne the burden and heat of day on countless fronts, as well as for the beginners, with the flow of graces from the Eucharistic Christ will meet us at every turn. Hardships in the conquest of self, denial of cherished affections, and wholehearted sacrifice of self, will be sweetened by uninterrupted union with Jesus, merciful and compassionate, our daily Communion Guest.

Nothing lifts the spirit more effectively and steels the courage of hard-pressed seculars, parents, men and women of all interests and occupations, more than the realization that our Blessed Saviour abides in our midst and takes us under His loving protection, in every need, provided we have recourse to Him. Christian homes will inevitably give forth the fragrance of Christian living to a skeptical world, if Christ is made the pulsing center of our activity and all our striving. He will instil fortitude and stout resistance against the evil assaults of the enemy.

What a marvellous training-school for children is a family hearth where the light from the Tabernacle in the church radiates faith, and hope, and love to every member. Where parents as well as religious Superiors and all lawfully constituted authority, representing Christ to those in their charge, show the clearest way to the abundant riches offered us freely in the Adorable Sacrament of the Altar. "Without Me you can do nothing," must replenish our faith and hope as we kneel in lowly adoration before the Tabernacle, or at the Holy Sacrifice of the Mass, or pause a moment in the assigned task during the day, to implore His assistance and grace. The slightest act of recollection or charitable submission to another's will, is of more value than a thousand worlds. Our Sacramental God will teach us His own gentle, selfless ways of doing all for His love alone.

The personal presence of Jesus in the Blessed Sacrament is a supreme gift. Here beats the Heart of Him who governs and disposes all things in heaven and on earth; here in our home He regulates everything in the minutest details. O my Jesus, *"portans verbo virtutis tuae,"* "who bearest me up through the Word of Thy Strength," who in all that happens to me, in every situation, hast the clear, concise, divinely designed plan, to promote me in virtue and competence for the service of my Heavenly Father.

Yet what shall we say of the incomprehensible acts of charity Jesus unceasingly bestows on us! He gives Himself to us daily as Victim of Immolation, when He enters our heart in Holy Communion, to be our food. It is the study of a lifetime. *"Quid retribuam Domino?"* "What shall I return to the Lord?" Faithful visits, personal intimacy with our beloved Saviour, Master, King and Friend, the Incarnate God, whose divine message we will earnestly ponder. Zeal in our whole life and attitudes in the House of God, silent happiness and contentment, in so far as it is possible according to the graces vouchsafed us. Jesus Himself will draw us ever closer to Him in this holy union in His living Presence in the Blessed Sacrament. The supernatural life demands sacrifice, and our lives of irrevocable surrender will be the recompense we make to the Heart of Christ our God.

Jesus remains with us, our Friend and Helper, in spite of our frailties, weakness, and faults. Yet strength flows to

us incessantly from the Saviour's Fountains, opened to us
in the Sacred Mysteries of the Eucharist. Strength of mind
and heart, clarity of vision and spiritual insight will lighten
for us the struggle that is inevitably ours as followers of
the Christ, who immolated Himself for sin by the shedding
of His Blood upon the cross.

"For what have I in heaven and besides Thee what do
I desire upon earth?"[11]

"*Ecce Deus, Salvator meus!*"

II. INTIMACY WITH GOD IN THE SPIRITUAL EXERCISES

"*Draw near to God and He will draw near to you.*"[12]
"*Let us rejoice and be glad that He has saved us.*"[13]

Prayer and mortification are the two wings that lift the
soul to God; the chief means of cultivating the spiritual
life. In the degree in which they are supreme in our striving
we shall succeed in holding aloof from all that is sinful
and disordered in our soul-life. In its stead we shall seek
to implant the virtues we so ardently desire, cultivate them
diligently, and bring them to full maturity through the
vital force of the grace Jesus imparts.

These are also the means of preserving the life of the
soul in fresh fervor and making it capable of greater
intimacy with God. In this union of love we shall grow
strong for the Christlife our apostolic activity requires of
us. Little wonder that spiritual masters invariably lay great

---

11 Ps. 72:25.
12 James 4:8.
13 Isa. 25:9.

stress upon a life of mortification and prayer, and strive to maintain this spirit alive in the souls of their disciples, men who are minded to go out in the strength of Christ in search of souls.

Even in prayer we should achieve this spirit, even though we are active in the midst of a world, with incessant mundane demands. Perhaps because of this circumstance, a more vigorous life of sacrifice will be within our reach. Union with God becomes all the more necessary for us if we would be useful instruments in His hands. To become true apostles of souls we must perseveringly cultivate that holy *"familiaritas cum Deo in spiritualibus devotionis exercitiis,"* "that holy familiarity with God in prayer and work," of which St. Ignatius so often speaks.

Intimacy with the Guest of our souls in the spiritual exercises! What are the requisites? As in any state of familiarity, they are twofold: the persons must associate with one another, be friends; then, the inner contacts must rest on the spirit of friendship, of justice and love.

1. THE SPECIAL FRIENDSHIP OF GOD

God must be our friend, and we, His. God is ever ready to bend down to men, and all who approach Him feel His goodness, love, and magnanimity. *"Accedite ad eum et illuminamini."* "Come ye to him and be enlightened."[14] In this light we take cognizance, however, to a greater or less degree, and the greater, the higher is the intimacy reserved for His special friends.

---

14 Ps. 33:6.

a) *The pure of heart*

Who are these friends of God? Proverbs gives the answer: *"Qui diligit cordis munditiam propter gratiam labiorum suorum habebit amicum regem."* "He that loveth cleanness of heart, for the grace of his lips shall have the king for his friend."[15] It is the king of which St. Paul says: "To the King of Ages, immortal, invisible, the only God, be honour and glory for ever and ever. Amen."[16] This purity of soul is the sparkling beauty and comeliness that wins for us His special friendship. The more radiant and intensified this beauty, the higher the degree of friendship.

If we would experience the delicate love of Christ and win His affection, St. Chrysostom counsels us daily to cultivate most assiduously this inner splendor of the soul. It should receive our daily most careful attention, he observes. Not only should we avoid what destroys inner beauty altogether, or even what impairs it, but we must aim at preserving purity of heart without the slightest stain. *"Homines divites in virtute, pulchritudinis studium habentes."* "Rich men in virtue, studying beautifulness."[17]

This is by no means an easy task. It exacts constant watchfulness and mortification. Because of the failings that still persist in spite of our vigilance, not a little patience and confidence are necessary. But the friendship of God is worth it all, and the condescending love with which the Infinite God bends over us, outweighs a hundred times the effort we expend. "Blessed are the clean of heart:

---

15 Prov. 22:11.
16 1 Tim. 1:17.
17 Ecclus. 44:6.

for they shall see God."[18] A foretaste of this bliss will repeatedly be our portion vouchsafed us in being friends of God.

b) Faithful souls, friends of God

"You are my friends if you do what I command you." The faithful fulfilment of the Most Holy Will of God. God has deigned to manifest His Will to us in the least details. If we desire to be friends of God and win His intimate confidence, we must approve ourselves by walking conscientiously on the way He has marked out for us. It leads invariably to His Sacred Heart. Our Holy Rule tells us not only what is His positive demand, but whatever pleases Him. His least wishes are there clearly indicated. "The religious," Our Lord told St. Margaret Mary, "who thinks to find Me on another way than that of exact observance of his Rule, deceives himself and removes farther away from My blessing and friendship."

"He who has My commandments and keeps them, he it is who loves Me."[19] And again, "If anyone love Me, he will keep My word."[20] There will be a bountiful reward— the love and intimacy of the Most Blessed Trinity. On the same occasion, Jesus Himself promised: "We will come to him and make our abode with him."[21] "He will be loved by My Father: and I will love him and manifest Myself to

---

18 Matt. 5:8.
19 John 14:21.
20 John 14:23.
21 John 14:21.

him."[22] What a marvellous recompense! Nothing more precious can be imagined than such knowledge and assurance, which is the heart of all spiritual goods, and is consummate holiness. *"Nosse enim te consummata justitia est."* "For to know Thee is perfect justice."[23]

2. INTIMACY WITH GOD IN PRAYER

Let us carefully fulfill the prerequisites for perfect friendship with God. Nothing more efficacious can be thought of than the conscientious discharge of our duty in the spirit of the Holy Rule and the solicitous custody of purity of heart. The cultivation of a tender friendship presupposes that the spirit of kindliness and love guide us in our spiritual exercises. Love must be the leading motive to the intimacies of our prayerlife. Love must support our earnest desires and help us persevere faithfully in the renunciation that love requires. The words of the Spouse in the Canticle suggest the light and encouragement that fill the soul in the friendship of Christ. "I sat down under His shadow, whom I desired: and his fruit was sweet to my palate."[24] She had longed to be with the soul's beloved, and when her desire of loving converse was fulfilled, she remained and enjoyed the sweet fruits of this intimacy.

"Intrans in domum meam conquiescam cum illa," says the Wise Man. He wills to enter his house, retire for prayer, and gladly, even eagerly converse with Eternal Wisdom, and will seek nothing else. "When I go into my house, I

---

22 John 14:21.
23 Wis. 15:3.
24 Cant. 2:3.

shall repose myself with her, for her conversation has no bitterness ... but joy and gladness!"[25]

a) *Ardent desire for prayer*

The Psalmist depicts the sentiments with which we should appear before God in prayer. "O God, my God, to thee do I watch at break of day. For thee my soul has thirsted ... in a desert land where there is no way and no water have I come before thee to see thy power and thy glory."[26] It is easy to cherish such sentiments once the love of God possesses the heart, if God is really our sole good, in very truth our God. "O God, my God, my soul thirsts for thee!" Such and similar aspirations rise spontaneously to our lips. It is the heart's desire to converse intimately with God. This longing will be all the more intense, the more complete our renunciation of earthly things and our total detachment, to find in God our greatest love. Even in time of dryness and aridity and other difficulties, the esteem and love of our spiritual exercises will remain unshaken.

Even if our heart were like a "desert land," without water, we should abide willingly in the Sanctuary with the Lord in prayer. Despite the sluggishness and depression of spirit, the indifference thrust upon us by nature, or the Evil Spirit, we still cherish the sincere and unabated desire for greater knowledge and love of God, *"ut viderem virtutem tuam et gloriam,"* "to see thy power and thy glory." The simple, yet trenchant *"Quo vadam et ad quid"*

---

25 Wis. 8:16.
26 Ps. 62:23.

of St. Ignatius, whither am I going and to what purpose, is a powerful and fruitful means in the matter of union with God in prayer. If in this manner we pray, we may hope to see our longing stilled, not seldom beyond expectation.

"*Qui adorat Deum in oblectatione, suscipietur, et deprecatio illius usque ad nubes propinquabit.*" "He that adoreth God with joy, shall be accepted, and his prayer shall approach even to the clouds."[27] It pierces them, goes to the throne of God, draws Him down to the soul: "*Ecce adsum, quia vocasti me!*" "Behold, here I am! for thou hast called me." To be called into the presence of God—a divine exaltation. Joy supreme! Dryness and distress of soul give way to a better understanding of God's condescension and merciful love. "The mercy of God is beautiful in the time of affliction, as a cloud of rain in the time of drought."[28] In order to taste these sweet delights, we must prepare our heart for these intimacies with God by unlimited confidence and trust in His divine friendship.

b) *Loving surrender in prayer*

Love must incite us to do carefully what the spiritual exercises require; to persevere patiently, resignedly, without haste or timidity in bearing whatever hardships we encounter at the time of prayer. Those are moments of trial and a challenge to our love of God. We must be filled with zeal and divine longing for the love of Christ; we must be ready for any sacrifice asked of us without reserve.

---

27 Ecclus. 35:20.
28 Ecclus. 35:36.

In his incomparable manual—the *Spiritual Exercises* —St. Ignatius has given us explicit instructions as to ways and means of achieving the life of prayer most profitably under all circumstances. The prevalence of the retreat movement of our day makes it relatively easy and within the reach of everyone in love with God and the interior life to acquire the genuine spirit of prayer. Solicitously cultivated, prayer that is strong and faithfully anchored in the Will of God is a powerful weapon of spiritual strength and courage. God is ever merciful and benign. He listens to our prayers with paternal interest, provided we come into His presence with wholehearted abandon and trust. *"Appropinquate Deo et appropinquabit vobis."*[29] "Draw near to God and He will draw near to you." O glorious promise! Our lives will be changed in this closest intimacy with the God of Love. The blessings He will bestow are worth the most ardent surrender to His demands of detachment and absolute abandonment to His all-holy designs. Interior joy and happiness will be our copious reward.

c) *Walking in the presence of God through love*

In truth, is not everything we do in the course of a day, literally the work of God? Beyond the material aid generously offered us, does He not bestow His supernatural help munificently? His grace renders our work pleasing to Him and enriches us and shapes our happiness; it helps us become Christlike. He, the Triune God, is with us always, in Him we live and move. "For in Him we live,

---

29 James 4:8.

and move, and are."[30] He is not present as a mere fantasy or figment of the imagination, or a lifeless statue, but rather as the infinitely loving and perfect God. His Heart overflows with love and solicitude that could never fill the heart of an earthly parent for the child, or a friend for his friend. What tremendous realities these! Must not the mere thought of them incite us to frequent visits and to intimate converse with our omnipresent God, who loves us to excess? Oh, the merit of repeated ejaculatory prayers and aspirations! How necessary they are, and what inner power they wield in the matter of spiritual living.

We need never fear that any time or attention devoted to silent, interior prayer will detract from the efficacy of our occupation. The contrary will come to pass from the very nature of the act, as experience clearly proves. What clarifies the mind, dilates the heart, evokes courage and trust, can never be an obstacle or a hindrance in the spiritual life. Does not Christ from the Tabernacle address to us the sweetly winning words: "Come to Me, all that labor and are burdened, and I will refresh you."[31] The momentary thought of God is, indeed, refreshing, drawing us closer to the secrets of His loving Heart.

Let us carefully foster union with God in the course of the busy day. Time and opportunities will not be found wanting. They arise naturally from the circumstances of our office, our bodily health, our inner sentiments. May love induce us to utilize them all, that we may more and more *live in God, with God, for God,* in filial surrender without anxiety or fear.

---

30 Acts 17:28.
31 Matt. 11:28.

It is a wholesome practice in the passing hours to substitute for useless speech or dissipation a few words with the God of my heart; a heart to heart message full of love and thanksgiving, a short aspiration to lift my soul to Him. In the silent stillness of recollection, communing with God, while I go about my duties, many faults will be hindered. Courage and love will prosper my endeavors toward virtue. I will feel free and rejuvenated in spirit in addressing myself to my dear Redeemer, with confidence and conformity to His holy Will. Losing myself in His Sacred Heart, the fountainhead of charity, the Godman, I will more easily carry out the Apostle's injunction to "put on Christ."

A *Fiat!* or *Suscipe!* or *Thy Will, O God, not mine!* These are tremendous levers to lift heart and soul. Never need we fear to encroach upon efficiency in the discharge of duty by momentary acts of recollection, directing our mind towards the Tabernacle, or invoking the Holy Spirit to enlighten heart and soul. It will rather be an enrichment of our spiritual life, a strengthening and refurbishing of our inner fortifications, in the charity Christ taught us with His dying breath.

Let us, therefore, strive for greater union with God in mind and heart, not alone in prayer, but in all our labors and activities throughout the day. This is what is meant by *walking with God*. It is living in closest intimacy with Him who dwells in our midst for love of us, who chooses our souls as the place of His delights.

"Draw near to God and He will draw near to you."[32]

---

32 James 4:8.